Mordecai C. Cooke, Metcalf Collection

Vegetable Wasps and Plant Worms

A popular history of entomogenous fungi, or fungi parasitic upon insects

Mordecai C. Cooke, Metcalf Collection

Vegetable Wasps and Plant Worms
A popular history of entomogenous fungi, or fungi parasitic upon insects

ISBN/EAN: 9783337381097

Printed in Europe, USA, Canada, Australia, Japan

Cover: Foto ©Andreas Hilbeck / pixelio.de

More available books at **www.hansebooks.com**

VEGETABLE WASPS

AND

PLANT WORMS.

A POPULAR HISTORY OF

ENTOMOGENOUS FUNGI, OR FUNGI PARASITIC UPON INSECTS.

BY

M. C. COOKE, M.A., LL.D., A.L.S.,

AUTHOR OF

"FREAKS AND FANCIES OF PLANT LIFE," "TOILERS IN THE SEA,"
"ILLUSTRATIONS OF BRITISH FUNGI," ETC.

WITH NUMEROUS ILLUSTRATIONS.

PUBLISHED UNDER THE DIRECTION OF THE COMMITTEE
OF GENERAL LITERATURE AND EDUCATION APPOINTED BY THE
SOCIETY FOR PROMOTING CHRISTIAN KNOWLEDGE.

SOCIETY FOR PROMOTING CHRISTIAN KNOWLEDGE,
NORTHUMBERLAND AVENUE, W.C. ; 43, QUEEN VICTORIA STREET, E.C.
BRIGHTON : 135, NORTH STREET.
NEW YORK: E. & J. B. YOUNG AND CO.
1892.

PREFACE.

——◆——

ONLY one attempt has been made to produce a
work of this kind in Britain, and that was
undertaken just thirty-five years ago. Mr. G. R. Gray's
"Memoir" was, moreover, privately printed, and was
necessarily exceedingly limited in its circulation.
During the intervening period many additions have
been made to the list of species, and more facts have
become known, so that another effort was desirable.
It will be evident that the subject may be approached
and viewed from two different positions. One aspect
will be associated with the entomophytes themselves
—an aspect which will commend itself to mycologists.
The other will be concerned with the hosts upon
which the fungi are parasitic, and all sympathy will
rest with them ; such a position as we would accord
to entomologists. In the work above alluded to
the subject was treated from the entomological side,
whereas my own antecedents would attract me to
the mycological side. In order, therefore, to com-
bine the two, as having a wider interest, I have

resolved to reproduce to a large extent, or, at any rate, to make a very free use of, Mr. Gray's entomological observations, in combination with my own mycological ones, inasmuch as I desire to lay no claim to special entomological knowledge, and find in these " Notices " just the information in which I confess myself deficient.

It appeared to me that the best arrangement I could adopt for this purpose would be to appropriate the method adopted in the original work, and whilst giving greater prominence to the mycological features of the entomophytes, to group them entomologically, in the several orders of insects, rather than adopt a sequence based solely upon the plants, irrespective of the animals. In order to present such a view as the mycologist only would accept, I have subjoined, at the close, an arrangement of the fungi according to their mycological affinities. By this means I have hoped to accommodate both classes of readers.

Lest exception should be taken to the large mass of references, in the form of foot-notes, I may remark that, as such a large number of facts had to be incorporated, I have adopted this method to assist investigators in the verification of the facts, and at the same time give a condensed bibliography of the subject, so that the student may have a guide to the literature, and follow it up, if he feels so disposed.

For all that relates to the *Entomophthoreæ*, a most important group in these latter days, I have made use of Mr. Roland Thaxter's able monograph of "The Entomophthoreæ of the United States," which is far in advance of anything we have on the subject in Europe.

It might have been possible to have included more of the *Schizomycetes* had I not resolved to draw the line at *Bacilli*, with the solitary exception of a passing reference to the "foul brood" of Bees.

In its present form I hope that the book will be welcome alike to the entomologist and the mycologist, and assist them in their respective studies.

M. C. COOKE.

CONTENTS.

VEGETABLE WASPS

PLANT WORMS.

ENTOMOGENOUS FUNGI.

INTRODUCTION.

THE two distinct aspects of this subject will be at once recognized by the two classes of readers which will possibly be attracted to the perusal of this volume. The entomologists will have the greatest interest in the orders and species of insects which suffer from the attacks of fungi ; whilst the mycologists will think but little of the hosts, and absorb themselves for the most part in the Entomophytes. For these two classes the introduction will be expected to exhibit more or less of a dual character, and, as the mycological has with us a preponderating influence, we give it preference.

There are four groups under which the fungi parasitic upon insects would primarily arrange themselves, and these, in the order of their importance, would be, first, the ascigerous, or *Cordyceps* group, which have mostly a fleshy stroma, a club-like shape, and sporidia contained in asci, including also those imperfect forms or conidial states which belong, or are allied to, *Isaria*. The second group would contain the *Laboulbeniaceæ*, small pollinia-like bodies, with diffluent asci, which attach themselves to various parts of the body of living insects, and do not seem to penetrate the cuticle. Thirdly, the *Entomophthoræ*, or innate absorption moulds, which absorb and replace the internal organs, and only appear on the surface after having killed their hosts. And, lastly, a miscellaneous collection of moulds, mostly of the kind found on dead vegetable and animal matter of all sorts, and, with a few solitary exceptions, such as the silkworm disease, not truly parasitic and destructive. Intentionally we exclude those minute and mysterious *Schizomycetes* which, under the forms of *Bacteria* or *Bacillus*, do not consider insects beyond the scope of their legitimate influence.

The first group consists of about five and forty entomogenous species, to which at first the generic name of *Clavaria* was applied, until their structure and fructification were ascertained, but which were afterwards transferred to the large genus *Sphæria* on account of their possessing the cells called perithecia, in which the sporidia were developed, enclosed in long delicate sacs or asci. When a division of *Sphæria* took place subsequently, a new genus termed *Cordyceps* was characterized, to which the entomogenous species, with some few others, were assigned, on account of their fleshy vertical stroma, and perithecia, with long filiform sporidia.

The general and typical form in *Cordyceps* is a somewhat club-shaped erect body, sometimes only a few millimetres and sometimes several inches in height, with a naked sterile solid stem, attached by threads of mycelium, and a thicker head, globose, oval, or elongated, which is covered on all sides with nearly globose perithecia, immersed in the substance, and only visible externally by their dot-like mouths or orifices. In a few instances the perithecia are only partially immersed, or nearly free, but such instances are rare. At first the perithecia contain only a minute drop of grumous gelatin, but finally this is differentiated into very long cylindrical asci, with a thin membrane, each containing eight long thread-like sporidia, which are commonly nucleate, then septate, breaking up finally into separate joints, each of which is a reproductive unit.

The vegetative portion, or mycelium at the base, pervades the body of the host-insect, commencing in many instances during life, and at length absorbing the whole interior, converting it into a fungoid mass. The external stroma, constituting the fungus proper, notwithstanding all that has been written to the contrary, is not developed until the whole interior is absorbed, and consequently the insect is dead. In cases where the larvæ, or pupæ, are buried in the soil, or rotten wood, the stroma, or club, elongates the stem, so as to bring the fruit-bearing portion above the surface into the light and air. Until the fructifying portion of the club is exposed, it remains without producing perithecia or organs of fructification.

Other fungi are produced on similar hosts, and under similar conditions, but these are not so firm and fleshy—much more branching, as a rule—and the surface is dusted with the powdery superficial spores. These are really compact moulds, of the genus *Isaria*, in which the stroma is formed of very thin filaments closely agglutinated into a common stem and branches, each filament producing a minute spore at its extremity. It is generally admitted that these moulds are not perfect and complete fungi, but the conidial stage of some more perfect fungus, and the entomogenous species are held to be the conidia of some species of *Cordyceps*. It is very difficult to trace their relationship, and in but a few instances has any good evidence been adduced ; in the rest it seems to have been taken upon trust, from analogy. In view, then, of this relationship, or reputed relationship, the entomogenous species of *Isaria* are bracketed with *Cordyceps*, as conidial forms. It must be confessed that the nature of the connection of *Isaria* with *Cordyceps* is very obscure and unsatisfactory. For some species of *Cordyceps* we are acquainted with no conidial form, and for some species of *Isaria*, even European, there is no evidence to connect them with any ascigerous species, nothing but bare supposition, founded upon the identity of the host.

The brothers Tulasne[1] consider that some at least of the Entomogenous fungi are represented under two different forms during their career ; for instance, they hold that *Isaria crassa*, as well as *Isaria farinosa*, is strictly united with the more perfect and complex form of *Cordyceps militaris*. They also remark that it would be interesting to ascertain what species of *Isaria* correspond with the three European species known as *Cordyceps entomorrhiza*, *Cordyceps gracilis* (which is only a slender form of *C. entomorrhiza*), and *Cordyceps myrmecophila*. It is not impossible, as some have suggested, that the more complete state of some of this class of parasites may be reserved for other climates. It is hinted by Mr. Gray that *Isaria sphe-cophila* may belong to some tropical species, which has been known under the name of *Guepes vegetantes*. Whereas, only recently, M. Cornu has expressed his belief that the *Cordyceps Ditmari*, since found in Europe, is the perfected condition of *Isaria sphecophila*.

---

[1] Tulasne, *Ann. des Sci. Nat.* (1857), p. 42; and "Selecta Fungorum Carpologia" (1861-65), vol. iii.

Tulasne has even hazarded the conjecture, or almost
a conjecture, that *Botrytis Bassiana* may eventually
prove to be the conidial form of *Cordyceps sinensis.*
That sphæriaceous fungi may appear in a conidial, or
imperfect state, in which only naked spores, or conidia,
are produced, has been demonstrated in some instances, and many others are suspected. A red
Stilbum, for instance, as the conidia of *Sphærostilbe
cinnabarina,* and often found growing in company;
species of *Fusarium* associated with some species of
Nectria, and undoubtedly the very common and well-
known *Tubercularia vulgaris,* passing gradually into
Nectria cinnabarina, on the same stroma, can scarcely
be controverted, so that for conditions known as
Isaria, or even as *Microcera,* to be suspected as states
of some species of *Cordyceps,* is by no means absurd,
or in the least degree improbable.

The second group, *Laboulbeniaceæ,* is one of great
interest, and there is no reason why some of the
species should not be found in Great Britain. It is
not unusual to see bees, and other insects, with the
pollinaria of orchids attached to their heads or bodies,
and entomologists will at times mistake them for fungi.
Species of *Laboulbenia* (see figures on Plate III.) have
a superficial resemblance to these pollinaria, in size,
form, and almost in colour, but hitherto the largest
number have been found on *Coleoptera,* adhering to
the legs, elytra, and body. They have no mycelium

penetrating the host, but are entirely superficial, being attached by a small obconical knob at the base of the stem ; hence they may be carried about by the same insect for an indefinite period of time. Their colour is mostly of some tint of brown, and their form more or less clavate. The upper portion is occupied by the perithecium, the cavity in which the spores are produced, and these latter escape by a perforation at the apex. The lower portion is narrowed into a stem, which has two cells, one above the other at the base, and above these several cells supporting the spore-cavity. The sporidia are mostly spindle-shaped, divided in the middle, at first contained in asci, which speedily disappear. Beside the upper portion of the clubs, and near the base of the perithecium, is usually a projection on one side, with thread-like processes proceeding from its apex, called the pseudoparaphyses (in rare instances they are found at the base of the stem). What their functions may be is still uncertain, but their number and form vary in different genera and species.

The third group are the *Entomophthoræ*, and the most common and familiar example will be found on the dead flies on the window-pane. These are deeply parasitic, and destructive minute fungi, often assuming the condition of an epidemic. "They are distinguished by the production of numerous hyphæ of large diameter and fatty contents, which ultimately emerge from the host in white masses of characteristic appearance, and produce at their extremities large conidial spores, which are violently discharged into the air and propagate the disease.   In addition to these conidia, the propagation of the fungus, after long periods of rest, may be provided for by the formation of thick-walled resting-spores adapted to withstand successfully the most unfavourable conditions.   These resting-spores, which may be either sexual (zygospores) or asexual (azygospores), finally germinate, and produce conidia that are discharged in the usual fashion, and serve to infect fresh hosts." [1]

Infection results from contact with one of the conidial spores which adhere to the surface of the host, germinates there, and by means of the germinating thread enters the body.   Infection as a result from the ingestion of spores with the food does not appear to occur.   After entering the body growth proceeds rapidly, and forms hyphal bodies (fig. 1), which are short thick fragments of variable size and shape, continually reproduced by budding, until the body of the host is more or less completely filled with them.   Having absorbed the contents of the body, the hyphal bodies germinate with rapidity, according to the humidity of the atmosphere.   Each hyphal body produces one

---

[1] Thaxter on "The Entomophthoreæ of the United States" (1888), p. 137.

or more threads, which either proceeds directly and
simply into the outer air, and produces its conidia, or
it branches indefinitely, each branchlet becoming a
conidia-bearer, producing spores at the extremity
(fig. 2). Usually the masses of conidia-bearers, when

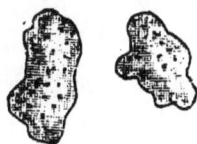

FIG. 1.—Hyphal bodies of *Empusa.*

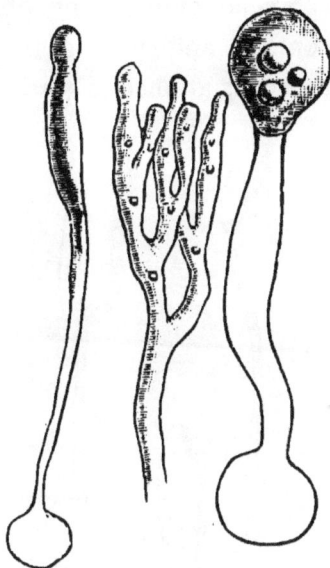

FIG. 2.—Conidia bearers of the
Entomophthoreæ.

in the external air, form tufts, or coalesce in a continuous spongy layer over the surface. Conidia are
formed by constriction, or budding, at the apices of
the threads and their branches, and are at first contained within the mother-cell. When fully matured,
the mother-cell is ruptured, and the conidium, or
spore, is forcibly ejected to a considerable distance.

The conidia are variable in size and form, often varying much in the same species. They are usually hyaline or slightly coloured, and commonly contain large fatty globules, the basal portion of the spore being always more or less papillate. The discharged spore adheres to any object with which it comes in contact, and if it chances to find a suitable host, proceeds at once to germinate; but failing in reaching a suitable host, a secondary conidium is formed, as a provision for further dissemination. The ordinary method is by the production of a thread of variable length, which grows upwards, swells at its extremity, and produces a conidium resembling that from which it is derived (fig. 3). Should this secondary conidium fail in finding a suitable host, then a third conidium is formed from the second, in the same manner. In some cases the secondary conidium is different in form from the primary, and is confined to definite species.

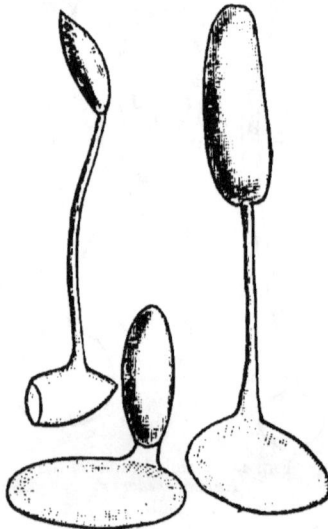

Fig. 3.—Secondary spores of *Entomophthora.*

Cystidia are sterile threads, longer than the conidia-bearers, sometimes very large, but their special office is unknown. Other modifications of the hyphæ, or threads, are the rhizoids, or rooting filaments, which serve to attach the host to some substratum ; they grow from the lower and outer portions of the fungus mass, and sometimes are expanded at their extremities into a discoid "sucker," by means of which they adhere.

The hyphal bodies, which produce the conidia-bearers, are also concerned in the production of resting-spores, either with or without sexual conjugation, and for the most part internally, within the body of the host. Non-sexual resting-spores (azygospores) are either formed by the conversion of a hyphal body into a resting-spore, or by direct budding from the hyphal body. They are usually spherical, of large size, surrounded by triple walls. Sexual resting-spores (zygospores) are produced by slightly varying modes, as a result of the conjugation of opposite threads. Threads, either within or without the body of the host, produce lateral outgrowths, at opposite points of two different threads, which meet midway between the two conjugating cells, and coalesce. The intermediate walls are then absorbed, and a connecting tube is formed, through which the contents are mingled. A bud is produced upon the connecting canal, which increases rapidly, and appropriates the contents of the two conjugating cells to form the zygospore (fig. 4). After this process is completed the empty hyphæ disappear. Sometimes, when the production of the zygospore is external, the spore is developed as a terminal swelling at the end of one of the conjugating threads.   Another mode of conjugation occurs in a single species, in which the hyphal bodies join laterally by means of short processes, and produce a bud at the point of union, which enlarges rapidly and absorbs the contents of

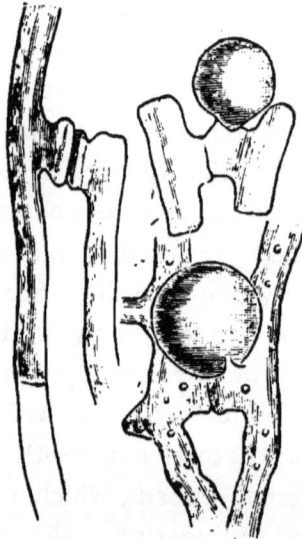

FIG. 4.—Resting-spores, or zygospores of *Entomophthora.*

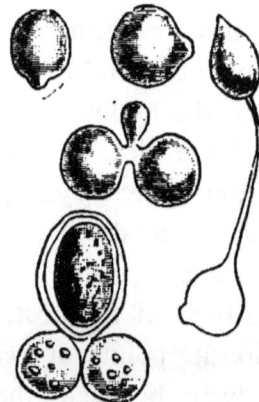

FIG. 5.—Conjugated hyphal bodies and spore.

the two conjugated hyphal bodies, producing a rest-ingspore (zygospore) (fig. 5).   There are also some other slight modifications in the production of resting-spores, in different species, but sufficient has been said to indicate the general character of the process.[1] The mature resting-spores are spherical, mostly smooth, and scarcely coloured, but brown in a few species. What periods of rest are required, what the conditions of germination, and what the results, are at present obscure. Some authors claim to have observed the process, whilst others have failed to obtain germination in any one instance.

The hosts belong to all hexapod orders, but the Diptera are the greatest sufferers; the Hemiptera come next, followed by Lepidoptera and Coleoptera, while the Neuroptera, Hymenoptera, and Orthoptera are about equally affected, being attacked by two or three species, the most productive localities for finding them being the margins of brooks in shady woods.

The last group of Entomophytes are, with the exception of two or three species, only saprophytes, and but a small selection of them will find illustration in these pages. They are moulds of different kinds, some being white moulds, or *Mucedines;* others black moulds, or *Dematiei;* but, excluding the species of *Isaria* and its immediate allies, which we have referred to as conidial forms of *Cordyceps*, they are of little importance, and not injurious to living insects (the *Botrytis Bassiana*, or mould of the silkworm disease, always excepted). Such genera as *Penicillium, Sterigmatocystis, Cladosporium, Verticillium,*

---

[1] For fuller details, consult Roland Thaxter on "The Entomophthoræ of the United States" (1888 : Boston).

and *Oospora* have no claim to the title of Entomophytes, and we have only alluded to such species as
have hitherto occurred exclusively on dead insects.
Of *Schizomycetes* we prefer to be restricted to a single
species, that of "foul brood," and without regret leave
the rest to more enthusiastic students of the *Bacilli*.

It is expedient that we now approach the other
aspect of our subject—the entomological—and in
doing so must place ourselves under the guidance of
Mr. Gray,[1] quoting, for the most part, his observations ; for to this aspect only an entomologist can
hope to do justice. Some of these observations will
fall in more naturally under the different orders of
insects, under which we have elected to follow Mr.
Gray as a basis of arrangement, but some general
notes apply equally to all orders. The first remark
applies to the condition of the host when parasitism
takes place. "It is necessary first to observe," he
says, "that life is certainly not extinct when the
insect first becomes the basis of these vegetable parasites, as has been indicated since the time of Father
Torrubia, in 1754 (in his case, it must be admitted,
under rather marvellous circumstances), although this
is now a very generally received opinion." Dr.
Mitchell [2] is quoted to the effect that "living insects,

---

[1] Gray, "Notices of Insects."
[2] Mitchell, *Silliman's Journal*, xii. 27.

while in health, become the bases of insect parasites,
and even remain for some time after they are attacked
in a living state, but gradually die as the parasites
advance to maturity. The chief or leading fact
intended to be herein established is the derivation of
nourishment by the vegetable from the *living* animal."
We have already admitted that the commencement
of parasitism takes place during the life of the host,
whilst disputing the assumption that the external
and complete development takes place until after
death, since previous to the latter consummation the
whole of the internal organism is replaced by fungous
mycelium, and hence animal organs and animal functions have ceased. " It may be further noticed," he
proceeds, "that most of the insects thus affected are
solely vegetable feeders, although there are a few
which feed on animal matter. It is also supposed
that the spores, or seeds, of the parasites may become
connected with the insect in two ways; either by
the insects swallowing the spores with their vegetable
food, or by their settling on some portion of the exterior surface, and thus finding their way into the
interior." In corroboration, Dr. Leidy[1] is cited to
the effect "that those insects which eat large quantities of vegetable solid food, especially such as eat
decaying substances, are very much infested with

---

[1] *Proc. Acad. Nat. Sci. Phil.* (1851), p. 210.

parasites." Holm considered, as far back as 1781, that the seeds (spores) were eaten with the food by the larvæ, and that they remained for some time in the intestines. M. de Quatrefages since observed that various medicines could be given to silkworms by sprinkling the leaves of the mulberry trees on which they fed, which shows that the spores, or seeds, may also be taken by the same means. That "the spores are taken in this mode is most probable," Mr. Gray continues, as they are "so infinitely minute that they can only be seen by the most powerful lenses, and therefore so light as to be wafted through the air by the slightest motion of the wind. When thus floating about they may either settle on the vegetation or fall on the ground, where they would become mixed with the soil, or vegetable matter, in which most of the insects in their earliest stages of life seek for nourishment, and by these means the spores may be taken in with the food, which is thought to be the most frequent way by which the fungus becomes connected with aërial animals. The idea that the spore finds, or bores, its way into the interior after it becomes attached to the external surface, is one which cannot be entertained with regard to ento-mophytes, when it is taken into consideration that not the slightest sign of any such operation on the outer surface of the insect can be observed, though various kinds of insects have been obtained, completely filled internally with the thallus (mycelium), and without any external appearance of the parasite ; nor can it be so with caterpillars, which have changed their skin on assuming the chrysalis state, after burying themselves in moss, etc., and which are found in the latter state to form the bases of fungi." On this point the remarks of Sir W. Hooker [1] are quoted, that in reference to the New Zealand entomophytes " the caterpillar is in the act of working the soil when the spores of the fungus are lodged in the first joint of the neck ;" and also of Professor Owen and Dr. Thompson,[2] " that the parasite fell upon and became connected with the caterpillar previous to its being buried in the earth, causing it to sicken and die, and then commenced the process of germination." These remarks, however, seem only to be quoted as in opposition to his own views. He then proceeds, " It is now allowed by most writers that the germination of the spore commences in the interior of the insect ; and it is also evident that it does not depend altogether on being nourished by the warmth and moisture of the interior of the insect, but rather on the insect becoming sickly and feeble by the effect of the heavy rains, that fall at stated periods in the intertropical regions, or from the extremely humid

---

[1] *London Journal of Botany*, ii. p. 209.
[2] *Medical Times* (1843), p. 65.

seasons which prevail occasionally during certain
months of the year in most extratropical countries.
This is especially applicable to those insects that
reside in the earth, or in decayed vegetable matter,
or in an exposed nest, as they must at such times be
saturated by the water, and thus become completely
enfeebled by its influence, after which the spore
rapidly germinates, and then the thallus (mycelium)
eventually expands itself throughout the interior of
the insect, and thus the plant gradually predominates
over the vital principle of the animal." [1]

"The same thing is supposed to occur, although
under other circumstances, with the silkworms, and
is thought to be occasioned by the leaves on which
they are fed being saturated during humid seasons
with a greater degree of moisture, and by the external dampness, penetrating into the apartments in
which the insects are confined, thereby affecting the
atmosphere with a degree of closeness and humid
warmth that is injurious to the insects, and causes
them to become sickly and feeble, and thus to fall
easy victims to the fungoid parasite or mould." In
support of this view the opinions are quoted of M.
de Quatrefages, that "silkworms fed on moistened
leaves speedily felt the effects of them, and very
few of them spun cocoons;" of M. Audouin, that

---

[1] See Waterhouse, *Proc. Zool. Soc.* (1839), p. 146.

"when live insects are attracted by fungi, it is only when they are confined in damp unventilated places."

Returning to his principal course of illustration, our author proceeds to say that "the thallus (mycelium) gradually develops itself and fills the outer case of the insect, to such an extent that it has been remarked that it seems entirely metamorphosed into a vegetable, with the exception of the skin and intestines, even occupying the orbits of the eyes, and to the points of the tarsi. The insect retains its natural form, although its internal parts are dried up by the growth of the fungus. The outer portion of the plant then forces its way through the skin or tissue at various places, through the joints of the body, and even, in some cases, through the hard surface of the head, thus exhibiting very great power of development; while progressing towards maturity, it also shows various peculiarities in the manner of its growth and form, which may in some cases be occasioned by the habit and position of the insect at the time it feels the effect of the inner plant, or mycelium.

"Many caterpillars, it should be noticed, are found in the same locality, apparently unaffected, by the insect not falling in the way of the spores while feeding, or by its health not having been so greatly enfeebled by the humidity as that of others around it to allow of the germination of the spores.

"When chrysalids form the bases of the parasite, it is supposed that the caterpillar had obtained the germ with its food previous to the change into the inactive state. It is still thought that extreme dampness is necessary for the development of the parasite, which the chrysalis is very liable to suffer from, as it either lies in the earth, vegetable matter, or moss, mostly without any kind of covering, or with only a slight cocoon, for some time before the period arrives to undergo its final transformation into the imago, or perfect state. The development in this case is in every respect similar to what it would be in and on the caterpillar; but it is more rarely met with.

"The spores, or seeds, it may be remarked, are probably equally taken during dry seasons along with the food, by the new series of insects that make their appearance in fungoid localities; but owing to the atmosphere being free from humidity, the insects are able to retain their health and energy, and are thereby rendered capable of throwing off quickly the remains of their food, as is the case with all vegetable feeders; sufficient time is consequently not allowed for the germination of the spore, and thus the insects escape, and undergo all their metamorphoses, and ultimately reach the perfect state, in which the insect after a short time leaves a new progeny, some of which may, or may not, form the bases of their fungoid enemies, at a period unfavourable to the insect, but more conducive to the development of the fungus.

"In connection with the statement that the development and growth of the internal mycelium are favoured by extreme moisture, an experiment may be referred to which was made by Dr. Leidy,[1] who placed some fragments of fungoid matter, taken from the interior of a mole-cricket, which did not appear externally, in a small glass case, along with some moist *Sphagnum;* these fragments after a time developed a series of cream-coloured stipites from three lines to an inch in length, varying in number in each fragment. It is probable that these productions would eventually have formed the outer development of the plant, had not the mole-cricket been discovered, and removed from its peculiar locality."

A further illustration is also given from the same authority,[2] "in a curious account of a portion of *Passalus cornutus* which had lain, half immersed in water, for two days, upon and around which no less than four kinds of vegetable parasites, consisting of filamentous fungi and algæ, were produced ; while on some Ascarides, which had been in water a few days,

---

[1] *Proc. Acad. Nat. Sci. Philadel.* (1851), p. 210.
[2] *Ibid.* (1850), p. 7.

he was able to observe in a single morning all the stages of development of *Achlya prolifera*. These plants, he considered, sprung from pre-existing germs, derived from a parent which had remained inert until circumstances favoured their germination."

Unfortunately the last account goes to prove very little, since it is doubtful whether any previous germs in the fragments of the insect, even if present, had anything to do with the development of the *Achlya prolifera* in water. To what extent any insects, or parts of insects, allowed to remain in water, may develop species of *Achlya* or *Saprolegnia*, is uncertain. It has yet to be demonstrated that the germs were not already in the water, awaiting the advent of any favourable host.

"It is well known," continues Mr. Gray, "that the fungus tribe are remarkable for the suddenness of their appearance ; this has occasioned some authors to suppose that some kinds of the parasites are in the first instance spontaneously developed while the animal is in a sickly state, or by certain organic changes in the fat, as in the silkworm, for example, so as to render its component parts capable of spontaneously producing mould, and that when once formed it is capable of being extended to others by spores. On the other hand, these opinions are thought to be untenable, as the plants are more probably propagated by seeds on their first development. Their germination is developed under particular and sometimes sudden circumstances, principally during the humidity of the spring and autumnal portions of the year."

It has been thought that the exposed position assumed by the diurnal Lepidoptera, in their three stages of life, preserves them from becoming the bases of fungoid parasites, as their chief time of existence is during the summer months, when the complete state of vegetation enables them to seek protection from the rains by resorting to the under side of leaves, trunks of trees, etc., and even should they become wet, the moisture is soon removed by the surrounding air, or by basking in the sunshine ; and thus they are kept sufficiently free from that extreme moisture which appears to be essential to produce that particular state of the insect which assists towards the development of the spores of the fungus, should they be taken in with the food.

" It may further be stated, in order to show that the parasitical fungi vary according to the habits of the insects, that those which reside in the earth, or in decayed vegetable matter, or bury themselves in damp moss, etc., generally become the bases of true fungi of the *Cordyceps* kind, while those which remain during some or the entire portion of their career exposed to the atmosphere, are usually affected by filamentous fungi of the genera *Isaria, Botrytis,*

Empusa, Stilbum, etc.   It may also be observed that
certain species of parasites never appear except on
particular species of insects, and even this depends
on the peculiar nature of the habits which they
assume at different periods of their existence, when
they become subject to a certain condition that is
highly necessary for the development of the parasite,
but these periods vary in the different orders : viz. in
Coleoptera it is during the larva and imago states ;
in Lepidoptera (nocturnal) during caterpillar, chrysalis, and imago ; in Hymenoptera during the pupa
and imago ; in Orthoptera during the imago ; in
Heteroptera during the imago ; in Homoptera during
the larva and pupa, and in one case only the imago ;
while in Diptera it takes place during the pupa (?)
and imago states.   Other circumstances also cause
the Entomophytes, in some countries, not to appear
for long intervals, even to the extent of several years,
though the insects which usually become their bases
may have numerously appeared, over and over again,
on the return of the usual allotted season of their
existence."   The drought, for example, is cited that
occurs in Australia after intervals of ten or twelve
years, and which prevails sometimes for a period of
two or more years, during which little or no rain
falls ; these may constitute the intervals that are
referred to as occurring between the times in which
fungoid parasites are found.

The geographical distribution of the insects which are at present (1858) known to become the bases of parasitical fungi varies in the different orders, and is exhibited in the following table :—

	Great Britain.	Europe.	Asia and Archipelago.	Africa.	Madagascar.	Australia.	Tasmania.	New Zealand.	North America.	South America.	West Indies.
Coleoptera ...	*	*			*			*	*	*	*
Lepidoptera ...	*	*	*			*	※	*	*	*	*
Orthoptera ...									*		
Hymenoptera ...	*	*	*	*						*	*
Heteroptera ...		*									
Homoptera ...								*	*		*
Diptera	*	*									
Arachnida ...	*								*		*

From this table it may also be perceived that the Lepidoptera, Coleoptera, and Hymenoptera of different localities are more suited by their habits of life to form the bases of parasitical fungi than any of the other orders of insects.

The foregoing remarks entirely refer to those parasites that germinate in the interior of insects. It will be necessary also to allude to those which have fungoid parasites adhering only to the outer surface of the living insect, of which, however, there are but few instances yet made known (since considerably augmented), and these are confined to species of the families *Brachinidæ, Gyrinidæ,* and *Staphylinidæ,* which reside either near to or in water. This circumstance leads one to suppose that aquatic or semi-aquatic habits are absolutely necessary for these insects to become the bases of the curious and extremely minute parasites which infest them.[1] These plants exhibit a very different formation, and thereby a total variation of habits, from all the other fungoid parasites. Water has in this case not only been the means by which the parasite became connected to any part of the outer surface of the insect, but it can scarcely be doubted to have afterwards assisted by its influence in the germination of the spores. It is generally thought to be one of the best means for the conveyance of the spores of some kinds of parasites (Algæ) into the interior of insects.

These remarks are concluded with the observation that "the results obtained from the histories of the various entomophytes seem to show that if the countries having humid primæval forests, or subjected to heavy rains, especially within the tropical portions of the world, were diligently searched by collectors, they would probably produce numerous examples of this curious phenomenon."

The Entomophthoreæ, which have been only of

---

[1] These observations which apply to the *Laboulbeniaceæ* would be modified in the face of modern additions to the family.

late the subject of special study, attack both larvæ
and pupæ, as well as imagines. In insects where the
larvæ and pupæ differ but slightly from the imago,
Mr. Thaxter observes that both these stages are
equally susceptible to the disease. He says that he
has seen one species that had developed upon
Hyphantria textor after pupation, but this occurrence
is certainly unusual. Amongst Lepidoptera he had
been surprised to find the imagines attacked in
numerous instances. Geometridæ, Noctuiidæ, and
Tineidæ may be affected, and he had even found
Colias philodice thus attacked. The species, or family,
of the host hitherto has been generally considered
a means of determining the species of parasite, in
most cases with some accuracy ; yet his observations
had shown that this is by no means the case, and
that specific distinctions, based largely upon the
character of the host, are of little value. The variety
of hosts attacked by a single species is sometimes
very great. In one instance (*E. sphærosperma*) he
had seen specimens upon larva of *Pieris*, on the
imago of *Colias*, Diptera of several families and
genera, *Phytonomus* larvæ (Coleoptera), the common
rosehopper, *Typhlocyba*, and *Aphis* (Hemiptera), on
ichneumons of several genera, and a small bee
(Hymenoptera), and on a species of *Thrips* (Thripidæ),
while in Europe it is recorded on *Limnophilus*
(Neuroptera).

In certain instances, where several of the Entomophthoreæ were found together, he had noticed two
species developed upon a single host. It is, therefore,
not always safe, where such proximity exists, to refer
the resting-spores that may occur in connection with
conidia to the same species of *Empusa*.

The habitat is also various. "Certain species are
found only by the margins of brooks in shady woods,
adhering to wet substances, such as moss, logs, stones,
etc., in the water, or along its margin, a constant
supply of moisture being apparently necessary for
their development. In other cases drier situations
are preferred, and the fungus readily withstands the
alternate dryness and moisture consequent upon the
variation of weather, producing its conidia repeatedly,
whenever the atmosphere was sufficiently moist, until
the conidia-bearers were exhausted. Many hosts,
before death, seek conspicuous positions, by crawling
upwards on grass, or other substances, whence the
conidia are discharged over a considerable area.
Perhaps the favourite position assumed by hosts
before death is upon the under side of leaves, in
shady situations, in woods, or about houses, where
a careful search during wet weather seldom fails
to disclose numerous examples. He had noticed
only one species which occurs on flowers attractive
to insects (namely, *E. muscæ*), which, although
common in all parts of houses, he had only seen in

nature on the flowers of *Solidago*, and certain *Umbelliferæ.*

"The period which ensues after the infection of a host until its death varies to some extent. In the larger hosts, such as flies or caterpillars, death may not take place for twelve days, although the usual period is from five to eight days. In minute hosts this period must be considerably shortened, owing to the ephemeral character of many forms known to be subject to the attacks of Entomophthoreæ. The first visible symptom of the disease is a general restlessness of the host. In caterpillars, for instance, the insect leaves its food-plant and wanders restlessly about; usually endeavouring to climb upwards before death, which is apparently quite sudden, and un-accompanied by contortions of the body. The host-insect thus remains clinging to the object on which it rests, or is fastened to it by rhizoids. Certain insects are fixed by the insertion of their probosces into the substratum on which they rest, as is the case with aphides. The house-fly is fastened by its proboscis, which adheres firmly to the substratum. Where rhizoids are developed, they often appear before the death of the host, and he had seen a geometrid moth, which was thus firmly attached to a pine needle, fluttering violently in its attempts to escape."[1]

[1] Thaxter, " Entomophthoreæ U.S.," p. 152.

HYMENOPTERA.

ANTS, WASPS, BEES, ETC.

SEVERAL families of Hymenoptera contain the hosts of particular species of Entomophytes, and in one instance at least (the "vegetating wasp") of considerable interest. In the family *Chrysididæ*, one of the species of *Chrysis*, from the Celebes, is spoken of as having minute parasites, which proceed from various parts of the thorax and abdomen, in the form of very minute, slender, semi-transparent filaments, with rounded heads, at the apex of each, of a yellow colour. It is impossible to say whether this is a *Cordyceps* or a *Stilbum*. "The insects are usually found in holes in rotten wood, which has been occupied by other insects, on which they, in their turn, are parasitic."[1]

"A species of *Pemphredon* is also named (forming part of the family *Crabronidæ*) as having been found in this country[2] attached to plants by a similar

---

[1] Gray, "Notices," p. 14.
[2] Stephens, *Proc. Ent. Soc.* (1851), ii. p. lxiv.

secretion to that which affects the common house-fly." This circumstance indicates some species of the *Entomophthoreæ*, which seem to be rare in their attacks upon *Hymenoptera*.

European Ant Club.

Cordyceps myrmecophila. Ces.[1]

This parasite was first recognized by Cesati on ants in Italy, and afterwards found in Northern Europe, North America, Ceylon, and Borneo. In Great Britain it has been found on an ichneumon, but apparently not upon ants. It attaches itself to the body, and is of very small size, with a long slender stem, not an inch in length, with an ovoid head. The whole plant is of a pale ochraceous white, and the internal structure conforms to that of *Cordyceps*, having long asci each containing thread-like sporidia, which break up into minute joints, from seven to eleven micro-millimetres long, and scarcely more than one broad. It has been reported that this species has occurred on some *Coleoptera*, but its original host was *Formica rufa* (fig. 6).

The examples named by Mr. Gray on species of

---

[1] Cesati, *Comm. Critt. Ital.* (1861), p. 61, pl. 4, fig. 2 ; Saccardo, " Sylloge," ii. No. 5010 ; Berk. and Br., *Ann. Nat. Hist.* (1851), No. 591.

Formica may be for the most part immature, or imperfect conditions of this Entomophyte. One, from St. Vincent,[1] is attached to a leaf by means of fungoid matter, while from between the hind part of the thorax and the fore part of the abdomen proceeds a very slender filament. In a second specimen, also attached to a leaf, a very long slender filament takes its rise from between the head and prothorax. The *Formica atriceps* from Santarem has a rather thick stem-like fungus from between the thorax and head above, which looks as if it were imperfect. A specimen of *Formica sexguttata* from Santarem, attached to a portion of a leaf by its abdomen and legs, bears, from the front of the head, above the labium, and from the prothorax, two slender filiform fungi; that of the latter is branched from the middle of its length, the ends gradually becoming very acute and hair-like. This latter may be an imperfect *Cordyceps*, or a species of *Isaria*, probably the latter, but from description it is impossible to say. These insects are described as neuters, residing chiefly in the nest, which they form underground, and wherein they perform all the labour of the community.

Fig. 6.—European Ant Club. *Cordyceps myrmecophila*, on ants (after Cesati).

---

[1] Gray, p. 14, pl. 4, fig. 7.

This species has some relationship to *Cordyceps Lloydii*, described hereafter, in the small terminal heads, but it differs from *C. unilateralis*, in which the capitulum is one-sided and attached to the stem above the middle, so that a pointed sterile continuation of the axis appears above the capitulum. In *C. australis* there is a sterile nodule about one-third down the stem, occupying the place of the capitulum in *C. unilateralis*, whilst the fertile head is oval and terminal. The two most nearly allied species, there-fore, are the present and *C. Lloydii*.

ONE-SIDED ANT CLUB.

Cordyceps unilateralis. Tul.[1]

This species was described by Tulasne from speci-mens in the Entomological Museum at Paris, growing upon *Atta (Formica) cephalotus*, collected by Trail in Brazil. It is also a very minute species, not more than half an inch in height, with a hemispherical head, attached on one side of the slender stem, about halfway up, so that the pointed apex of the stem rises above the head like a spur ; it is reddish turning

FIG. 7.—*Cordyceps unilateralis* on ant from Brazil.

---

[1] Tulasne, "Selecta Fungorum Carpologia," iii. p. 18, pl. 1, figs. 3, 4 ; Saccardo, "Sylloge," ii. No. 5027.

black, but paler in the upper portion. The one-sided capitulum is about the size of a split vetch-seed, the surface rough with the apices of the immersed perithecia (fig. 7). It has been stated[1] that this species occurred also on *Camponotus atriceps* in Brazil, on *Echinopta melanarctos* and *Polyrhachis merops* in the Celebes ; but the suggestion that it is the same species as the one described under the name of *Cordyceps Lloydii*, found on *Camponotus atriceps* in British Guiana, does not seem to be tenable.

BRAZILIAN ANT CLUB.

Cordyceps australis.   Speg.[2]

This rather peculiar little species was found upon *Pachycondyla* (*Formica*) *striata*, amongst moss on the trunks of trees, in Brazil, by Dr. Puiggari. The stem is about half a centimetre long, and purplish ; about one-third of the way down grows a small brownish sterile head, whilst the top of the stem is dilated into a subglobose or oval fertile head of a yellowish colour, smooth when fresh, but finely re-ticulated when dry. The internal structure is that

---

[1] *Ann. and Mag. Nat. Hist.* (1886), p. 317.

[2] Spegazzini, "Fungi Argentini," iv. p. 208 ; Saccardo, "Sylloge," ii. No. 5028.

which pertains to the genus, having immersed perithecia containing long asci, with thread-like sporidia breaking up into frustules, from five to ten micromillimetres long.

It will be observed that the characteristic specific difference relied upon in the diagnosis of this species is the peculiar sterile cauline nodule, which corresponds in position to the capitulum in *Cordyceps unilateralis.* The subglobose head, otherwise, would indicate a relationship to *C. myrmecophila.* It has never been figured, and we have seen no specimen. If only one specimen were found, it is just possible that it was an abnormal development of *C. unilateralis,* in which the perfection of the cauline capitulum was arrested, and a supplementary small capitulum at the apex followed the disturbance ; but this is merely a suggestion of possibility.

GRENADA ANT CLUB.

Cordyceps Sheeringii. Massec.[1]

A curious and unique little *Cordyceps* was collected by Colonel Sheering in Grenada, on the body of an ant, the clubs being gregarious, and springing from all

---

[1] Massee, in "Annals of Botany," vol. v. p. 510, fig. 4 (1890-91).

parts of the body. The stem is slender, flexuous, and not more than one centimetre high, bearing a globose capitulum, of an ochraceous colour, and not exceeding two millimetres in diameter (fig. 8, No. 1). The perithecia are immersed in the capitulum (Nos. 2, 3). But the great peculiarity of this species is that the cylindrical asci contain comparatively short, thread-like sporidia (60 × 1½ μ), which have only five septa, and not breaking up into joints, as in most other species (Nos. 4, 5).

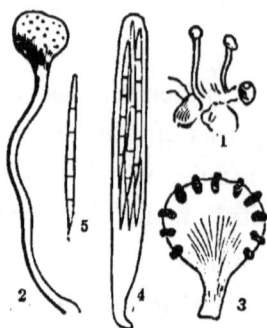

FIG. 8.—*Cordyceps Sheeringii* on ant from Grenada.

GUIANA ANT CLUB.

Cordyceps Lloydii. Fawcett.[1]

The occurrence of a new Entomophyte on ants has recently been recorded, with the following description : Stroma solitary, pale ochrey white, springing from the joints, head or capitulum depressedly globose, about one and a half millimetre broad, seated on a thread-like stem, which is thickened below the middle, about four and a half millimetres long, and about

[1] Fawcett, on an Entomogenous fungus, *Ann. Nat. Hist.* Oct. 1886, p. 316 ; Saccardo, " Sylloge," vol. supp., No. 7512.

half a millimetre thick below the middle, and a quarter of a millimetre at the top and bottom. Internal structure as in other species, but, the thread-like sporidia being immature, showed no tendency to separate into frustules. On the body of *Camponotus atriceps* by the river Puruni, in Guiana. "The ant has the appearance of having been attacked by the fungus while yet alive. The growth of the fine threads of the mycelium through the body

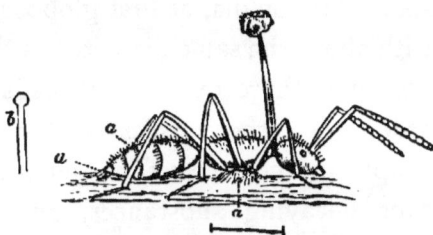

FIG. 9.—Guiana Ant Club. *Cordyceps Lloydii* (from "Annals of Natural History").

would gradually exhaust it, until at last they have grown out at the joints of the thorax and abdomen, and attached it to the leaf on which it was standing, while the capitate stroma has then grown up between the head and thorax " (fig. 9).

ANT MOULD.

Sporotrichum minimum. Speg.[1]

This snowy white mould was found upon the putrescent body of *Atta* (*Formica*) *Lundii* in a rotten

---

[1] Spegazzini, "Fungi Argentini," iv. No. 324; Saccardo, "Sylloge," iv. No. 506.

trunk in the Argentine Republic. It was effused over the insect, at first in a powdery and then a cottony white stratum, forming minute tufts. The threads were creeping and densely interwoven and branched, very slender, scarcely two micromillimetres in diameter, sparingly septate, and hyaline. The spores, or conidia, at first globose, then a little ovoid, with about the same diameter as the threads, scattered here and there over the threads, in no determinate order. All the species of these moulds are very simple in their structure, generally forming patches over decaying substances, and variable in colour, with minute spores, mixed indiscriminately with the slender threads. They are in no case destructive, but always saprophytes, and do not merit the title of parasites.

ANT STILBUM.

Stilbum formicarum. Cooke and Massee.[1]

A species of ant (*Formica*), the name of which is undetermined, has been sent from Victoria, in Australia, bearing upon its body a very pretty little *Stilbum* (plate 1, fig. 12), with elongated slender stems, from five to eight millimetres in length, black, and flexuous, slightly thickened towards the base, and

---

[1] Cooke and Massee, in *Grevillea*, vol. xviii. (1889), p. 8.

bearing at the apex an obovate rose-coloured capitulum or head, with elliptical conidia, ten micromillimetres long, and three broad.   The black stems and clavate rose-coloured head are very characteristic, forming a pretty little species, of which several occurred on the body of each dead insect.   The number of species of *Stilbum* found upon dead insects is confined to about four, of which *Stilbum Buquetii* has been longest known.   That species is found upon various dead insects, but the stem is not black or smooth, and the capitulum has a different form.   It is our impression that they are all of them saprophytic, but some species of *Stilbum* have been found to be related as conidial forms to sphæriaceous fungi.

European Wasp Club.

Cordyceps odyneri.   Quelet.[1]

Dr. Quelet has described an Entomophyte on the larva of *Odynerus* from the Vosges (fig. 10).   The stem is slender, from ten to twenty millimetres long, pruinose and pale grey, arising from a white mycelium. The head, or capitulum, ovoid and olive-grey.   Perithecia half immersed, and comparatively few.   Sporidia

---

[1] Quelet, 14th Supplement " Champignons de la France," p. 10, pl. 12, fig. 28 ; Saccardo, " Sylloge," vol. supp., No. 7513.

thread-like, and septate. This is a very minute species, and would be readily overlooked by a collector. Unfortunately many of the species of *Cordyceps* are almost the rarest amongst fungi, so that anything like a critical estimate of species cannot be undertaken in such a dearth of specimens. All that we can hope to do is to continue the record.

FIG. 10.—European Wasp Club. *Cordyceps odyneri* (af.er Quelet).

Gray has remarked that Mr. F. Smith found *Odynerus parietum* in Battersea Fields, having a fungus growing from the front of the prothorax. This intimation leaves us very much in the dark, and it would be assuming too greatly upon such evidence to suggest its being the present species ; nevertheless the fact may be kept in mind, to instigate further search in other localities.

VEGETABLE WASP.

Cordyceps sphecocephala.   Klotsch.[1]

Before proceeding with this parasite, it is advisable to attempt a rectification of names. The name under which it has pleased Professor Saccardo to record it is *Cordyceps sphecophila,*[2] but it is not the precise name

---

[1] Tulasne, " Selecta Fungorum Carpologia," iii. p. 17, pl. 1, figs. 5—9.
[2] Saccardo, " Sylloge," ii. No. 5015.

employed by Klotsch. When Mr. Berkeley described
this species,[1] he explained that the name attached
by Klotsch was *Sphæria sphecocephala*, which was
apparently a wrong transcription of Kunze's *sphærocephala;* but, as the name was a good one, he proposed
to retain it, and therefore described it as *Sphæria
sphecocephala*, which afterwards became *Cordyceps
sphecocephala*, the name adopted also by Tulasne.
We cannot approve of these changes in old names,
and in this instance do not hesitate to protest against
it, as an unwarrantable multiplication of synonymy,
whatever the excuse may be.

This species is a small one, rather tough, pallid,
with a long twisted stem, and a shortly
club-shaped head (fig. 11). The asci are
produced within perithecia immersed in
the head, and the long filiform sporidia
are septate, but do not so readily break
up into the short joints so usual in this
genus. It has been found on the
bodies of various species of *Vespa* and
Polybia in the West Indies and in South
America, and represents the rather celebrated "vegetable wasp" which had a
romantic history a century ago, some
particulars of which we shall record as a contribution

FIG. 11.—*Cordyceps
sphecocephala* on
wasp.

---

[1] Berkeley, in Hooker's *Journ. Bot.*

to a history of pseudo-scientific romance.   Edwards,[1] in his "Gleanings," gives the following narrative :—

"The vegetating wasps figured on the plate are from 'Apparato para la Historia Naturali Espanola,' in folio, Madrid, 1754.   I have inserted these figures and history as a companion to the vegetating insects in the foregoing plate.   The Spanish author, Father Torrubia, a Franciscan friar, has treated his subject extremely well, and as a man of letters, but yet it is not quite divested of some vulgar errors.   I remark this the rather as characters are necessary to be noted, when extraordinary phenomena are set forth.   I shall now proceed to his account, which seems to bear great analogy to the insect described in the immediately foregoing chapter.   'Being,' says Father Torrubia, 'at a gentleman's country seat, two leagues from the city of Havana, in New Spain, on the 10th of February, 1749, I found some dead wasps in the fields (however they were entire, the bodies, wings and all, and, indeed, were perfect skeletons).   From the belly of every wasp a plant germinated, which grows about five spans high.   The natives call this plant *Gia;* and as it is full of sharp prickles, their vulgar notion is that the said prickles owe their growth to the bellies of the wasps.'   The author further says he made many microscopical and other observations on them,

---

[1] Edwards, "Gleanings in Natural History," p. 265, pl. 336 (1758).

but does not relate what they were; however, he firmly believes the whole affair. This is his account. In his fourteenth plate he figures the wasps and plants, which I have copied in my plate, as shooting from their bodies, and springing from the earth. I am obliged to my friend, Mr. Emanuel Mendes da Costa, F.R.S., etc., for pointing out to me this curious insect, and translating this extract from the Spanish. Upon the whole of what is said by the Spanish author, I am of opinion that the insect he describes is no other than what I have figured in the foregoing chapter; for the Spaniards have not yet attained to any perfection in natural history, and I believe the good father might mistake the bunch of protuberant parts from the fungus for dried leaves."

This account is summarized in the "History of Insects,"[1] with the remark that "Edwards, in his work on birds, has copied the figures. They are represented as having taken possession of the plant, and are flying away with their booty attached to their bodies, though the original observer stated that he found them dead in the field." To which is added, that "some others were found in the island of Dominica; they had very much the appearance of the drone. After they buried themselves in May, they began to vegetate toward the end of July, or rather

---

[1] "History of Insects" (Murray's Family Library), ii. 296.

they are found so about that time.   When the tree
has arrived at its full growth it resembles a coral
branch about three inches high, bearing several little
pods, which are supposed by the inhabitants to
' drop off and become worms, and from thence flies.' "

In a note to his memoir, Mr. Gray thus described
the plate in question : " Torrubia, in his ' Apparato,'
gave a representation of two wasps lying on the
ground with a tree growing out of the base of the
abdomen, while three other wasps are flying round
the trees that are growing from the ground, having
a similar tree affixed to each insect.   Each tree is
furnished with numerous trifoliated leaves."

In an American work[1] we find a reference to these
instances of plant-insects, not indisposed to condone
the native romance.   "Westwood," it says, "states
that he has seen a species of *Clavaria*, both of the
undivided and branched kinds, which had sprung
from insects, and were four times larger than the
insects themselves.   In truth, it cannot then be
denied that Piso may not have seen a plant of a
proportionate magnitude which had likewise grown
out of a mantis.   The pupæ of bees, wasps, and
cicadas have been known to become the nidus of a
plant, to throw up stems from the front part of the
head, and change in every respect into a vegetable,

---

[1] Cowan's " Curious Facts," p. 91.

and still retain the shell and exterior appearance of
the parent insect at the root. Specimens of these
vegetated animals are frequently brought from the
West Indies. Mr. Atwood, in his account of
Dominica, describes a vegetable fly as follows : ' It
is of the appearance and size of a small cockchafer,
and buries itself in the ground, where it dies ; and
from its body springs up a small plant, resembling
a young coffee tree, only that its leaves are smaller.
The plant is often overlooked from the supposition
people have of its being no other than a coffee plant,
but on examining it properly the difference is easily
distinguished ; the head, body, and feet of the
insect appearing at the foot as perfect as when
alive.' [1] Also, it is added, that Dr. Colin, of
Philadelphia, has mentioned, on the authority of a
missionary, a 'vegetable fly' similar to the last
mentioned, on the Ohio River." [2]

Tulasne, under this species, quotes as authority
the description by Abraham Halsey,[3] in which he
refers to a specimen from Guadeloupe, communicated by Dr. Madianna, where he says "it is known
amongst the inhabitants by the name of *la guêpe
vegetale*, or vegetable wasp. The clavula rises somewhat flexuously, or spirally, and the capitulum,

---

[1] Smith's "Nature and Art," vol. x. p. 240.

[2] *American Philosophical Trans.*, vol. iii., Introduction.

[3] *Annals of the Lyceum of New York* (1824), p. 125.

instead of being globose, is ovate. The most remarkable particular, however, respecting this fungus is the fact communicated by Dr. Madianna, that he has noticed the wasp *still living* with its incumbrance attached to it, though apparently in the last stage of existence, and seeming about to perish from the influence of its destructive parasite."

"It may be doubted whether the vegetable ever predominates over the animal life while the vital principle of the latter is in full energy, but that the larvæ, in a feeble state, may have afforded a fit recipient for the seed of the fungus, while their complete evolution was retarded by some cause, until the final transformation of the insect, is certainly not improbable. In this respect they may offer some analogy with the entozoical worms, which are most commonly observed to prey upon animals of debilitated or languishing health. A congener of this fungus, and nearly allied to it, is also remarkable for selecting for its nidus the larvæ of insects. I am not aware that it has been found in circumstances to support the inference that it was the cause of the death of the larvæ."

In collecting all the scattered notes and references to this phenomenon, we become conscious of a great deal of repetition of the same observations under a different phraseology, as well as the expression of a variety of opinions and suggestions. Nevertheless,

on such an interesting subject, we have been desirous
of bringing together as much as we could of the
literature of the subject. It would hardly have
been anticipated that the article "Dry-rot" in a
Cyclopædia[1] would have yielded the following:
"Dry-rot occurs also in animals. Specimens of
Hymenopterous insects resembling wasps have been
brought from the West Indies, with a fungus growing
from between their anterior coxæ, and it is positively
asserted by travellers that the insects fly about whilst
burdened with the plant. Upon opening the bodies
of the wasps they are found filled with the mycelium
of the fungus, up to the orbits of the eyes and the
points of the tarsi, the whole of the intestines being
obliterated. In such cases it is to be supposed that
the mycelium of the *Sphæria* first kills the wasp by
compressing and drying up the body, and then,
continuing to grow, occupies the whole of the cavity
of the shell of the insect."

The following extract, however, is somewhat more
original than the rest: "An interesting account has
been given by a gentleman, who, while botanizing in
America,[2] found lying on the ground a wasp's nest,
which had, by some means unknown to him, been
separated from a branch of a laurel, near which it

---

[1] "Dry-rot" in English Cyclopædia (1854), ii. p. 395.
[2] Mitchell, *Silliman's Journal,* xii. p. 22 (1827).

had fallen. The creatures were in a strange condition after this disaster to their dwelling ; some were
flitting about over their cells, and by the softness of
their wings, and the faintness of their colours, were
easily known to have been hatched but a short time.
Many of them were lying dead on the ground, and
on examining these he instantly perceived vegetables
proceeding from their bodies, which were uniformly
attached to the thorax. He collected about fifty of
the vegetating wasps. On inspecting the nest, he
found a considerable proportion of the cells empty ;
this, however, was not the case with them all, for
there were still some that contained young wasps in
the state of larva (pupæ). He drew them from their
cells and satisfied himself that there was an incipient
vegetation, and moreover that its progress had kept
pace with the growth of the insect. Yet in some
instances the vegetation is considered to commence
only when life has ceased. In confirmation of this
opinion, it is related that in Trinidad a wasp was
found apparently in a perfect condition, glued somehow by one of its wings to a leaf of a tree. From
all parts of its body issued filaments from one to
three inches long ; they were shining black, and
resembled the plant called Spanish beard." [1]

---

[1] "History of Insects" (Murray's Family Library), vol. ii. p. 298
(1838).

In illustration of the foregoing extract, Mr. Gray adds, " The nest of this insect is composed of finely gnawed wood, which is reduced by the insect to a kind of paste, and then is formed into a nest of a variable number of hexagonal cells, the number depending on the number of insects forming the community. The cells are arranged in a single tier; and after numerous cells are constructed the nest itself partakes also of a hexagonal shape. As the tier is not enveloped in an outer case, as is usual with other wasps, the openings of the cells are entirely unprotected, and are thereby exposed to the atmosphere. It is in these open cells that the insect resides during the first two periods of its existence, but it is during the larva-state that the minute germs of fungi may get conveyed to the insect with its food,[1] which consists of vegetable matter, as the insects have been found with an incipient vegetation previous to leaving the cells. These nests often become saturated and detached by the heavy tropical rains, as they are only united sideways to the small branch of a tree by a slender pedicle, and thus fall on the decayed vegetables that clothe the ground of the primæval forests of tropical

---

[1] Mr. Mitchell thinks that under particular circumstances the body of the insect, while yet alive, becomes the soil or base upon which vegetables fasten themselves, and from which they derive support (*Silliman's Journal*, xii. p. 23).

E

countries, which may assist the growth of the parasite."

There is a figure published in the *Gardener's Chronicle* for 1882,[1] which is of interest. All the account of it is contained in the following words. Alluding to *Cordyceps sphecocephala*, it says, "This

FIG. 12.—Wasp with *Cordyceps* (from *Gardener's Chronicle*).

fungus seems to have no place at present in the lists of British fungi, yet it seems probable that the fungus now exhibited, growing from the body of a bee, is no other than that species." It exhibits several slender clubs growing from different parts of the body, certainly bearing some resemblance in form to the typical *C. sphecocephala* (fig. 12).

We return now to the figures given of this entomophyte, in addition to those already alluded to. That in Mr. Gray's memoir, which occurred on *Polistes americana* from the West Indies,[2] calls for no special remark. The other, on *Polistes rubiginosus* from St. Vincent,[3] is precisely the same species. The *Polistes mexicana* from Trinidad bears something evidently different, but what it is impossible to say. Dr. Madianna relates that it was "in an apparently perfect

---

[1] *Gardener's Chronicle*, March 18, 1882, p. 377, fig. 57.
[2] Gray, pl. 4, fig. 6.   [3] Gray, pl. 4, fig. 4.

condition, glued somehow, by one wing only, to a leaf of a tree. From all parts of its body issued filaments from one to three inches long. They were wholly different from the *Sphæria*, being black, shining, and resembling the plant called Spanish beard, or *Tillandsia usneoides.*" [1]

There is the same uncertainty about the following: " A specimen of *Polistes* is contained in Westwood's collection,[2] having two fungi about two inches long proceeding from the under part of the thorax, one of which has an ovate head at the apex, of a pale-green colour. The insect is imperfect, and has become black, probably from the effect of the fungus. Another imperfect specimen of this genus is represented,[3] having short branched fungi at the base of the wings. Both these examples are too imperfect to apply any specific names to them, but they were no doubt brought from Tropical America." The fungus on the latter is possibly an imperfect *Cordyceps sphecocephala.*

HUMBERT'S WASP CLUB.

Cordyceps Humberti. Rob.[4]

Recognizing the differences between the entomo-

---

[1] Gray, p. 15. [2] Gray, pl. 5, fig. 6. [3] Gray, pl. 4, fig. 5.
[4] Tulasne, " Selecta Fungorum Carpologia," iii. p. 18; Saccardo, "Sylloge," ii. No. 5045.

phyte found on *Icaria cincta* from Western Africa,
and those on the wasps of the West Indies, Robin
separated them as distinct species, which was afterwards recognized by Tulasne. In illustration of
this species, the figure is cited which appeared in
Saussure's work,[1] reproduced by Mr. Gray in his
memoir (pl. 4, fig. 3), which is thus described : Some
of the clubs short and stout, thickened upwards into
an ovate oblong, rough capitulum; others slender and
much elongated, ending in a small ovate capitulum
(fig. 13).   " The insect," says Mr. Gray, " is also in the
imago state, and it is the first African insect that has
been observed to form the basis of a parasitical plant.
It is most remarkable for bearing apparently two
kinds of fungi.   One, which is represented by two

FIG. 13.—Humbert's Wasp Club. *Cordyceps
Humberti* (after Saussure).

examples only, proceeds
singly from the base of
each wing; they are short,
rather   thick,   with   a
prominent   club-formed
termination.   The other
kind consists of four rather long and very slender
filaments, arising from the third joint of the abdomen.
Each filament has a slight indication of a club-like
termination, apparently trifoliated ; they are altogether
different from those at the base of the wings, yet

---

[1] Saussure, " Mon. Vesp. Soc.," p. 39, pl. 5, fig. 9.

they may be the same fungus under a different manner of growth. The insect has retained its proper colour, and is affixed longitudinally to the branch by means of its tarsi and the apex of its abdomen."

Orange Wasp Isaria.

Isaria Saussurei, pro tem.

The entomophyte figured by Saussure[1] on *Polistes americana,* and reproduced by Mr. Gray in his "Notices,"[2] is probably the *Isaria* condition of *Cordyceps sphecocephala,* and which represents the insect "attached longitudinally to a branch by means of the tarsi; it wants the wings, although it is in the imago state. The parasite proceeds from the joints of the upper surface of the thorax and abdomen, in the form of numerous slender filaments from two lines to three quarters of an inch in length. The thorax and abdomen are black, except at the tip of the latter, which is red, while the plant is of an orange colour. It is stated by M. Saussure to have been brought from the Antilles and Cayenne."[3] The simple fact of its form and orange colour is insufficient to give this parasite a proper diagnosis in the

---

[1] Saussure, "Vesp. Soc.," pl. 11, fig. 5.
[2] Gray, pl. 4, fig. 2.   [3] Gray's "Notices," p. 14.

genus *Isaria;* but as no microscopical examination can be made, the only resort is to place it under a provisional name (fig. 14).

Still more uncertainty prevails as to the position of that entomophyte which led Felton[1] to describe its host as a new species of wasp under the name of *Vespa crinita.* This, again, has the appearance of an *Isaria,* and may, after all, be only an imperfect condition of the above, but it is impossible to settle such questions by guessing. In this instance it was also *Polistes americana* which was the host.

It was furnished with very long and extremely

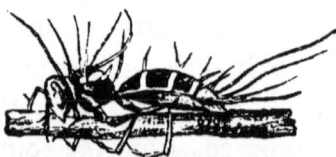

FIG. 14.—Orange Wasp Isaria, *Isaria Saussurei* (after Saussure).

slender filaments, that proceeded from the various sutures of the head and thorax, and from the joints of the abdomen and legs. They are of various lengths, being longest on the head, thorax, and abdomen. Felton says that all the hairs are of a light-brown colour, and seem to be stiff, but their ends are quite soft, like papillæ, and from thence thicker. These are sometimes, it is said, found in clusters of many individuals matted together.

---

[1] Felton, *Philos. Trans.*, vol. liv. p. 54, pl. 6.

Hornet Club.

Cordyceps Ditmari.   Quelet.[1]

This entomophyte was found, and described, by Dr. Quelet, in 1877, on the body of a wasp in the Jura, and was considered by M. Cornu to be the perfect condition of *Isaria sphecophila ;* but, as having a distinct appearance to the entomologist, we have kept them distinct.   The head, or capitulum, is ovoid, three to four millimetres thick, of a yellow straw colour, with a flesh-coloured tinge, dotted with the purple ostiola of the immersed perithecia.   The stem is slender, and either simple or forked, pale lemon yellow, darker at the base.   The splitting off of the cuticle forms a double fringed collar round the stem in some cases.   The internal structure is that usual in the genus, and the long thread-like sporidia separate into slender, rod-like joints about twelve micromilli- metres long (fig. 15).

FIG. 15.—Hornet Club. *Cordyceps Ditmari* (after Quelet).

---

[1] " Quelques espèces de Jura " (1877), p. 330, pl. 6, fig. 14 ; Sac-cardo, " Sylloge," ii. No. 5024.

BORNEAN ENTOMOPHYTE.

Cordyces gentilis.   Cesati.[1]

This entomophyte is noteworthy as having been found in Borneo on some sphæcoideous host, stem very variable in length according to the depth at which the matrix was deposited, being very long when amongst chips, fragments, and refuse, always slender and flexuous, becoming black, smooth, terminating in a cylindrical head or capitulum, one centimetre and a half long and two millimetres thick, rather acute at the apex, and very pale tan-coloured, dotted with the darker ostiola, or mouths of the immersed perithecia.

Another Bornean species is very doubtful, as it is uncertain whether it was entomogenous or not. (*Cordyceps adpropinquans.* Cesati.[2]) It seems to have been described from a figure only, and is said to have been cæspitose, branched at the base, and of the colour of *Cordyceps militaris*, with a pale-grey stem.

HORNET ISARIA.

Isaria sphecophila.   Ditm.[3]

This is the conidial form, possibly, of some *Cordy-*

---

[1] Cesati, "Myceti Borncensis" (1879), p. 14 ; Saccardo, "Sylloge," ii. No. 5020.

[2] Cesati, " Myc. Born.," p. 14 ; Saccardo, "Sylloge," ii. No. 5056.

[3] Ditmar, "Deut. Crypt. Fl.," t. 57 ; Fries, "Sys. Myc.," iii. ; Saccardo, "Sylloge," iv. No. 2787.

ceps, and M. Cornu has expressed the opinion that
it is *Cordyceps Ditmari* of Quelet, but as yet this is
only conjecture. It is gregarious in habit, the
stroma consisting of very long, rigid, thread-like
prolongations, of a pale umber colour, smooth towards
the base, nodulose in the middle, and attenuated
towards the apex, and somewhat downy, sprinkled
with the naked conidia, and of a greyish colour. The
conidia themselves are large for the genus, elliptical,
ten micromillimetres long, tinged with brown. The
figure given by Dr. Gray [1] certainly belongs to this
species, but he does not say if it was found in Britain ;
only that it "occurred on the well-known Hornet, or
Vespa crabro, which was taken out of rotten wood
during summer, being attached to the under surface of
the thorax and abdomen, in a series of filiform fungi,
measuring from two and a half to near four inches in
length, gradually becoming acute at the tips, while at
an inch from the base is a knot-like projection from
which the remaining portion of each of the stems
seems to spring."

SAW-FLY ENDOPHYTE.

Empusa tenthredinis. Fresenius.[2]

This is apparently a rare species, both in Europe

---

[1] "Notices," pl. 4, fig. 8.

[2] Fresenius, "Ueber die Entomophthora," p. 205, figs. 51-58 ;
Thaxter, " Entomophthoræ U.S.," p. 162, pl. 15, figs. 49-55.

and in the United States. Mr. Thaxter found it early
in September upon a small *Tenthredo* larva, feeding
upon *Scutellaria*, in a swampy situation among woods.
The larva when found was hanging flaccid by its
prolegs, and the conidial threads were just beginning
to emerge in small tufts over its body (plate 4, fig.
42).   The conidia are broadly ovoid, tapering slightly
towards the apex, and with a prominent, rather narrow
papillate base (25 × 35 to 35 × 55μ).   Fertile
threads simple, coalescing over the host.   Secondary
conidia like the primary.   Resting-spores unknown.
In this species the insect is attached to the matrix by
its legs.

APIDÆ.

THE BEE FAMILY.

Mr. Gray thus slightly notices bee diseases :
"The family *Apidæ*[1] may here be referred to, as
the larvæ of British bees, covered with a fungoid
parasite, have been discovered by Mr. F. Smith
while digging into their nests, which they form
either in wooden posts or in banks of earth.   They
have, however, been more particularly found so
affected in the colonies of *Anthophora acervorum.*

---

[1] Gray's " Notices," p. 15.

This latter insect forms in chalk-pits a nest of such amazing extent, that in the middle of April a dark flickering shadow is cast on the ground from the countless insects assembled."

Subsequently, however, a more explicit notice was appended, to the effect that Mr. Timpron Martin, of Liverpool, records [1] that three hives were placed in a dry attic in October; each hive was enveloped in a piece of calico, the four corners of which were brought together over it, and thus formed a loop, by which it was suspended from the ceiling. This mode of treatment is supposed to have given more air to the bees in the interior than they could have had through the summer, while the hive was placed on a stand. The hives were taken down about the 14th of March; the bees in two of them were found to be in a healthy state, but all the bees in the third hive were dead. In the last-mentioned hive there was abundance of honey when it was opened, and it was clear that its inmates did not die from want; but it was noticed that there was an appearance of mould on the combs. It was thought that the bees might have died during the early part of February, but they were certainly alive in the hive in January.

---

[1] *Proc. Liverpool Lit. and Phil. Soc.*, 1857–8; *Proc. Linn. Soc.*, 1858; *Ann. and Mag. Nat. Hist.*, 1858, p. 387.

The Rev. H. Higgins supposed that the bees might probably have died from the growth of a fungus, and he obtained some of the bees for examination, which were transmitted in a dry state, and were found, by means of a lens, to have no indications of vegetable growth. On examining, however, a portion under a microscope, the head and thorax were clean; but a portion of the sternum had innumerable very minute linear, slightly curved bodies, showing the well-known oscillatory or swarming motion. In the abdomen of several bees, which showed no external appearance of the growth of any parasite, there was obtained an abundance of well-defined globular bodies, resembling the spores of a fungus. No trace of a mycelium was visible; the plants had come to maturity, fruited, and withered away, leaving only the spores. But it appears uncertain whether these spores were developed before or after the death of the bees.[1] This can have no relationship with the "foul brood," hereafter described, although the disease may have been caused by some other of the *Schizomycetes*, which have probably more to do with the diseases of the lower animals than we have hitherto given them credit for.

---

[1] Gray's "Notices," p. 22.

EUGLOSSA PARASITES.

It is difficult also to account for, or determine, the curious parasites found on the bodies of two species of *Euglossa*.[1] It was stated that from the basal portion an elongated portion was produced, which was bent backwards, and rested on the dorsum of the abdomen; in one of the specimens the appendage was divided at the extremity into two branches (fig. *a*), and in the other it was dilated into two uniform lobes (fig. *b*). Professor West-

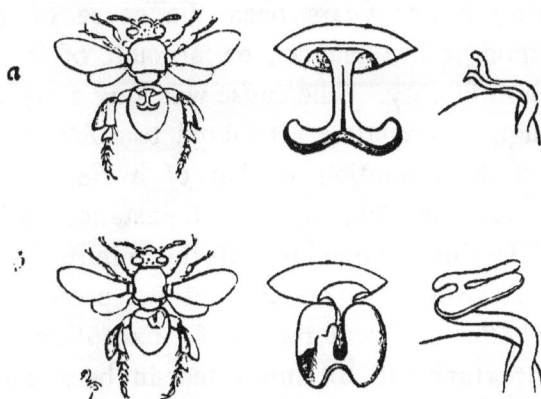

FIG. 16.—Parasites on *Euglossa* (after Westwood).

wood thought them to be most probably vegetable substances in different stages of development. Pos-

---

[1] *Trans. Ent. Soc. London* (1841-43), vol. iii. p. 4, pl. 6, figs. 1, 2; Tulasne, " Fungi Sel. Carp.," iii. p. 20.

sibly they were Orchid pollinia. These specimens
were exhibited at one of the meetings of the Entomological Society.

Foul Brood.

Bacillus alvei.   Cheshire.[1]

It has been claimed for "foul brood" in bees that
the disease is one of great antiquity, having, presumably, been referred to by ancient writers as early
as the Christian era. Whether this be so or not, it
has during recent years been the cause of great
alarm amongst bee-keepers, on account of its pre-
valence and fatality. The cause was long a mystery,
and though at one time attributed to a *Micrococcus*,
the latest determination is that of a *Bacillus*. It
was not our intention, in the first instance, to have
included in this volume any of the minute *Schizomycetes*, parasitic upon insects, but the present case
seems to offer sufficient reasons for exception, in its
great importance to all interested in bees, that a
short account appeared to be indispensable.

The *Schizomycetes* occupy a kind of border-land
on the outer edge of fungi, and their importance in
animal diseases is only beginning to be properly

---

[1] Cheshire and Cheyne, "Disease of Hive-bee known as Foul
Brood," in *Journ. Roy. Mic. Soc.* (1885), vol. v. p. 581.

recognized; but no one can predicate their future history, and their widely extended influence over the health and life of humanity, as well as of the lower animals. Already six hundred and fifty described species are recorded in systematic works, and their number increases nearly every day. They are characterized as destitute of mycelium, typically one-celled, extremely minute, variable in form, multiplying indefinitely by subdivision, and having two forms of spores. When it is said that they include the species of *Bacillus*, *Bacterium*, and *Micrococcus*, it will be admitted that their study verges upon the infinitely minute, and equally important factors in life, health, and disease.

Foul brood has created such havoc amongst bees, that we find one bee-master lamenting that in 1848 "a fearful pestilence made its appearance in my apiary, which spread so fast that it contaminated every stock and artificial swarm that I possessed." He lost in one year more than five hundred stocks from the foul brood. Another note of alarm was sounded in this country in 1870, when it made its appearance amongst the bees of a large bee-master,[1] who thus gave expression to his dismay : " At first I could not tell what was amiss, for the bees became quite dispirited. If any were seen working, it was

---

[1] *Gardener's Chronicle*, Oct. 9, 1875, p. 459.

only with a lazy kind of effort which seemed to indicate disease. I then removed those which were infected to a distance of nearly three miles, thinking it was possible to save them ; but I had my trouble for nothing, for they gradually dwindled away, until before the autumn all became so weak that I buried both hives and bees, to stop the spread of the foul brood. I find, from experiments, that if a healthy colony is fed with honey from a diseased stock, they will be quickly infected. Again, the disease is spread more by robbing than all other causes com- bined. When a stock is weak, the neighbouring colonies, as well as those at a distance of a mile or so around, will prey upon it ; but if a few bees from an infected stock are placed in a healthy hive, they seem to carry the infection with them, although they are strong and healthy ; but we must bear in memory it is the young brood in the cells which become diseased and putrefy, and not the old bees. Some authors have proposed to remove the queens, and, thus preventing breeding, the disease could not spread from hive to hive. The better plan is to destroy the stock if they are diseased. It is a hope- less task to attempt to cure them by any means ; they only make matters worse by keeping them on the stand. . . . Many causes have been assigned for this disease. Some talented and thoughtful bee- keepers have supposed it was caused at first by the brood being chilled ; thus dying, they decay in the cells, and become a putrefying mass. This theory has long disappeared. Microscopical science has revealed the true secret, which is a kind of mould (fungus), the spores from which may float about in the atmosphere, and when they find a suitable nidus they speedily generate the foul brood, so called. . . . We must not forget that the disease infects the brood in the cells, inducing putrefaction, thus causing a most intolerable stench to issue from the diseased hive. The cells are filled with a dark-coloured, half-liquid mass, resembling treacle."

Soon after this period investigations were being pursued in Germany with the view of discovering the immediate cause of foul brood and its cure. One of the most prominent names was that of Dr. Schön-feld, who thought that a species of *Micrococcus* was the cause of the mischief. This, therefore, was a summary of the conclusions derived at that time : " Since Dr. Prensz and Vogel have given the decided assurance that there are always found Micrococci in foul brood, and since I have practically proved that healthy brood can be infected by Micrococci, so can there be no longer doubt that where foul brood appears as an epidemic, there the infection is pro-duced, and carried into effect by *Micrococcus*."

This was the position in 1885, when Cheshire and Cheyne demonstrated the cause of the disease to rest

F

chiefly with a *Bacillus* which they denominated
Bacillus alvei. The following summary[1] of their
observations will exhibit the grounds for this conclusion : If a comb be removed from near the centre
of a healthy hive during the summer months, its
cells will normally be filled with eggs, larvæ, and
pupæ, in every stage of development. The eggs, as
left by the ovipositor of the queen or mother, adhere
commonly by the end to the base of the cells they
occupy, and, favoured by the high temperature constantly maintained within the hive, the germinal
vesicle at about the end of three days matures into
a larva ready for hatching. These eggs are liable to
the disease even before they leave the body of the
mother, but most careful microscopic examination
is needful to make this apparent. On the contrary,
the larvæ, which are constantly fed by the workers,
so change in appearance soon after infection, that
a practised eye at once detects the presence of the
disease. Whilst healthy their bodies are of a beautiful pearly whiteness, lying, at first floating, in the
abundant pabulum the nurses are ever at hand to
supply. As they grow they curl themselves at the
bottom of the cells until these become too strait for
their occupants, which now advance the head to be
in readiness for the cocoon-spinning which follows

---

[1] *Journ. Roy. Mic. Soc.*, August, 1885, p. 582.

upon the close of the eating stage. When the disease strikes the larvæ, they move uneasily in their cells, and often then present the dorsal surface to its mouth, so that mere posture is no insufficient evidence of an unhealthy condition. The colour changes to yellow, passing on by degrees towards a pale brown, whilst the skin becomes flaccid and opaque ; death soon occurs, when the body, now

FIG. 17.—Honeycomb with foul brood (after Cheshire and Cheyne).

shrunken by evaporation, lies on the lower side of the cell, increasing in depth of tone, until in a few days nothing more than a nearly black scale remains. Should the larvæ, however, escape contamination until near the period of pupahood, they are sealed over in the usual way by a cover made of pollen grains and wax, which is pervious to the air. The cover furnishes a screen, on which part of the cocoon is soon after spread, but the inhabitant of the cell is marked out for death, and before very long the capping or sealing sinks and becomes concave, and in it punctures of an irregular character appear, and this is nearly conclusive sign of the diseased condition of the colony. The sense of smell is also appealed to, as a peculiar, very offensive, and extremely characteristic odour now escapes from the diseased combs. The bees in addition lose energy, but become unusually active in ventilating their hive by standing at the door, heads towards home, and flapping their wings persistently, so that a strong out-current, and, as a necessary consequence, a corresponding in-draught, are set up. Should any attempt be made at removing a dead larva, which has assumed a deep-brown tint, its body, tenaciously adhering to the cell wall, will stretch out into long and thin strings like half-dried glue. The disease is terribly infectious, and once started, soon spreads from cell to cell, and not unfrequently from stock to stock.

Should a speck of this tenacious coffee-coloured matter be examined by a quarter-inch, it would be found to contain countless swarms of very minute bodies, which dance in the field with a pronounced Brownian movement. These have been supposed to be Micrococci in consequence of some reported experiments made in Germany by Dr. Schönfeld. Mr. Cheshire endeavoured to repeat those experiments. The results showed that in foul-broody matter no Micrococci necessarily existed, that the disease could not be communicated easily to flies, as alleged, but that every dead larva of the fly contained Micrococci innumerable, and that when bee-larvæ were artificially infected with foul-broody matter, the bacillus nature of the disease was incontestable, while no *Micrococcus* could be discovered.

We need not follow the details of the experiments, which are on record, but confine ourselves to results. It had always been assumed that the disease affected larvæ only, but this was found to be an error. Amongst other examinations was a bee. " The stomach and colon were exceedingly small, and the amount of fluid I could obtain truly microscopic ; but this was full of active bacilli, of the same size and character I had previously discovered in the larvæ." Continuing the investigation, he found "that a large proportion of imago workers and drones die of this disease if they are raised in infected stocks," and, what is of equal importance, that the ovaries of queen-bees contained the bacilli in more or less profusion.

The means by which the disease is propagated are also detailed, in the paper in question, which, with the means of cure, appeal rather to the bee-keeper than the general reader. "Microscopists will have no difficulty in accepting the idea of these organisms being carried about in air-currents, when it is remembered that a single cubic inch of material would form a quadruple line of these bacilli from London to New York. Ordinary dust-motes are to such organisms as hen's eggs to sand-grains. Nor is their multitude less remarkable than their minuteness. He had examined many larvæ, which must at least have contained 1,000,000,000 ; so that the means by which they are disseminated must be altogether too varied." On the question of infection Mr. Cheshire says, "Although I would not dogmatize, my strong opinion is that commonly neither honey nor pollen carry the disease, but that the feet and antennæ of the bees usually do. I also think it probable that, occasionally at least, nurse-bees infected bring the disease-germs to the mouth in feeding the larvæ, and then, turning foragers, leave a germ or germs on the nectary of a flower, which, visited by another bee, becomes the means of infection to it. The malady is thus carried into other, and perhaps somewhat distant, apiaries."

As to cure, phenol is recommended. This was mingled with ordinary sugar syrup of a density most suitable for feeding purposes in the proportion of one to five hundred by weight of the syrup, and this was then poured into the comb in which brood was being raised. The nurse-bees immediately accepted the medicated food, and as a result the malady in the very worst cases disappeared, the exceptions being those in which the queen herself was badly diseased.

As to the bodies themselves which constitute this fungus, the bacilli are stated to measure about three and a half micromillimetres in length, and about one in breadth, rounded or slightly tapering at the ends, often with a clear space near one end. The spores are described as oval, and somewhere about two by one micromillimetres in size. The production of spores from the rods or bacilli is thus decribed: "The first thing noticeable is that the rod begins to swell, and becomes spindle-shaped. This swelling, which generally affects the middle of the rod, but may in some cases be most marked towards one end, increases in size, and the centre of the swelling gradually ceases to take on the stain. The capsule of the spore apparently also is formed within the rod, and is not merely the outer part of the rod. In three or four hours the rod is seen to have almost or completely disappeared, leaving the spore lying free, or within the faint outline of the original bacillus."

COLEOPTERA.

BEETLES.

SEVERAL species of Cordyceps have been found on beetles of the different families in this order, and especially the *Melolonthidæ*, on larvæ and imagines; and, in some instances, the presumed conidial or *Isaria* forms. We have only attempted approximately to follow the arrangement of families, in which entomologists will be most interested, and this process they will be able to continue for themselves. *Laboulbenia* is also represented by some of the oldest species in that genus of external parasites, which do not culminate in the destruction of their host, and some species of more recent date. Of the true entomophytal moulds, belonging to the *Entomophthoreæ*, this order has a limited share; the perfect insects offering great resistance to their attacks, by reason of their hard covering, are less subject than those of other orders, but even these have not altogether escaped. A few accidental moulds, which are superficial, or confined to dead insects, have been added, but with no other claim but their habitat for their introduction.

GREY BEETLE CLUB.

Cordyceps cinerea. Tul.[1]

Some species of *Carabus* has, in France, been attacked by a *Cordyceps*, described by Tulasne under the above name. The larvæ, as well as the perfect insects, are reported to have been observed with this parasite upon them. The stems are flexuous and linear, dark brown at the base, but pale grey above, and very long, with an acute branchlet about the middle, and the apex swollen into an ovoid, or nearly globose head or capitulum, about the size of a pea, of a rather violet-grey colour, and smooth. The enclosed sporidia are of the usual thread-like character, breaking up into short truncate joints, six to eight micromillimetres long, and from one and a half to two thick.

"The larvæ and perfect insects of this family reside beneath stones, under the bark of trees, between clods of earth, in decaying vegetables, and in moss growing at the base of trees (plate 1, fig. 6). They undergo their final metamorphosis in the

---

[1] Tulasne, "Selecta Fungorum Carpologia," iii. 16, pl. 1, fig. 11; Saccardo, "Sylloge," ii. No. 5026.

autumn; on the approach of winter they hibernate in moss until the return of spring, when they may be seen wandering about paths, etc., in search of their prey, which consists of herbivorous larvæ and beetles."

It has been affirmed that a larva, possibly of a species of *Carabus*,[1] was discovered on the Pyrenees, about two thousand four hundred feet above the sea-level, with *Cordyceps entomorrhiza* growing upon it, but this identification cannot be confirmed.

BEETLE ISARIA.

Isaria eleutheratorum.   Nees.[2]

One of the numerous species of *Isaria* has been credited with parasitism on the dead bodies of some species of *Carabus*, but whether it is the conidial form of *Cordyceps cinerea* or not, is still undetermined. This fungus grows in tufts, the component filaments of which are thread-like, twisted and compressed, with short branches, the whole being whitish, and powdery or downy. The upper portion becomes powdered with the ovoid conidia, which are produced, naked, at the tips of the delicate hyphæ which compose the stroma, and are from six to

---

[1] Lucas, *Ann. Soc. Entom. de France* (1849), vii. p. 40; Robin, "Veg. Par.," p. 661.

[2] Nees, "System der Pilze," p. 86, fig. 84; Saccardo, "Sylloge," iv. No. 2789; Saccardo, "Fung. Ital.," pl. 844.

seven micromillimetres long, by three and a half broad. It has been found in France, Germany, and Italy. Vahl[1] records that the imago of *Carabus hortensis* had been found dead, and in a state of decay, whilst to the mouth, thorax, side of the sternum, at the joints of the legs, and at the joints of the abdomen, were attached a species of *Clavaria*, for which he proposed the name of *Clavaria setiformis*. There is every reason to suppose that it was only the *Isaria* above named. It must be remembered that the main distinction between *Isaria* and *Cordyceps* consists in the former producing only minute naked spores, or conidia, on the external surface; and in the latter the fructification consists of long thread-like sporidia, in asci, which latter are enclosed in cysts, or perithecia, imbedded, or partially imbedded, in the substance of the clubs. It is easy to determine them in the specimens themselves, but not always so easy from figures, deficient in detail.

WHIP-END BEETLE HANGER.

Laboulbenia nebriæ. Peyritsch.[2]

Found on the elytra and abdomen of *Nebria*

---

[1] Vahl, "Naturhist. Selsk. Skrivt." (1792), ii. p. 50.
[2] Peyritsch, "Mon. Laboulbenia," p. 445, fig. 29; Saccardo, "Sylloge," vol. viii. No. 3613.

brunnea and *Nebria villæ* in Austria. The whole length of the parasite, exclusive of the long appendages, is three hundred micromillimetres. It becomes black; the perithecia are oblong, darkest upwards; appendages, or pseudo-paraphyses, of unequal length—the larger ones simple or forked, with many articulations, brown, and many times longer than the perithecia (to 700μ long), the smaller ones shorter than the perithecia, with a terminal and lateral branch, and curved (plate 3, fig. 31). Comparing this species with all the other known forms, it may readily be distinguished by the long arms, or appendages, often erect, and either single, or only forked near the base, which give to the parasite a most distinct appearance. What are the peculiar functions of these appendages, whether short or long, in any of the species, is at present unknown; but, in some form or other, they seem to be always present, although sometimes reduced to a very rudimentary condition. They cannot be confounded with what are termed *paraphyses* in ordinary ascigerous fungi.

COMMON BEETLE HANGER.

Laboulbenia Rougetii.   M. and R.[1]

Mr. Gray has observed that three species of the

---

[1] *Ann. Soc. Entom. de France* (1849), vii. p. 40; 1850, p. 51, pl. 3, fig. 1.

genus *Brachinus,* namely, *Brachinus crepitans, Brachinus sclopeta,* and *Brachinus explodens,* have been found by M. Rouget, during spring and autumn, to be infected, while living, on the surface of their antennæ, thorax, elytra, and legs, with a very curious minute yellow-coloured fungus, which has been named *Laboulbenia Rougetii.*[1] M. Rouget says they are obtained on the mountains in the environs of Dijon, in dry as well as in low and moist places.

The genus is a very singular one, and its affinities are still somewhat doubtful, although belonging to the *Ascomycetes.* Altogether there are about thirty-four species, with twenty-five others closely related, and all parasitic on living insects. The perithecium, or fertile cell, or conceptacle, is teat-like at the apex, and pierced with a pore, through which the sporidia are discharged ; it is seated upon a rather thick stem, which is two-celled below and many-celled above. Curious arm-like bodies, called pseudo-paraphyses, accompany the perithecia externally. The perithecia themselves contain the hyaline sacs, or asci, which hold the spindle-shaped, two-celled colourless sporidia. This is a brief outline of their structure as a genus.

The present species is about two hundred and fifty

---

[1] Montagne and Robin, *Ann. Sci. Nat.* (1849), p. 233 ; Robin, " Veg. Par.," p. 622, pl. 8, figs. 1, 2 ; Saccardo, "Sylloge," viii. No. 3695.

or three hundred micromillimetres long, somewhat top-shaped, and deep yellowish brown, with a triangular, or rather an obconical, black nodule at the base, by which it is attached to the insect. The appendages at the side, or pseudo-paraphyses, are simple or slightly branched, jointed, and pale yellowish (about fifty micromillimetres long). The sporidia are spindle-shaped and bicellular, with a thick outer wall (about sixty micromillimetres long). The structure will be better understood by reference to a figure. It is probably found elsewhere beside France and Germany, but being small has evidently escaped notice.

These entomophytes, carried about on the bodies of living insects, adhere to them by means of the discoid base. There is no mycelium, or rooting filaments, and no evidence of any penetration of the surface of the insect, so that they are purely and essentially superficial; and whatever inconvenience they may cause to their host, they are by no means destructive or injurious. Perhaps, if we might suggest an analogy, they appear to be analogous to pediculi, or those *Anoplura* which infest birds and other animals, save that they are fixed to a definite spot. It is rather notable that no decided record is extant of their occurrence in the British Isles, and yet there is no reason against it. Their detection must be anticipated rather from entomologists than myco-

logists, since the latter are not addicted to the microscopical examination of beetles.

Flagellate Beetle Hanger.

Laboulbenia flagellata.   Peyritsch.[1]

This little entomophyte has occurred on the elytra
and feet of *Bembidium lunatum, Anchomenus albipes,*
and *Anchomenus marginatus* in Austria.   The whole
fungus is not more than five hundred micromillimetres
long, of a pale yellowish-brown colour, with a teat-
like apex, and a black nodule at the base.   The
appendages, or pseudo-paraphyses, at the side are
slender and thread-like, from four to seven, either
simple or branched at the base, all about equal in
length, but longer than the perithecia, septate and
hyaline.   This is one of the most graceful in the
group to which it belongs, bearing several long
flexuous appendages ; but these, though more numerous, are not half the length of those which adorn
Laboulbenia nebriæ.   It is not uncommon for two
individuals to be attached to a single discoid base
(plate 3, fig. 35).   From their very minute size they
are scarcely to be detected, except under a lens, and
that is insufficient to demonstrate their true character.

---

[1] Peyritsch, "Mon. Laboulbenia," p. 247, figs. 1–3 ; Saccardo,
" Sylloge," viii. No. 3607.

The length of the appendages, and their whip-like character, gave rise to the specific name of *flagellata.* Under what conditions they attach themselves, especially to the surface of beetles, is a mystery, and their life-history is comparatively unknown.

Thick Beetle Hanger.

Laboulbenia vulgaris.   Peyritsch.[2]

A rather common species of *Laboulbenia* on various species of *Bembidium* and upon *Deleaster dichrous* in Austria. It is dark brown, turning blackish. The appendages, or pseudo-paraphyses, of unequal length, and numerous. The arm which supports them is nearly of the length of the perithecium, and of the same colour. The sporidia are spindle-shaped and straight or curved, two-celled, and uncoloured.

It is not unusual for two of these individuals to have only a common disc, or base of attachment. In its appearance and general character it is more distinct than some of the other species, as the pseudo-paraphyses are very much reduced in size, although the projection which bears them is unusually large. In its young state the whole plant is a simple narrow club, with no appendages whatever, and only divided

---

[2] Peyritsch, "Mon. Laboulbenia," p. 248, figs. 17–28; Saccardo, "Sylloge," viii. No. 3612.

by transverse septa. The colour also intensifies with age, so as to become nearly black ; probably if they had maintained their yellow tint, or in the case of yellow species, they may have been confounded by collectors with pollinia, to which they offer a superficial resemblance.

Fan Beetle Hanger.

Laboulbenia luxurians. Peyritsch.[1]

A very minute species of *Laboulbenia* has occurred on the elytra and feet of *Bembidium varium* in Austria, which is not more than two hundred and twenty micromillimetres long, of a dark-brown colour. Lateral appendages, or pseudo-paraphyses, numerous, curved, and diverging in the upper part like a fan, only about half the length of the perithecia. Of course, like the rest of the genus, it is found on the living insects, and carried about by them attached to their persons.

Excepting its very minute size, this may at once be distinguished from *Laboulbenia vulgaris* by the fan-like tuft of short appendages borne at the apex of a shorter lateral arm. The top of the fan does not extend more than halfway upwards of the

---

[1] Peyritsch, "Mon. Laboulbenia," p. 248, figs. 10-14 ; Saccardo, "Sylloge," viii. No. 3611.

G

perithecium (plate 3, fig. 30). In all the species, as far as yet known, the most important character relied upon appears to be the appendages, or pseudo-para-physes, taken perhaps in connection with the general external form, which varies but little in the genus *Laboulbenia* itself. The fructification, or sporidia, not having as yet assumed that paramount impor-tance which has been assigned to them in other families, do not enter into specific characterization.

CURVED BEETLE HANGER.

Laboulbenia anceps.   Peyritsch.[1]

This little parasite much resembles *Laboulbenia flagellata*, and has been found on the feet of *Ancho-menus viduus* in Austria. The description is rather imperfect, so that it may eventually prove to be the same species. It is of the same pale yellow-brown colour. The appendages, or pseudo-paraphyses, at the side are in a cluster, and curved like a bow, each being about of equal length to the perithecium, and hyaline (plate 3, fig. 29). This is all that can be said about it as a species, except, perhaps, that the bundle of pseudo-paraphyses is longer than in *L. fascicu-lata*, and not so long as in *L. flagellata*, whilst they

---

[1] Peyritsch, "Mon. Laboulbenia," p. 247, pl. 1, fig. 7; Saccardo, "Sylloge," viii. No. 3609.

are all curved outwards in one direction. We are not responsible for the suggestion that it may be a variety or a condition of *L. flagellata,* or even of *L. Rougetii,* to which latter it has a still greater superficial resemblance. It must be borne in mind that the special study of these singular entomophytes is of very recent date, so that, up to a few years since, nothing was known of them beyond the two species described in Robin's work on " Vegetable Parasites." Their rarity, or local distribution, peculiar habitats, and minute size have all contributed to keep their history obscure.

Tufted Beetle Hanger.

Laboulbenia fasciculata. Peyritsch.[1]

A small species of *Laboulbenia* has been found on the elytra and feet of *Chlænius vestitus* near Vienna. It is said to be rather smaller than *Laboulbenia anceps* (about three hundred and seventy micromillimetres long), and, like it, of a pale yellow-brown. The lateral appendages, or pseudo-paraphyses, are more numerous, collected in a bundle, in a brush-like manner, and diverging at the apex, hyaline and septate, about equal in length to the perithecium (plate 3, fig. 33). Comparing it with *L. luxurians,* it may be said that

---

[1] Peyritsch, " Mon. Laboulbenia," p. 248, figs. **8, 9** ; Saccardo, " Sylloge," viii. No. 3610.

the lateral appendages are longer, rising quite to the
height of the apex of the perithecium ; and, as compared with *L. anceps*, that they are more numerous,
somewhat shorter, and more divaricate, bending in all
directions. As the appendages in all these allied
species are fasciculate, the name is not a very good
one, but the things themselves are of more importance
than the names. As the beetle itself is not an uncommon British insect, it is not impossible that the parasite
may come to light some day, when entomologists
are made aware of its existence, and commence to
look for it. It might even be found in existing
collections, for the parasites adhere firmly, and are
so minute as to be readily overlooked. A little club,
less than half a millimetre in length, is not much
more than a robust hair.

STAPHYLINE CLUB.

Cordyceps memorabilis. Ces.[1]

It was in 1861 that Cesati first described and
published figures of this entomophyte, under the name
of Racemella, which was found growing upon the body
of one of the Staphyline beetles in Italy (fig. 18). The
species is a very small one, and has this peculiarity,

---

[1] Cesati, in *Comm. Critt. Ital.*, i. 65, pl. 4, fig. 1 ; Saccardo,
"Sylloge," ii. No. 5032.

that the perithecia are not immersed in the substance
of the club, but are seated upon the surface. The
clubs are simple, or sometimes forked, from six to
eight millimetres long, of an orange colour, beset
at the apex with the obversely pear-shaped perithecia, which are reddish orange, and smooth, enclosing the asci, which contain the usual long thread-like
sporidia, breaking up ultimately into very minute
joints. This parasite is a very curious one, and
deserves the name of *remarkable*, as the specific name
indicates. Up to the present it does not appear to
have been found again, and
is therefore an exclusively
Italian species. Another
species, growing on *Sphingidæ*, resembles it in the free
perithecia, but is not to be
confounded with it. The
occurrence of parasites upon

Fig. 18.—Staphyline Club. *Cordyceps
memorabilis* (after Cesati), enlarged
three times.

the *Staphylinidæ* is much more uncommon than one
would expect.

These insects, says Mr. Gray, reside in damp
places on the margins of rivers, beneath dead leaves,
and under the bark of decaying trees. Their food
consists of decaying animal and vegetable matter,
especially fungi, in which some of the species chiefly
pass their existence.

The figure which we have given is enlarged three

or four times, and is a copy of the original by Cesati. It will be observed that a number of clubs arise from the same insect, which is very much enveloped in mycelium.

Common Beetle Hanger.

Laboulbenia Rougetii. Robin and Mont.[1]

M. Rouget has recorded three species of *Staphylinidæ* as affected by this parasite, namely, *Goerius olens*, *Pæderus riparius*, and *Ophonus brevicollis*. But this entomophyte has already been alluded to in detail, and in this, as also in similar cases, it will be unnecessary to repeat remarks and descriptions already given (see *ante*, p. 76).

M. Lebert[2] has stated that *Gærius olens* is also subject to a disease, which shows itself in spots, in each of which fungi are to be found occupying the outer ring or its interior. What this disease may have been we are in no position to guess.

---

[1] Mont. and Rob., " Veg. Par.," p. 622, pl. 8, figs. 1, 2 ; and p. 639, pl. 10, fig. 2.

[2] Lebert, *Berlin Entom. Zeit.* (1858), p. 170.

HORNED BEETLE HANGER.

Heimatomyces paradoxus. Peyritsch.[1]

This is another of the *Laboulbenia* group of parasites, bearing a different generic name on account of a very trifling difference in structure; that is to say, the perithecium is produced at the apex into a lateral horn. It occurred upon *Laccophilus minutus* and *Laccophilus hyalinus* in Austria.

In this species the stem is short, the perithecium three times as long as the stem, and thickened below, produced at the apex into an acute or obtuse horn. The pseudo-paraphyses, with few joints, bilobed at the tips. In this instance the sporidia are large (40—$48 \times 6\mu$), curved and hyaline.

There is sufficient distinctness and character in this parasite to make it a prominent feature amongst its allies, some six or eight of which (plate 3, fig. 32), to the uneducated eye, present a degree of sameness, only varied in minute points. Here, by means of the prominent horn, we recognize a new departure, sufficient for identification by other than mycologists. It is one of two parasites, belonging to the same family, occurring on the same insects. There can scarcely,

---

[1] Peyritsch, "Mon. Laboulbenia," p. 258, figs. 35-39; Saccardo, "Sylloge," viii. No. 3619.

however, be any suspicion of their not being perfectly
distinct.

CLAWED BEETLE HANGER.

Chitonomyces melanurus. Peyritsch.[1]

This is another minute entomophyte, technically
removed from *Laboulbenia* on account of slight
differences.   It has been found on the same insects
as *Heimatomyces;* that is to say, on *Laccophilus minutus* and *Laccophilus hyalinus* in Austria.

The perithecia are three-lobed at the apex, three
times as long as the short yellowish stem.   The
pseudo-paraphyses become blackish with two pellucid
lines, the apex spirally incurved.   The blackish
pseudo-paraphyses and yellow perithecia and stem
are notable, and the sporidia are very small (plate 3,
fig. 34).   Instead of a bundle of pseudo-paraphyses at
the side, the one organ in this species, which takes
their place, is black, with a curved hook or claw at the
apex.   This must not be confounded with the curved
hyaline trichome, seen in the figure, proceeding from
the pore of the central lobe of the perithecium.   The
stem also is remarkably short, as it is in *Heimatomyces*, and the perithecium proportionally long.

---

[1] Peyritsch, "Mon. Laboulbenia," p. 250, figs. 30-34 ; Saccardo,
"Sylloge," viii. No. 3618.

WATER-BEETLE HANGER.

Laboulbenia Guerini. Rob.[1]

Amongst the *Gyrinidæ* it is recorded that a species named *Gyrites sericeus*, from the cascades of Caraccas, had this very minute parasite attached to the surface of the thorax, between the thorax and abdomen, and the margins of the elytra. This, Mr. Gray remarks, is the only true aquatic insect which has hitherto been recorded as having a parasitic fungus attached to it. The insects of this family pass their larva and perfect states in the water; but when the larva is about to assume the pupa-state, it creeps out of the water up the stems of some plant that grows on the margin, and then envelops itself in an oval cocoon, which is pointed at each end.

This minute entomophyte is a little over four hundred micromillimetres long, bay-brown, with a nodule at the base. The perithecia are rather conoid and pierced at the apex, and about one-third of the entire length. The curious appendages, or pseudo-paraphyses, are in a tuft, and numerous, forked, and jointed in a bead-like manner, separating readily at the joints, pale-coloured. Sporidia spindle-shaped and two-celled. Observations on the form and

---

[1] Robin, "Veg. Par.," p. 624, pl. 9, figs. 1–3; Saccardo, "Sylloge," viii. No. 3606.

structure have been given under *Laboulbenia Rougetii.*
It will be seen, on comparison of figures, that it is
unusual for the lateral appendages to be forked as
they are in this species.

BEETLE HANGERS.

Species of the *Laboulbeniaceæ.*

During the past year or two a large number of
new species of those peculiar parasites which we have
termed " Beetle hangers " have been described for the
first time, as infesting various kinds of insects.[1]   The
peculiarities of these new forms are of more scientific
than popular interest, and it would serve no useful
purpose to enter upon minute details.   We shall,
therefore, confine ourselves to their enumeration.

On *Harpalus Pennsylvanicus* Mr. Thaxter has
found *Laboulbenia harpali,* which occurs on the
inferior surface, always on the left side of the anterior
inferior face of the abdomen ; *Laboulbenia elegans* in
single tufts on the inferior surface of the thorax,
always on the right side ; *Laboulbenia arcuata,* and
Laboulbenia conferta ; all four on the same species of
beetle.

---

[1] Notes on U. S. Laboulbeniaceæ, by Roland Thaxter, in *Proc.
Amer. Acad. Arts and Sciences,* 1890, and " Supplementary Notes "
in the same journal, 1891.

On *Platynus cincticollis* he has seen *Peyritschiella curvata* and *Laboulbenia elongata*, the latter being the largest species known, as well as a small species, named *Laboulbenia fumosa*, on the elytra of the same beetle. Later on he discovered another species, which he has called *Peyritschiella minima*, on the same host.

On *Platynus extensicollis* the same author has indicated two species, called respectively *Laboulbenia paupercula* and *Laboulbenia scelephila*. On *Patrobus longicornis* also he has found a large species, in Connecticut and Maine, which he names *Laboulbenia brachiata*. On *Bembidium*, in addition to the species previously known, he has found *Laboulbenia truncata*.

To these must be added *Cantharomyces verticillata* on *Sunius longiusculus* in Illinois, and *Cantharomyces Bledii* on *Bledius assimilis* in the same State; *Zodiomyces vorticellaria* upon *Hydrocombus palustris*; *Hesperomyces virescens* on *Chilocorus bivulnerus*; and *Laboulbenia casnoniæ* on *Casnonia pennsylvanica*. Although the mere mention of these names can convey no definite ideas, yet we felt incumbent to render the catalogue as complete as possible, even at the risk of offering incomprehensible names. One fact will at least become evident, that the order of *Coleoptera*, or beetles, are favoured with a large proportion of the numerous species of that interesting group of insect-fungi, termed the *Laboulbeniaceæ*.

LAMELLICORN PARASITES.

Mr. Gray has alluded to entomophytes on large lamellicorn larvæ, and others have been met with, in too incomplete a condition to determine to what particular species of *Cordyceps* they may belong. As to the insects, he says, "From the formation of their antennæ, they are placed provisionally in the family *Dynastidæ*, although, from our own imperfect knowledge of the peculiar characters of the various larvæ, it is impossible to affix any generic or specific names."

These larvæ[1] are usually found in tropical countries, buried a few inches beneath the surface of the soil, which generally consists of leaves, fibres, and roots of plants in a state of decomposition, and are especially fond of places that are used as potato-patches by the inhabitants, even on the elevated plateau of the Andes, to the height of two thousand four hundred feet above the sea.   They form themselves chambers in which they reside, by feeding on the decayed vegetable matter that surrounds them.   They remain for four or five years in their larva-state before they undergo their change into the pupa, previous to their final metamorphosis into the perfect insect ; so that it may be easily supposed that the larvæ have ample time to get infected with the germ of the fungoid

---

[1] Gray, "Notices," pl. 1, figs. 5, 6.

parasite, especially during rainy seasons. There can
be no doubt that it commences its growth internally,
as specimens have been met with having the fungus
just bursting forth from the mouth and other parts
of the body, "resembling a green pea," but the most
usual place is from the pectoral surface of the thoracic
segments, and from between the segments, and from
the spiracles of the abdomen, the specimens varying,
however, much in position, number, and mode of
growth. These larvæ, from their unwieldy proportions, lie on their side within the chamber amidst
the decaying vegetable detritus, and thus cause the
fungus to partake of various contortions arising from
the limited space in which it is confined, from its
incapability to make its way through the vegetable
detritus, or from the depth it might be when growing. It invariably projects upwards towards the
surface of the earth, even should it commence its
growth from the side of the jaw, or of the abdomen,
in which the larva lies. The larvæ are usually found
dead, and sometimes partially decayed ; but this
latter circumstance may greatly depend on the length
of time during which they have lain in the damp
soil after death, their death having been occasioned
in the first instance by the growth of the parasite.
On the other hand, it has been recorded by Mr.
Mackay[1] that the larva obtained at Maracaibo,

---

[1] Mackay, *Proc. Zool. Soc.* (1839), p. 146.

where it is known to the natives under the name of Projojoy, "was alive when first found," and it is added that "this is by no means a solitary instance in which these vegetable productions have made their appearance on living insects."

Though the larvæ of these insects are numerous, and easily found in some localities, yet it may be remarked that periods of several years often elapse before specimens with fungi are again discovered, which seems to depend entirely on the return of a wet season at certain periods of the year, producing a certain condition of the insect which appears to be essential to the development of the fungoid parasite.

Again, he adds, further on, that Mr. Jervis had mentioned that "he was acquainted with a Scarabæus (*Dynastes ?*) apparently in the perfect state, which had been found in the hotter parts of New Grenada, having a fungoid excrescence attached to it. The natives gravely assured him that this excrescence would be transformed into, or become, a large tree, called 'Diomato,' a name which is applied to a species of *Diospyros*, remarkable for its hard and beautifully veined wood."

Proceeding with the record of these instances of doubtful forms, we may mention that Professor Westwood exhibited to the Entomological Society,[1]

---

[1] *Trans. Ent. Soc. London* (1841-43), iii. p. 5, pl. 6, fig. 6.

in 1838, a large lamellicorn larva from South America, from the pectoral surface of the thoracic segments of which a long and slender curved vegetable production was produced, nearly equalling the entire body in length (fig. 19).

FIG. 19.—Parasite on Lamellicorn Beetle (after Westwood).

Whether having any relationship to this family or not, Mr. Gray has noticed that a large kind of brown beetle is recorded by the Rev. Mr. Taylor,[1] under the New Zealand name of "Mumutana," as abundant amongst the sand-hills in the vicinity of the sea. This insect, he says, is sometimes found completely filled with the nut-like substance, but in no instance has he noticed any plant shooting from it.

Another instance is alluded to in another work, in which it is stated[2] that Mr. Drury had a beetle in the perfect state, from every part of which small stalks and fibres sprouted forth; they were entirely different from the tufts of hair that are observed in a few Coleopterous insects, such as *Buprestis fasci-cularis* of the Cape of Good Hope, and were certainly

[1] Taylor's "New Zealand," p. 423.
[2] Donovan's "Insects of China," p. 19.

a vegetable production.   No one can speculate from such a vague note whether the parasite was a *Laboulbenia,* or an *Isaria,* or anything else.

MAY-BUG CLUB.

Cordyceps melolonthæ.   Tul.[1]

A species of *Melolontha,* which the Americans term "May-bug," the larvæ of which are found in great profusion in meadows at certain seasons of the year, when it is not unusual to find some which have attached to them a vegetable sprout.   In some instances this sprout is three inches in length; it generally proceeds from between the head and the under part of the thorax, and in a few instances from the mouth.   There is generally one to each grub, though some are found with two; and the larvæ were not only dead, but in a state of decay, and the sprout rising above the ground indicates where they are found.   It is a vulgar but prevailing notion that such grubs are changed to briars.[2]

This entomophyte is the species named by Tulasne *Cordyceps melolonthæ,* the clubs of which are either

---

[1] Tulasne, "Selecta Fungorum Carpologia" (1865), t. iii. p. 12, pl. 1, fig. 32 ; Saccardo, "Sylloge," iv. 5044.

[2] "History of Insects" (Murray's Family Library), vol. ii. p. 296 (1838).

solitary or in pairs, on buried larvæ of species of
Melolontha, and the same author refers to this parasite
the description and figures of Fougeroux de Bonderoy, and the descriptions hereafter alluded to by
Mr. J. Cist. The clubs are in themselves simple and
swollen above into a clavate head, being very similar

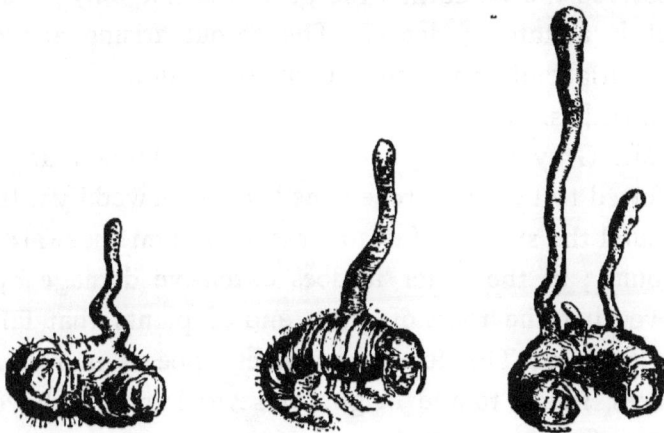

FIGS. 20 to 22.—May-bug Club. *Cordyceps melolonthæ* (after Fougeroux de Bonderoy).

in habit to *Cordyceps Miquelii,* on Cicada. The knowledge of this species is up to now very imperfect, for
the well-matured heads with ripe sporidia have not
yet been found, or at least recorded.

It was in 1824 that Mr. J. Cist[1] related his observations on the entomophyte which is now known
under the above name. "It is not unusual," he says,

---

[1] Cist, on "May-bug," in *Silliman's Journal* (1824), viii. p. 270, pl. 4.

" to find a number of the larvæ which have attached to them vegetable sprouts, in some instances three inches long. These excrescences generally proceed from the space between the head and under part of the thorax, and in a few instances from the mouth." He further remarks that "in every case where he observed the vegetation the grub was not only dead, but in a state of decay. The sprout arising above the surface of the ground is the indication where the animal lies."

Mr. Gray thought it was the same larva that is referred to by Mr. Mitchell[1] as "found in wood-yards, around the stumps of dead trees, and often in sward-ground ; in the latter it does extensive damage by devouring the roots of grass, and of plants that fall in its way. The fungus at times appears in many places, rising to the height of several inches above the surface of the earth."

According to Gray, the larvæ were considered by Count Dejean to be those of *Ancyloncha puncticollis.* In the description given in a few words by Tulasne, he simply says, "on buried larvæ of *Melolontha,* commonly called ' May-bug,' in North America."

The observations of Fougeroux de Bonderoy on these parasites, contained in the same memoir as those on the vegetable fly of the Carribeans, viz.

---

[1] *Silliman's Journal,* vol. xii. p. 26.

Cordyceps sobolifera, are of some interest as far as they go, and are often alluded to, so that by quoting them we shall have fairly exhausted the memoir.

"The grub," he says, "resembles those which produce beetles ; it is of the size of the larvæ, which turn, after their metamorphosis, to a small kind of cockchafer ; its body is composed of many close-set rings ; its large and scaly head is of short length, and there are seen upon it two jaws, or falces, set somewhat forward, and two small antennæ composed of three articulations. The grub has some hair distributed upon the rings of the body. It has six feet, of which the two near the head are slightly the smallest, and more within the body of the animal.

"It cannot be supposed that the grubs of which we speak are those which produce, by a second metamorphosis, the nymphs of the Cicada, because, according to the account which M. de Reaumur has given of these grubs, they have no resemblance to those which we are describing, since the Cicadæ upon leaving the egg pass into the state of hexapod larvæ, the two very large nippers of which show their great affinity to the forms which they will take as nymphs ; these nippers make them to differ essentially from the larvæ we are describing now. Here, then, is a second insect upon which the Clavaria is found, and this is an interesting fact in the history of this singular vegetation.

" From the state of preservation in which I have these insects, it appears that the plant has grown some time upon the living animal, for the Clavaria upon some of these insects is two inches in length. The larvæ are entire, very sound, and not dried up. In fact, we know how short a time is requisite for the perfect production of a fungus."

Mr. Gray remarks of the above quotation that the larva most probably belongs to *Rhizotrogus* or *Ancyloncha*. " The parasite on this larva is represented by the author as growing from a broad base of thallus, which is deposited *externally* on the upper side of the larva, in which respect it differs from most others that have been recorded. In proof of his opinion, he states that in some specimens which had been preserved in spirit of wine the plant had separated from the body of the larva, and exhibited the under surface of the basal part of the stem or thallus of the parasite, fluted as if occasioned by only lying close to the outer surface of the abdominal segments of the insect. This mode of separation, however, may have been entirely caused by the action of the spirit upon the Entomophyte ; but as the larva retains in some measure its perfect form, it may be inferred that its interior was previously filled with the thallus, and that, as in other recorded Entomophytes, it was not until after this had taken place that the fungus showed itself externally, as is evidently exhibited where it is represented bursting forth between two of the dorsal segments of the thorax. The manner of growth of the parasite may probably be caused by the position of the insect at the time it was exhausted by the progress of the thallus internally, the point of external growth being the nearest portion to the surface of the earth. The latter remark is also applicable to the other figures, which at the same time afford evidence that the plant had grown above the surface of the soil. It is usual to find only one parasite on each larva, although in some two, and in others even three, have been noticed, varying much in length and form."

We have it on the authority of Mr. Gray that " some larvæ were discovered near S'a Fe de Bogota by the late Mr. Stevens, which may possibly belong to the genus *Ancyloncha*, but certainly to a smaller species than those just noticed. These larvæ bear a great similarity to those mentioned by Mr. Cist, and, like them, the parasite invariably arises from beneath the head and the prothorax. In one specimen it had just made its appearance, in another it is about two inches long, while in a third it reaches to about six inches in length, of nearly equal thickness throughout, and having the tip somewhat acute and of a light colour. These examples were no doubt discovered, like those observed by Mr. Cist, by the principal portion of the fungus appearing above the surface

of the vegetable soil."[1]   From the figure of one of
these, it is evidently a young and imperfect form of
a *Cordyceps*, with a slender flexuous stem, but without
having the capitulum properly developed.   It has
a much more attenuated form, and seems to suggest
a species of *Cordyceps* distinct both from *Cordyceps
melolonthæ* and *Cordyceps Ravenelii.*

There is a record in the *Boston Proceedings*[2] of a
Cordyceps on *Melolontha* from the Philippine Islands,
which may be alluded to here, although, if it had
been mature, it might possibly not have been referred
to this species.   The specimen was found in 1866
on Mount Mahahai, an extinct volcano, about fifty
miles from the city of Manila ; it was found about
three thousand feet above the level of the sea, in a
clearing in the forest, which had been made a coffee-
plantation ; the soil was black and rich, and quite
moist from the daily heavy rains which prevail at
this season of the year.   The caterpillar when found
was dead, somewhat dry, though not decayed, and
was lying on its side, the under surface resting in
the moist rich soil.   The attention of the gentleman
who picked it up, and who gave it to me, was
attracted by the peculiar colour and aspect of the
vegetable growth, which reminded him of the delicate

---

[1] Gray, "Notices," p. 4.
[2] Kneeland, on "A Caterpillar Fungus," in *Proc. Boston Soc. Nat.
Hist.* (June, 1867), vol. xi. p. 120.

roots of a hyacinth, as seen growing in water; their size was about that of the hyacinth roots, but the colour was more yellowish, and the structure more tough and elastic; the plant was living when found. The larva on which this parasite was 'growing is, according to Messrs. Osten Sacken and Scudder, that of a Lamellicorn beetle of the family *Melolonthidæ*, and coming near *Melolontha*, or the May-beetle, or May-bug.

The body of the specimen appeared filled with the fungus, and it had burst out in six different places, from the head to the tail, in filaments about an inch and a half in length. The fungus was so far perfect, but it had not proceeded to fructification, although Mr. C. J. Sprague considered it a *Cordyceps.* It must be rare, as none of the natives or foreign residents had ever noticed anything of the kind before.

The remarks of Mr. Sprague on this insect parasite when submitted to him do not contain much in supplement to the foregoing account. He says, " I have no belief myself that the fungi investing insects are at all peculiar to them ;" but this opinion is no longer tenable in respect to the species of *Cordyceps*, whatever it may be of moulds. He proceeds to say, "But I am not prepared to say that the *Isaria* may not develop into *Sphæria* under favourable circumstances. These things are so strange in their growth, that a certain form may for centuries never appear as other than a warty excrescence, never producing asçi and spores, but propagating itself by mycelium, and then it may take an ascoid growth quite dissimilar from its long non-developed appearance. Until you have asci and spores, you can never decide beyond any doubt as to the species of a fungus. You may even mistake as to its genus. The mycelium accommodates itself to its matrix, and takes on, therefore, excessively varying forms. This fungus is like *Cordyceps entomorrhiza* in habit, so much so that it has no peculiar characters to distinguish it. It has no perithecia, and consequently no fruit. It has not reached a development which warrants a name. I should say that it has all the appearance of *Cordyceps*, but, in the absence of all fructification, it is impossible to further name it." He concludes by reiterating his opinion against the "belief in the exclusive attachment of certain fungi to certain insects. Fungi," he says, "grow on everything organic. Some species have as yet been detected on certain things; but this is so peculiar an exception, I place no reliance on the mere fact of an individual discovery of this sort. Should you place the larvæ of all sorts of insects under the same favourable conditions, I believe that the same fungus would grow from them all," etc.

Mr. Gray has two figures in his memoir which

present a great resemblance to forms of *Cordyceps melolonthæ,* occurring on larvæ of Lamellicorns. One [1] represents a young larva, " which does not exhibit the appearance of having the body so entirely filled with the thallus internally, yet from the dorsal portion of the thoracic segments, where the thallus is spread over the surface, grows a long thick fungus, of the length of two inches and a quarter, having a somewhat lengthened clavate head. Another [2] example consists only of the head and thorax of the same kind of larva, but which is not in any way infested with the thallus ; though from the pectoral portion springs a lengthened stem of a fungus, which is curiously divided, as if cut into two slender branches for about half its length, each of the branches being much curved, and furnished with an oblong head at the apex. Both these fungoid parasites have evidently grown for some part of their length above the soil, and they exhibit an entirely different habit from any previously described. They were brought from New Grenada."

A parasitic fungus which has recently been very destructive to the larvæ of the cockchafer in certain districts of France, was from the first believed to be a near ally of the muscardine. M. Giard thinks that it is a form of another fungus, found on the same

---

[1] Gray, " Notices," pl. 1, fig. 9.   [2] Gray, pl. 1, fig. 10.

host, which is *Isaria densa,* whereas the mould has been named *Botrytis tenella,* but M. Giard contends that the mould, even in its simplest form, is rather an *Isaria* than a *Botrytis.*[1]

CAROLINA BEETLE CLUB.

Cordyceps Ravenelii. Berk.[2]

Similar kinds of larvæ to those of *Ancyloncha* are found in South Carolina during the spring and summer months. "But their parasites differ entirely from those usually found in this kind of insect both in their manner of growth and general appearance. They are composed of a long and somewhat thick stem with a lengthened and subclavate head, and plainly evidence that part of the fungus had been exposed above the surface of the vegetable detritus."[3] These larvæ have been affirmed to be those of a species of *Ancyloncha* or of *Rhizotrogus,* and the parasite described under the above name is said to be brownish, with an elongated flexuous stem, which is compressed and sulcate, at first rather downy, becoming smooth (plate I, fig. I). The head, or capitulum, is three quarters of an inch long, cylindrical,

---

[1] "Comptes Rendus" (1891), p. 1079.

[2] *Cordyceps Ravenelii.* Berk. and Curt., *Journ. Linn. Soc.* (1857), p. 159, pl. I, fig. 4 ; Saccardo, "Sylloge," iv. No. 5035.

[3] Gray, "Notices," p. 4.

attenuated upwards, enclosing, as usual, the perithecia with their asci and sporidia. The latter are
thread-like, breaking up into small frustules two and
a half or three micromillimetres in length. The
entire height of the fungus is not more than two
or three inches, and hitherto it has only been found
in South Carolina and Texas. Altogether this parasite bears some resemblance to the celebrated "plant-
worm" of the Chinese.

CEYLON MAY-BUG CLUB.

Cordyceps Barnesii. Thw.[1]

Unfortunately, our information of this Ceylon
species is exceedingly limited, it having been found
only by Dr. Thwaites and Beccari, but it is recorded
as occurring on buried larvæ of *Melolontha*. The stem
of the parasite is cylindrical and velvety, with a somewhat cylindrical club-shaped head, the apex of which
is sterile. The conidial form has also been found,
which assumes rather a *Stilbum* shape, with a branched
stem, and globose heads bearing minute conidia two
and a half micromillimetres long. The entire length of
a usual-sized club is about two to two and a half
inches, of which the fertile head occupies about half an

---

[1] Berkeley and Broome, "Ceylon Fungi," No. 977; Saccardo,
"Sylloge," ii. No. 5052.

inch, or a little more, and is somewhat thicker than the stem, of a reddish colour, whilst the stem is yellowish white (plate I, fig. 2). One important peculiarity is that the capitulum is terminated at the apex by a little sterile horn, or apiculus, present in all the specimens, and sometimes curved. The perithecia are prominent, but immersed, and the fructification is entirely that of the genus. When dried there is but the slightest indication of a velvety stem, or at most only a little mealiness. In the Kew Library there is an original coloured drawing of the species when living, whence our figure is derived.

Nothing can be said of the so-called *Lycogala fragilis*, which was stated by Holm[1] to have occurred on a broken and decayed specimen of *Melolontha vulgaris*, infesting the sides of the body and legs with small round spots. It was certainly not a *Lycogala*, but it might have been a *Laboulbenia*, or even *Leocarpus vernicosus.*

In the family *Cetoniidæ* Mr. Gray calls attention to two instances, recorded by M. Reiche,[2] "one of which occurred on a species of *Cetonia*, from Madagascar, having a fungus proceeding from its head ; while the other was on a species of *Gymnetis*, having

---

[1] Holm, " Acta Hafn " (1781), p. 258, fig. 5.
[2] *Bullet. Soc. Entom. de France* (1849), p. lvi.

a similar production on the thorax. As he gives neither further description nor figures of these two entomophytes, they must remain thus briefly noticed."

TAILED BEETLE CLUB.

Cordyceps stylophora. Berk. and Br.[1]

Of the Coleopterous larvæ which suffer from this entomophyte, Mr. Gray[2] has given the following information: "In South Carolina," he says, "there have been observed during the autumnal months several larvæ, which showed that they were but slightly buried in rotten logs, as they had roots springing from around the base only of the stem. These insects, judging from the figures, may possibly belong to the *Elateridæ.* The parasite differs in form from any of those previously known, being long, slender, and with the middle of each stem swollen, to contain the enclosed perithecia, but the stem is sometimes found perfectly simple," and then in its barren state (fig. 23).

FIG. 23.—Tailed Beetle Club. *Cordyceps stylophora,* on larvæ.

---

[1] Berkeley and Broome, *Journ. Linn. Soc.,* vol. i. p. 158, pl. 1, fig. 3.

[2] Gray, "Notices," p. 4.

The stem is from a half to three quarters of an inch long, and a quarter of a line thick, smooth, about as long as the cylindrical head, which is produced upwards into an acuminate sterile process, as long, or longer, than itself. The perithecia are immersed in the cylindrical head, which thus holds a central position. On the whole, this *Cordyceps* is a very characteristic one, and is found attached to larvæ buried in rotten logs. It is unusual for the axis to be prolonged beyond the capitulum, or head, but in this species it is carried to an extreme; as in *Cordyceps Barnesii*, it is quite rudimentary—almost an apiculus.

Cape Beetle Club.

Early in the present year (1891) Dr. McOwan sent over to this country, from the Cape of Good Hope, three larvæ of some Coleopterous insect, and, we are assured, belonging to the family *Elateridæ*, with a *Cordyceps* growing from the front of the head, but unfortunately in an imperfect condition. Two of the specimens had the terminal capitulum broken, and in all of them the perithecia were only commencing formation. The stems are from one and a half to two inches long, and the clavate head about half an inch. In habit and appearance it approaches *Cordyceps Barnesii*, but without the sterile apiculus at the apex.

It is certainly an interesting species, both from its locality and its host, but it would be folly to apply a name without evidence of fructification, although there is not the slightest reason for doubt of its being a true *Cordyceps*, and not referable to any described species at present found in this order. The indications of the perithecia are immersed in the substance of the club, at its periphery, and not at all superficial. In one instance there is a second club in process of growth. The lower portion of the stem is slightly velvety.

BEETLE ENDOPHYTE.

Entomophthora lampyridarum. Thaxter.[1]

An American *Entomophthora* on beetles, especially on the imago of *Chauliognathus Pennsylvanicus*, has recently been discovered. The affected beetles were found firmly attached by their mandibles to grass or leaves in open fields. Unfortunately, for lack of material, the description is not quite perfect, but the species is relied upon as distinct.

The conidia are regular, ovoid, slightly tapering towards the apex, with an abrupt, broad, slightly papillate base, contents granular, without large oil globules (average $15 \times 35\mu$). The conidia-bearing

---

[1] Thaxter, "Entomophthorae U.S," p. 169, pl. 17, figs. 161-172.

threads digitate, or divide like the fingers; secondary conidia either like those of the first generation, or more commonly elongated, cylindrical, rounded at either end, and borne vertically on hair-like spore-bearers. Resting-spores unknown.

"The melon-shaped secondary conidia are produced in great abundance, even in a fairly moist atmosphere, and, in only one or two instances, I observed a second form like the primary condition in process of formation. In many cases the more common secondary conidia were larger than the spores from which they were produced, and this, together with the apparent thinness of the spore-wall, seems to indicate that they are not as resistent as is usually the case with secondary conidia when borne on hair-like spore-bearers. It will be noticed that the secondary spore-bearers are much less thread-like than is usually the case."

WEEVIL CLUB.

Cordyceps curculionum.   Tul.[1]

It is generally known amongst entomologists that specimens of *Curculio* are collected in tropical countries, and sent home with the collections, which

---

[1] Tulasne, "Selecta Fungorum Carpologia," iii. p. 20; Robin, "Veg. Par.," p. 650; Saccardo, "Sylloge," ii. No. 5013.

have club-shaped parasites attached to them. Foreign collectors, or collectors abroad, have generally a keen eye to the monetary value of such "varieties," and are seldom satisfied with their weight in gold to part with them. The golden opportunities are perhaps rather too rare. The Rev. F. W. Hope exhibited one of these, in 1836, from Brazil, at the Entomological Society. From between the prothorax and elytra two very long and clavate fungi had been produced, one of which was entire, the other branched.[1] This gives a general idea of the character of this

fungus, to which Tulasne gave the name of *Cordyceps curculionum.* The fertile stem is almost erect or curved, and whitish, with a brownish tint below. The head is shortly clavate or egg-shaped, rather acute at the apex, two to two and a half millimetres long and one and a half to two milli-

Fig. 24.—Weevil Club. *Cordyceps burculionum* (after Tulasne).

metres thick, of a yellowish-grey colour, and granular with the perithecia (fig. 24). The internal structure corresponds with other species, the long thread-like sporidia breaking up into joints, eight or nine micromillimetres long, and about one and a half thick. They have been collected in Brazil, Peru, and we read that a

---

[1] *Proc. Ent. Soc. Lond.* (1837–40), vol. ii. fig. 3.

I

species of *Curculio*, in the perfect state, from Mexico had long slender filaments attached to various parts of its body; and another specimen was remarkable for having one on the rostrum, which gave it an appearance of an additional horn.[1]

Mr. Gray has figured several in which growth seems to have been arrested before the club-heads had been developed; as, for instance, on *Heilipus celsus* from Cayenne,[2] on *Heilipus brachypterus*[3] and *Heilipus hylobioides*[4] from Brazil, on a species of *Heilipus* from Ega, and on *Chalcoderma*[5] from Para. These insects, he says, "have the fungus protruding from the proboscis, the joints of the body, and along the suture of the elytra; while from between the thorax and elytra spring one, two, or even three long slender excrescences; and others sometimes proceed from different parts of the body. The apical portion of these fungi is usually tapering and light-coloured." He then refers to others, in which the capitate heads are developed, as in *Heilipus* from Lima, *Dionychus* from Brazil,[6] and *Auchonus* from St. Vincent. He says that "the lengthened fungi noticed on these insects also proceed from between the thorax and elytra, but they have at the apex of each projection

---

[1] "History of Insects" (Murray's Family Library), ii. 296 (1838).
[2] Gray, "Notices," pl. 1, fig. 15.   [3] Ibid., pl. 5, fig. 4.
[4] Ibid., pl. 5, fig. 11.   [5] Ibid., pl. 1, fig. 14.
[6] Hope, *Journ. Proc. Ent. Soc.*, ii. p. iv. pl. 8, fig. 8.

a clavate head of a pale colour. In some examples the stem has been observed to be branched." These are the perfect *Cordyceps*, as described by Tulasne. A specimen of *Calandra* is referred to by Kirby and Spence[1] as having a fungus projecting from the rostrum.

"The insects of this family, which are very numerous in tropical countries, live entirely on vegetable substances, and many of them are apterous; they are not unfrequently seen on the leaves, or in cracks and cavities in the bark of trees, and in the interior of stems of plants. Some species are, however, found by turning over the partly decomposed leaves on the ground and the rotten trunks of fallen trees; such localities probably facilitate these insects becoming during rainy seasons the bases of the different kinds of fungoid parasites."[2]

It is not improbable that the Coleopterous insect alluded to by Mr. Gray as belonging to the family *Erotylidæ* (the *Erotylus tæniatus* of Columbia) was attacked by a form of this same *Cordyceps*. "It is remarkable for producing occasionally from the head, from between the head and thorax, and from the sides of the body, a number of very 'slender vegetable appendages,' the apex of each ending in a small

---

[1] "Introd. to Entom." (1826), iv. p. 208.
[2] Gray, "Notices," p. 4.

tuberculated head of a yellowish colour.[1]   The figure resembles *Cordyceps curculionum.*

The species of this genus are seen flying about during the day in the dense forests of the tropical regions of the New World. When in repose, they seek the leaves of plants ; while in the larva state, however, they live under the bark of trees or in fungi, but they chiefly feed upon decayed vegetable matter.

BEETLE STILBUM.

Stilbum Buquetii.   M. and R.[2]

A minute capitate compound mould, of the large genus *Stilbum*, attacks various insects in tropical countries. The erect compound threads are very gregarious, each complex stem bearing a capitate spherical reddish head, which is covered with the oblong naked conidia, or spores. The stems are thick and black, downy, composed of a number of delicate threads, which are agglutinated together into a common stem ; in this respect resembling *Isaria*, but differing in having a distinct capitulum, or head. The species of this genus are common on vegetable substances, but rarely attach themselves to insects, or other

---

[1] Parry, *Journ. Proc. Ent. Soc.* (1847), p. iv.

[2] Montagne and Robin, "Veg. Par.," p. 640, pl. 9, figs. 4, 5; Saccardo, "Sylloge," iv. No. 2678.

animal substances. Another species is recorded in North America, *Stilbum ramosum* (Peck [1]), on "insect larvæ," but it is not stated to what order of insects the larvæ belonged.

Gray says that the species of Curculionidæ, which are subject to become the bases of this fungus, are *Hypsonotus clavulus*[2] from Brazil, *Pycnopus bufo*[3] from Brazil, and a species of *Rhyssomatus* from the Amazon. "These insects," he says, "have the thallus surrounding the abdomen, and sometimes extending between the thorax and elytra, from which spring numerous short excrescences, having tuberculated heads of a yellow colour" (plate 2, fig. 25). In external appearance the species of *Stilbum* much resemble miniature species of *Cordyceps*, but of course differing in internal structure.

LITTLE HELOPS CLUB.

Cordyceps helopis. Quel.[4]

One of the most recent additions to the parasites of the Coleoptera is this species, found upon *Helops*

---

[1] Peck, "Twenty-sixth Report N. Y. State Museum," p. 78; Saccardo, "Sylloge," iv. No. 2696.

[2] Robin, "Veg. Par.," p. 640, pl. 9, figs. 4, 5.

[3] Gray's "Notices," pl. 1, fig. 12.

[4] Quelet, "Diagn. Nouv." (1879), p. 235, *Cordyceps larvicola ;* Quelet, "Espèces Nouv." (1878), ii. p. 292, t. 3, f. 1 ; Saccardo, "Sylloge," ii. No. 5025.

caraboides in the Jura, and afterwards in other places
in France. It occurs on the putrescent larvæ, and
has thus been described : The head, or capitulum, is
oblong, from five to six millimetres long, fleshy and of
a tawny saffron-yellow, dotted with dark purple points.
The stem is slender and flexuous, shining white,
marked with rosy streaks (fig. 25). The elongated
sporidia break up into nearly cubical joints from two
and a half to three micromillimetres in
diameter. Very slight information is
given of this handsome species, but from
the description and figure it would certainly
seem to be quite distinct from any before
known. These minute species are very
liable to be overlooked, especially when
growing upon the ground, or amongst
dead leaves with no more than the head
exposed above the surface, and then not
so large as a grain of wheat—perhaps
something like an ant's egg (as they are
called) set on end. The larvæ or pupæ

FIG. 25.—Little
Helops Club.
*Cordyceps he-
lopis* (after
Quelet).

are generally more or less buried, and in
this condition the entomophyte is developed, thrusting the stem upwards, and forming a
capitulum as soon as the apex reaches the air. It
requires close searching to find much larger species
than the present by its only visible portion.

Tarichia uvella. Krassilstchik.[1]

Under the above name a fungus has been described as growing on Coleopterous larvæ, producing a mass of brick-red spores, cohering in small grape-like clusters. These spores are said to be round, papillate (8–10μ diameter), surrounded by a wall of no great thickness. In fluid these spores germinated in four days, producing septate hyphæ, which, after a week, grew out of the culture fluid, and produced single terminal, cylindrical, uncoloured spores (9 × 3μ). What it may be is uncertain, but not apparently related to *Empusa*, to which it was at first supposed to be allied. With only such meagre information, this is never likely to be more than one of the mythical names scattered over the pages of botanical literature, representing nothing but an incident of individual experience. It is to be regretted that such names are not permitted to be forgotten, but as this has been alluded to again so recently it cannot be ignored. Whether the original object is still in existence is unknown.

---

[1] Krassilstchik, *Mem. Soc. Nat. Nou. Russ.* (Odessa, 1886), xi. p. 95; Thaxter, p. 190.

White Beetle Mould.

Sporotrichum densum.   Link.[1]

On dead insects, both beetles and wasps, this mould has been observed in Germany, and it appears also to have occurred in Australia. As is usual in this genus, it forms a rather thick and dense stratum, composed of sparingly branched hyaline threads, bearing here and there, scattered over them, minute globose conidia, or spores. It has been suggested whether it has not some affinity with the well-known silkworm disease (*Botrytis Bassiana*), but this we see no good reason to suspect. The species of *Sporotrichum*, like moulds of some other genera, will flourish on almost any kind of decaying vegetable and animal matter, some of them like this; only having been found two or three times, and in each case on insects, it follows that they should be supposed to occur only on insects. No species of the genus is known to have occurred on living matter, as they are saprophytes pure and simple, and then probably only as the stroma or conidia of some fungus of higher organization, possibly the *Sphæriacei.*

---

[1] Link, "Obs. Myc.," i. p. 11; Nees, "Syst. Pilze," fig. 45; Saccardo, "Sylloge," iv. No. 507.

Woolly Beetle Mould.

Sporotrichum globuliferum. Speg.[1]

On the decaying bodies of certain *Coleoptera,* as, for instance, *Monocrepidis* and *Naupactus xantho-graphus* in South America, this mould has been recorded. It forms tufts of one millimetre and a half in diameter, white and floccose, penetrating into the interior of the insects. The threads are creeping, sparingly jointed, hyaline, from three to four micro-millimetres thick, closely branched and anastomosing, bearing here and there clusters of the globose, or nearly globose, spores, which are two and a half micromillimetres long, and one and a half to two in width.

The remarks made under the previous species are applicable also to this, which is not entitled to rank as a parasite, but rather an accidental development upon one out of many forms of decaying animal matter.

Globose Endophyte.

Empusa apiculata (var. *major*). Thaxter.

This variety of *Empusa apiculata* was found on the imago of a Coleopterous insect, *Ptilodactyla serricollis,*

---

[1] Spegazzini, "Fungi Argentini," ii. p. 42; Saccardo, "Sylloge," iv. No. 505.

in North Carolina. The type-form occurred on Lepidoptera and Diptera.

In this variety the conidia are more nearly spherical (38×45 to $55 \times 60\mu$), with the basal papilla smaller in proportion to the body of the conidium than in the typical form, the description of which must be sought in the order *Lepidoptera* in the present work.

LEPIDOPTERA.

BUTTERFLIES AND MOTHS.

"THE Lepidoptera are divided into two sections, the first of which embraces the *Rhopalocera*, or diurnal Lepidoptera. These, however, have hitherto remained unrecorded as being the bases of parasitical fungi, or even of filamentous species or moulds (*Colias* only having been since announced as the host of one of the species of Entomophthora), and this notwithstanding the fact that most of these insects pass their existence, and undergo their metamorphoses, as it may be said, in the air, where the spores of these singular plants are stated to float, and thereby, in the opinion of some writers, get affixed to insects in their different stages of life ; notwithstanding also that their food entirely consists of vegetable matter, which is supposed to be one of the chief channels by which the spores are conveyed into the interior of insects, where they are thought to be dormant until some extraordinary coincidence awakes them into active life. Yet this section of Lepidopterous insects has, so far as is known (with the one exception), escaped from becoming the bases of these fungoid parasites." [1]

The Nocturnal Lepidoptera, or *Heterocera*, have by no means been so fortunate, for the number of entomophytes associated with them is very large, and the parasites themselves the most imposing of the whole series. The species of *Cordyceps* alone, not less than twenty, including the well-known *Cordyceps Robertsii* of New Zealand, the *Cordyceps Gunnii* of Tasmania, the very large *Cordyceps Taylori* of the Murrumbidgee, the Chinese "plant-worm," and the rather common British species *Cordyceps militaris* and *Cordyceps entomorrhiza*. Species of *Isaria* appear also to affect Lepidoptera more than any other order. The small species of *Laboulbenia* are remarkably absent, and the number of species of *Entomophthora* but few. This deficiency is in part compensated by the silkworm diseases, which have no parallel in any other order. The Lepidoptera must be held to be the most prolific in *Cordyceps* and *Isaria*, and almost exclusively so ; and these occur on larvæ, pupæ, and imagines. Entomologists may be able to account for this circumstance better than those who concern themselves more with the entomophytes than with their hosts.

---

[1] Gray, "Notices," p. 5.

Sphinx Isaria.

Isaria sphingum. Schw.[1]

When Mr. Gray[2] wrote his "Notices," he was able to enumerate many species of *Sphingidæ* which had been known to act as hosts to parasitic fungi, mostly of the *Isaria* form. Since then others have been recognized, leading to the conclusion that almost any species in that family are liable to attack. Those referred to by Mr. Gray were *Pachylia achemenides* of Surinam, *Macrosila collaris* of St. Domingo, *Sphinx Carolina* of North America, *Anceryx ello* of Para, *Anceryx pinastri* of Europe, *Smerinthus populi* of Europe, a species of *Sphinx* from Jamaica, and another from Guadeloupe. The majority of these have been referred to the present species, and we have determined it as occurring on *Spirama retorta*, and a species of *Hypena*, from Darjeeling.

All these insects, he says, are infested in their imago, or perfect state, and are usually found, principally during or after the rainy season, attached to a leaf or trunk of a tree, sitting with their wings at rest, as if they had been suddenly exhausted by some peculiar action that progressed internally. This even-

---

[1] *Isaria sphingum*, Schwein, "Syn. Car.," No. 1298; Robin, "Veg. Par.," p. 610; Saccardo, "Sylloge," iv. No. 2781; *Isaria sphingophila*, Link, "Sp. Plant." (1824), ii. p. 114.

[2] Gray, "Notices of Insects," p. 5, pl. 3, fig. 12.

tually shows itself in the form of a fungoid matter or mould, entirely covering the external surface of the body and the principal nervures of the wings ; at the same time, the margins of the latter and the basal joints of the legs become firmly attached to the leaves or trunks of trees ; the fungus then grows rapidly on the head and thorax, and especially from the joints of the abdomen, in the form of slender filaments of various lengths and thicknesses. The parasite varies in different specimens. In some the filaments are rather thick and sometimes flattened, especially at their base, reaching, in the longest example, to the length of about nine lines ; while in others they are slender and minutely branched on the sides, attaining the length of an inch and a half to two inches. There seems no doubt, from the position in which these are discovered, that the parasite was, as observed by Dr. Halsey,[1] evolved whilst the Sphinx was yet in a state of existence, " but the fungus does not become fully developed externally until after the death of the insect ; and it is usually more or less in a state of decay,

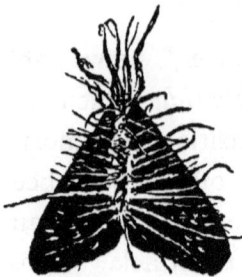

FIG. 26.—Sphinx Isaria. *Isaria sphingum*, on imago of Hypena (*Science Gossip*).

---

[1] *Annals Lyc. New York* (1823), p. 125. See also Cramer, "Papilio Exotic," t. iii. (1782), p. 135, pl. 267, figs. A, B; Ernst, " Papillons d'Europe," t. iii. (1782), t. cxv. fig. 162.

dependent upon the length of time it has remained on the leaf or trunk after the development of the parasitical mould before it was discovered. The caterpillars of this family pass their life exposed to the atmosphere, in the same manner as the Diurnal Lepidoptera, which appears equally to protect them from the attacks of parasites. The chrysalides, on the contrary, bury themselves in the earth, to await their final metamorphoses, yet they also have not been found affected with fungoid parasites."

Sphinx Club.

Cordyceps sphingum. Tul.[1]

Although the *Isaria* form, which bears naked spores, or conidia, had been known for many years, it was Tulasne who first discovered the perfect condition which bears the above name, although it is thought that an indication of this had been manifest to M. Lebert[2] in 1858, when he called the production which he then described *Acrophytum tuberculatum*, without recognizing its true character and affinities.

The stroma of the parasite rises from a thin, pale ochraceous crust over the matrix, in thin, rather rigid tapering processes, chiefly from the joints of the abdomen, and resembling the *Isaria* (fig. 27). The

---

[1] Tulasne, " Selecta Fung. Carp." (1865), iii. p. 12, pl. I, figs. 1, 2.
[2] Sieb. and Koll., *Zoolog. Zeit.* (1858), ix. p. 448, pl. 17, figs. 13-17.

perithecia are not immersed, but free on the surface of the crust, or attached to the stroma, either slightly cæspitose or crowded together in a spike, of a pale-reddish colour (fig. 28). In the interior are produced the long characteristic asci, with the thread-like sporidia.

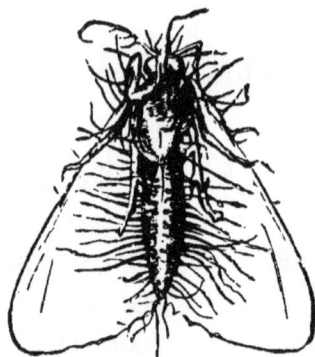

FIG. 27.—Sphinx Club. *Cordyceps sphingum,* on imago *Spirama retorta (Science Gossip).*

FIG. 28.—Fertile stipe of *Cordyceps sphingum,* magnified.

This perfect condition has been found in Switzerland, North America, and in Brazil, and is said to occur also on *Orthoptera.* The superficial perithecia, seated on the stroma, and only slightly immersed at the base, is not a common feature in *Cordyceps,* but it is very marked in this species, and in *Cordyceps memorabilis,* as well as *Cordyceps superficialis.* They are less immersed than usual, becoming free in the upper portion, in *Cordyceps Robertsii, Cordyceps acicularis,* and *Cordyceps Ravenelii.*

RED ISARIA.

Isaria cinnabarina. Preuss.[1]

The pupa of *Sphinx ligustri* has been the subject of attack from *Isaria cinnabarina* in Germany. The stroma is cæspitose, from six to eight millimetres high, of a deep flesh-colour, approaching scarlet; the stems and clubs are indistinct from each other, but repeatedly branched, everywhere equal in colour, floccose and powdery; the conidia ovate, and of the same red flesh-colour. There is only one record of its appearance, the first and last, above described, and therefore it is not possible for us to add any information beyond that on the record. It has not been figured, and no one knows anything of it except the individual responsible for its name. It may be remarked that red species of *Isaria* are not common, the majority of those which are entomophytes being white, or whitish, so that a red species is not likely to escape notice in the future, any more than it is likely to have done in the past, without record.

The erroneous notion, once entertained, that *Sphynx*

---

[1] Preuss F. Hoyersw., No. 343; Saccardo, "Sylloge," iv. No. 2780.

K

Carolina was the host of *Cordyceps Robertsii* was soon
dispelled, and it is only alluded to here as an exploded
figment. It is rather remarkable that so few parasites
have been recorded on the *Sphingidæ;* practically,
indeed, only one, for *Isaria sphingum* and *Cordyceps
sphingum* are different states of the same thing, and
Isaria cinnabarina hardly deserves to count.

HEPIALIDÆ.

As this family contains so many of the caterpillar
fungi, their special descriptions may be preceded
by some general observations which are contained
in Mr. Gray's memoir. "In this family," he says,
"the horny shields partake more or less of the
character of the transverse scales on the separate
segments of the thorax, as is exemplified in the caterpillars of the European species of *Hepialus*. It may
be remarked that more than one-third of the described
species of this family are found in what are designated
the Australian regions, viz. New Zealand, six ; Australia, nine ; and Tasmania, ten—making in all twenty-
five species. As their metamorphoses are at present
unknown, it is impossible to appropriate with certainty
the generic and specific names to all the caterpillars
on which parasites are found." [1]

"Certain localities of Australia and Tasmania [2] are
more favourable for procuring these caterpillars with

---

[1] Gray, "Notices," p. 5.   [2] Ibid., p. 8.

their parasites than others. The occasional humidity of the country greatly encourages the appearance of this singular fungus; at least it is always after their tubes have been filled by the heavy rains, which fall in immense quantities at lengthened intervals, that the entomophytes are found."

In this country it is reputed that *Cordyceps entomor-rhiza* is more commonly found on the larva of *Hepialus* than on any other insect, albeit it was Mr. Gray's opinion that the larva figured by Dickson for this parasite was coleopterous, belonging to the family *Silphidæ*.

NEW ZEALAND VEGETABLE CATERPILLAR.

Cordyceps Robertsii. Hook.[1]

The first succinct account of this entomophyte we have met with was the report of its exhibition at one of the meetings of the Entomological Society in 1836,[2] when the caterpillar was presumed to be that of a *Sphinx* feeding on the sweet potato (*Convolvulus batatus*), an error which probably originated with Dieffenbach, as this passage occurs in his "Travels."[3]

---

[1] Hooker, "Icon. Plant.," i. pl. 11 ; *Journ. Bot.* (1841), iii. pl. 1 ; Colenso, *Lond. Journ. Bot.* (1842), i. p. 304 ; Berkeley, in *Lond. Journ. Bot.*, ii. 209.

[2] Children, *Proc. Ent. Soc.* (1836), p. 6 ; Evans, ibid. (1838), iii. p. 4, f. 4.

[3] Dieffenbach, "Travels in New Zealand," ii. 284.

The caterpillars feed on *Convolvulus batatas;* the *Sphæria Robertsii* is found parasitical on this cater-

pillar, which only occurs at the roots of the rata tree (*Metrosideros robusta*). It was called by Thompson the "bulrush caterpillar" soon after, and seems somehow to have got the name of *Sphæria larvarum*,[1] soon followed by that of *Sphæria Robertsii*, and somehow *Sphæria Forbesii*,[2] which soon dropped. Whilst mentioning synonyms, it may be observed that Corda figured it in his "Icones" under the name of *Sphæria Hugelii*, and when the old genus *Sphæria* was split

FIG. 29.—*Cordyceps Robertsii* on New Zealand caterpillar.

---

[1] Westwood, *Journ. Ent. Soc.* (1836), p. vi.
[2] *Lond. Journ. Bot.* (1848), vii. 578.

up into smaller genera, this, with all similar entomophytes, came under the genus *Cordyceps*, for which
Tulasne endeavoured to substitute *Torrubia*, but it
settled down to *Cordyceps*.

The report of the exhibition at the Entomological
Society, by Mr. Children, of specimens of a caterpillar
from New Zealand, from the back of the neck of
which a long dry vegetable protuberance had been
produced, was to the following effect : " The grub of
New Zealand in appearance resembles that of a
large caterpillar.   It lives entirely on the sweet
potato (*Convolvulus batatas*, or Kumera of the New
Zealanders).   During the season it continues healthy
and active, but ultimately dies ; it retains its natural
appearance, but becomes dry and hard, when an
appendage sprouts from the tail from four to six
inches long, resembling a small twig." With the
view of exciting inquiry into the particulars of the
growth of this vegetable, which was believed both
by Messrs. Robert Brown and J. Bennett to be most
probably a species of *Clavaria*, he mentioned that
O. F. Muller had published a memoir on the subject
of vegetable excrescences found upon animals, all of
which, however, were dead at the time of their discovery ; but that Dr. Mitchell had published a paper
in *Silliman's Journal*, in which he stated that he had
noticed many similar instances, especially in a wasp's
nest, the larvæ of which were not full grown, but that

incipient vegetation had commenced in the bodies of these larvæ, which, however, continued growing, as well as the vegetable substance within their bodies, until the latter burst out and killed the larvæ subsequently to its attaining its size. The circumstance of the growth of mould on the outside of living chrysalides was also mentioned, as proving that it was not essential that the animals should be dead, and also that the introduction of the germs of a plant, or the larvæ of Æestridæ, into the stomach of an animal, had not the effect of destroying their vital properties, and therefore that it was not contrary to nature that the *Clavaria* found upon these caterpillars had grown within their bodies whilst still living.

When described and figured, for the first time, under the name of *Sphæria Robertsii*, only the following notes were given, after stating that it came from New Zealand. " It is there not uncommon, always growing on the dead larvæ of a peculiar insect which feeds on the sweet potato (*Convolvulus batatas*), and in all the specimens I have seen it springs from the back of the neck, just below the head. The larva, though probably when living of a very soft or fleshy character, when dead becomes perfectly hard, and almost horny, so that were it not for the colour it would appear to form one substance with the parasite. Although my specimens are simple, yet there is on

each an appearance that would indicate the stipes
to be sometimes branched. The whole plant is of a
perfectly black colour, and both the stipes and head
are much elongated." The supposed indication of
branching is the little nodule on the stem, which is
present in all specimens, and does not develop further.
The whole plant being of a black colour might possibly refer to badly preserved specimens, but is not
applicable to the many specimens we have seen. As
to the contents of the caterpillars, the remarks of
Professor Westwood here following will suffice.[1] " He
stated that he had examined the internal appearance
of one of these caterpillars, and that the interior was
filled with a hard dry whitish matter, like the kernel
of a nut, and that a very slender tortuous black line
ran down the centre of the body. Dr. Buckland
considered that the substance found in the interior
of the body of the caterpillar was vegetable, burning
with the odour of hay, without any smell of animal
matter, being, as he apprehended, analogous to the
subterraneous plant (mycelium) which produces for
its fruit the common mushroom."

Bearing also upon this subject, an extract was
published from a letter by Dr. J. D. Hooker,[2] then
upon a voyage of discovery in the South, to the

---

[1] *Trans. Entom. Soc. London* (1841-43), iii. p. v.
[2] Hooker's *Journal of Botany*, vol. ii. p. 209.

following effect : "About *Sphæria Robertsii* I collected all the information and as many specimens as
I could, but am still much at a loss to account for its
development. They are found in spring generally
under tree-ferns ; the caterpillar is buried in the
ground, as is the lower portion of the fungus. Now,
both these fungi (*i.e.* this and *C. Taylori*) belong to
caterpillars which bury themselves for the purpose
of undergoing the metamorphosis; and both Mr.
Taylor and Mr. Colenso hold the same opinion, that
in the act of working the soil the spores of the fungus
are lodged in the first joint of the neck, and the
caterpillar settles head upwards to undergo its change
when the vegetable develops itself. 'I do not remember,' you have remarked in your 'Icones,' 'that
the entire body of the insect is filled with a pith or
corky vegetable substance, and that the intestines are
displaced, which my specimens in spirits show well,
and then what does the muscular fibre of the animal
become ? It must, I suppose, be all turned into vegetable, for the skin of the creatures remains quite sound
all the time. This change may take place from the
displacement of one gas and development of another ;
it also occurs in the dark, and is hence somewhat
analogous to the formation of fungi on the timber-
work in mines. However this may be, the whole
insect seems entirely metamorphosed into vegetable
with the exception of the skin and intestines." To

this M. J. Berkeley adds, " As in silkworms attacked by *Botrytis Bassiana*, it is most probable that the caterpillar lingers a short time till the vital organs are clogged up with the mycelium. It does not appear that in any case it has made any progress with its cocoon."

Before entering fully upon the entomological aspect, as interpreted by Mr. Gray, we will quote the remarks of Dr. Pereira on this point, made in 1842. " Dieffenbach suggests that the insect is a species of sphinx which feeds on the sweet potato (*Convolvulus batatas*); but the absence of any spine or horn on the last segment of the larva is an objection to this suggestion. Mr. Doubleday thinks that it may be *Hepialus virescens*, which is found at the root of the rata tree. He has a caterpillar apparently identical with that on which the fungus grows, and which is believed to be the larva of *Hepialus virescens*." [1]

With this suggestion as to the relation of the host, we revert to the account given in the "Notices" of this caterpillar and its affinities. "It has [2] the prothorax entirely covered. The mesothorax has an interior and a posterior transverse shield, with a somewhat quadrate spot of the same horny substance on the lower part of the side; while the metathorax

---

[1] Pereira, in *Pharmaceutical Journal* (1842), vol. ii. p. 592.
[2] Gray's " Notices of Insects," pp. 6, 7.

is furnished with a narrow anterior transverse shield, with a subtriangular and a subquadrate small shield on each side beneath it. The anal segment of the body is also apparently protected by a horny covering."

These caterpillars are usually found in certain districts during spring beneath the "rata" and the tree-ferns that grow in a light porous and peaty soil, under which the caterpillar burrows perpendicularly in search of its food, consisting of the young and fibrous roots of those trees, and afterwards forms horizontal chambers in passing from one root to another. These roots generally extend to a distance from, and form a circle round, the trunk ; the moisture that drops off the leaves keeps the soil in a certain degree of softness, which is beneficial in several ways to the insects. These reside entirely in the earth during the first two states of their existence, as caterpillar and as pupa, and it is not until the third, or perfect state, that they are seen flying about, or settling on the plants in the neighbourhood of their late abode. The perfect state is known to entomologists under the name of *Charagria virescens.* It is of a buffy white satiny colour, with green irregular lines distributed over the surface of the upper wings, while the under wings are of a greenish white. There is also a second species, named *C. rubroviridans,* which is of a larger size, and has the under wings of a pale rusty colour. The caterpillars of both these species may readily become the bases of this fungoid parasite, as their habits are altogether similar."

" The female deposits her eggs in the crevices of the bark of trees and between the fronds of the tree-ferns near the surface of the earth, which the insects of this family are enabled to do by the attenuation of their abdomen and its great capability of extension, which allows it to become an ovipositor of considerable length. As soon as the young comes into existence, it burrows into the earth in search of its food, and it is certain that the caterpillar does not pass any portion of its life on trees, as is supposed by some writers; but the insect remains in the earth during the first two stages of its existence. It is probable, therefore, that the parasite becomes connected with the caterpillar by means of the seed being taken with the food, and thus passing into the interior of the insect, which had previously become sickly and weakened by the rains which fall at times in great quantities, saturating the earth around it. It is certainly only after such atmospheric influences that the germination of the plant predominates over the growth of the insect, which is found of various ages with the fungus in different stages of growth."

Taylor says that the New Zealanders' name for this plant-caterpillar is " Hotete," " Aweto," " Weri," and " Anuhe." The natives eat the plants, which when fresh have the flavour of a nut, and also use them when burnt as colouring-matter for their tattooing, rubbing the powder into the wounds, in which state it has a strong animal smell.[1]

"The interior of the insect becomes completely filled by the inner plant, or thallus (mycelium); after which the growing head of the outer plant or fungus, passing to a state of maturity, usually forces its way out through the tissue of the joint between the head and first segment of the thorax. The fungus grows to various lengths, reaching in some examples to the length of ten or more inches ; of course, this depends in a great measure on the depth to which the cater-pillar may be buried at the commencement of the outer growth of the fungus. It is stated that this caterpillar settles head upwards to undergo its change, when the vegetable develops itself.

"But it is evident that the caterpillars are subject to the full development of the parasite at various periods of their growth ; certainly some of them, from their size, are attacked long before they are sufficiently matured to place themselves in that position which it is necessary for them to assume before they undergo their final metamorphosis. This idea may have originated from the specimens having the parasite usually projecting forwards, but it may

---

[1] Taylor, *Tasmanian Journal* (1842), p. 307.

readily be observed, on examining them, that the base of the plant invariably rises perpendicularly from its origin before it is bent, as if the caterpillar had become stationary in a horizontal position in consequence of its being affected by the internal thallus, and the plant had then naturally made its way directly upwards through the peaty soil to the surface, which it would eventually appear to surmount by two or three inches, which portion becomes granulated when matured. It may be added, from information conveyed to the writer, that the fungus, after appearing above the earth, has been gradually withdrawn through the loose soil with the caterpillar attached when the latter has been found in the living state; of course, in such a case the caterpillar was not buried far in the soil, and therefore the fungus was short and easily removed.[1]

" The stem of this parasite, it may be remarked, is sometimes slightly coated on the part which is near the surface of the earth with a white woolly matter; the stem is also slender, and somewhat weak in proportion to some others, and it appears to be often broken when a new stem arises from or near the same place—which, it is said, is ‘ not known to occur in

---

[1] A similar caterpillar has been found perfectly changed into a vegetable substance, but in want of the external fungus, numerous examples of which were dug up in a garden at New Plymouth, New Zealand (Taylor, " New Zealand," p. 424).

any other plant with which we are as yet acquainted in the vegetable kingdom.' "[1]

The figure by Corda[2] represents the plant proceeding in a perpendicular manner from the "tail,"[3] or anal portion of the caterpillar. Such examples must be rare ; for though a great many specimens of this entomophyte have been examined by the writer, yet he has never met with it in a single instance. A specimen has also been recorded "with an undeveloped stipes growing out of the tail of the caterpillar, as well as one from the back of the head."[4]

Great confusion has existed as to this caterpillar. "One writer evidently confounds it with that of the *Sphinx Carolina*, which cosmopolitan insect is extremely common in New Zealand, as elsewhere, feeding on the *Convolvulus batatas*, to the great annoyance of the natives, who cultivate that plant for food. This insect, when in its perfect state, is the one referred to by the same writer[5] as attracted by the scarlet flowers of the 'rata,' flitting from blossom to blossom, seeking the honey which abounds within them. A wood-boring larva has also been sent from New Zealand as the same as that with which the

---

[1] *Medical Times* (1844), p. 200.
[2] *Sphæria Hugelii*, Corda, " Icon.," vol. iv. p. 44, t. ix, f. 129.
[3] *Journ. Proc. Ent. Soc.* (1836), ii. p. 6.
[4] *Tasmanian Journal* (1849), p. 75.
[5] Colenso, *Lond. Journ. Bot.*, i. p. 304.

parasite is connected. These mistakes probably originated through the misinformation conveyed to travellers by the natives."

Amongst the features presented by this *Cordyceps*, it is worthy of note that the stem is always very long and slender in proportion to other species, and that there is a little nodule or projection on one side of the stem, scarcely half-way up. The fertile portion is also very long and cylindrical, the perithecia being arranged around the central axis, closely packed together, nearly free, and not immersed in the stroma, as in the majority of species (fig. 29). The perithecia are very small, and densely packed together, so that the peculiarity is not so observable as it would be if the perithecia were larger and not so densely packed together. There is often a suggestion of a cuticle covering the perithecia in the young condition, which is probably the case.

AUSTRALIAN VEGETABLE CATERPILLAR.

Cordyceps Gunnii. Berk.[1]

Although collected some years previously, in Tasmania, this entomophyte was first made known in

---

[1] Berkeley, in Hooker's *Lond. Journ. Bot.* (1848), vol. vii. p. 563, pl. 22; Currey, *Linn. Trans.*, xxii. pl. 45, figs. 1, 2; Saccardo, "Sylloge," ii. No. 5030.

1848, when it was described and figured, since which period it has been several times found both in Tasmania and in parts of Australia. "The stem, with caterpillar attached, is from five to eighteen inches long, rarely branched, flexuous, rugged below, cylindrical, solid, white, collecting particles of sand by means of a few downy threads. The head is from two to three inches long, one-third to one quarter of an inch thick, perfectly cylindrical, or lanceolate, obtuse, or a little acute at the apex, sometimes compressed, yellow below, with the top of the stem becoming black above. The mouths of the perithecia scarcely projecting; sporidia breaking up into truncate (almost quadrate) joints." This description is accompanied by an extract from

FIG. 30.—*Cordyceps Gunnii*, from Tasmania.

the letter of Mr. Gunn. "The caterpillar burrows in the ground to various depths, from four inches to one foot, and the fungus seemed to fill up the hole made by the caterpillar, which in all cases is erect (we figure one in which it was at angles with the caterpillar). The caterpillar and stipes varied from five to eighteen inches in length, and were white, except about two or three inches which projected above the surface of the ground, and were shaded off from the white colour below the ground to yellow at the surface, and thence to a deep olivaceous black at the extremity."

The specimen figured differs from those ordinarily seen in some important particulars (fig. 30). It was from a dried specimen, selected for its short stem, and it is smaller and less robust than usual; moreover, the parasite rises at right angles from the caterpillar, whereas it is usually continued in a line with the body. The specimens figured by Berkeley[1] are of the more usual size and proportions, and that given by Gray[2] is also equally good (plate 1, fig. 4). There is also to be found in the fructification of this species a good feature not to be overlooked, in that the linear sporidia are broader than usual, and break up into quadrate joints; in other species, as a rule, they are

---

[1] Berkeley, in Hooker's *Journal* (1848), pl. 22.
[2] Gray, "Notices," pl. 11, fig. 6.

L

considerably longer than broad.   It is found not only
in Tasmania, but in many parts of Australia, especially in the south, and though constantly obtained
by collectors without the caterpillar, and sometimes
only a fragment of the stem, there is no difficulty in
its identification.

As to the insect which is subject to the attacks of
this entomophyte, we could not presume to write with
authority, although Berkeley supposed it was a *Cossus*
or *Hepialus*, but fortunately we can fall back upon
Mr. Gray for his opinion on the subject, and the
evidence on which it was based.

First of all, as to a caterpillar bearing a species of
Cordyceps, doubtless only a variation of *C. Gunnii*,
with an abnormal head, Mr. Gray says, "Among a
series of Entomophytes from New Zealand (?) was
found one;[1] but whether it had been accidentally
placed among them for preservation, or had come
with them from that country, is unknown.   It, however, differs greatly from its companion in the horny
shields on the thorax, each segment of which is
strongly protected in front by a somewhat crescent-
shaped shield ; that on the prothorax is the largest,
while the other two gradually decrease in size ; the
one on the metathorax has beneath it on each side
a spot of the same kind of horny substance.   It may

---

[1] Gray, pl. 2, fig. 6.

be remarked that in the formation, and position, of the shields it approaches very nearly to those seen on the caterpillar of *Hepialus lupulinus* of Europe. It is probable that the habits and food of this caterpillar are similar to those of *C. Robertsii;* but in this case it evidently endeavours to seek the mouth of its perpendicular tube after it becomes affected by the internal germination of the seed of the fungus, which eventually checks its progress when near the orifice, where it remains stationary, after which the external growth of the fungus takes place while the insect is in an upright position, causing it to burst forth apparently through the suture above the labium, and thus it grows on the same plane with the caterpillar. Its growth having taken place in a ready-formed tube, also allows of the free development of the stem, which so increases in thickness as to split the head into two equal parts ; while a portion of the fungus, when fully developed, always appears above the orifice, and the end spreads out into a palmate form."

Then follows an account of the normal form of the same. "The caterpillar of *Cordyceps Gunnii* was found in Tasmania.[1] The prothorax is almost entirely covered by a horny shield ; the mesothorax is furnished with a semicircular shield in front, and a lengthened subtriangular spot of the same horny

[1] Gray, pl. 5, figs. 7, 8.

substance on each side close to the posterior margin ; while the metathorax has a moderately-sized sub-quadrate spot on each side, of a less horny substance. Another caterpillar [1] was brought from Victoria, and differs from the former in possessing an additional narrow semicircular shield in front of the metathorax. Another caterpillar is also known to the writer, which is found in New South Wales ; but it is only furnished with a semicircular shield on the front of the mesothorax, and with a small subquadrate spot on the side of the metathorax, both of which are apparently of a less horny substance than that which entirely covers the prothorax.

" Such variations of the shields are observed in those found in the European species of the genus *Hepialus.* The similarity of their modes of life, how-ever, causes these three caterpillars to become the bases of the same kind of fungus parasite ; and it is probable that these caterpillars are all referable to species of the genus *Pielus,* or of some closely allied forms." [2]

" Certain localities of Australia and Tasmania [3] are more favourable for procuring these caterpillars, with their parasites, than others. The occasional humidity

---

[1] Gray, pl. 2, fig. 7.   [2] Gray, " Notices," p. 7.
[3] Melbourne and Hunter's River ; but it is in the neighbourhood of Launceston, Tasmania, that the greatest number of specimens have been found.

of the country greatly encourages the appearance of this singular fungus ; at least, it is always after the tubes have been filled by the heavy rains, which fall in immense quantities [1] at lengthened intervals, that the entomophytes are found. The caterpillars that become the bases of the fungi vary much in size, reaching in some examples to the length of four and a half inches ; this may be considered to show that the caterpillars become possessed of the germ of the parasite at various periods of their age, and that it must be obtained while residing in the burrows, wherein they pass the chief portion of their existence, and which they form. quite regardless of the nature of the soil, whether it be composed of sand or clay. The tubes are sometimes made to the depth of two or three feet, and are lined when formed with a coarse web, which greatly facilitates their progress within them ; and these tubes are sometimes extended in a horizontal position, while seeking for the various roots that are buried beneath the soil, and which constitute their food. When the caterpillar feels the effects of the inward growth of its enemy, it no doubt, from the position of the plant, which is longitudinal with the insect, seeks the orifice of its perpendicular tube, but it is apparently checked in

---

[1] The fall of rain on one occasion, in Tasmania, during February, 1854, was equal to eight and three quarter inches in thirty-eight hours.

its progress at a distance from the opening, which distance is shown by the length of the fungus on the different specimens of the entomophytes, reaching in some examples to a foot and more. After the thallus (mycelium) has filled the interior, the outer portion of the plant invariably bursts forth about the head and prothorax, which two portions are usually covered by the mycelium from which the parasite takes its rise; it then appears for about two or three inches above the earth, ending in a lengthened oval velvety head, of an olivaceous black colour, while the stem beneath the ground is white, shadowing off into yellow above it. In some cases two, and in others three, fungi take their rise from the same base. It may be further remarked that the caterpillar is sometimes discovered coated with a white mould; and it may be added that chrysalides were also found by Mr. Hawkes at Franklin Village, Tasmania, each of which had a fungus growing from it. The germ from which the fungus sprung had probably been taken by the caterpillar before its metamorphosis into the chrysalis state, and, the rainy weather happening to set in soon after, caused the germination of the spore."

Tasmanian Vegetable Caterpillar.

Cordyceps Hawkesii. Gray.[1]

This entomophyte is, in many particulars, distinguished from *Cordyceps Gunnii*, and, like that species, is found in Tasmania. Mr. Gray was the first to point out its distinctive character and apply to it the above name. The entire length of the club and its host is from five to nine inches, of which the club does not occupy an inch; it is cylindrical, slightly narrowed and truncate at the apex, dotted with the immersed perithecia. The stem is irregular, flexuous, from two to four or five inches long, but slender, and for a great part of its length clad with a fulvous woolly coating (plate 1, fig. 8). It is not thicker than a straw in many specimens, and altogether of a much more slender habit than *C. Gunnii*. Two clubs arise together from the same spot in some instances, or from different parts of the same caterpillar, and occasionally there are three or four clubs on one individual. The internal structure is undoubtedly the same as in this genus, but the dimensions of the sporidia are not named.

The specimens were obtained by Mr. Hawkes in Tasmania in the month of April, and after him the

---

[1] Gray, "Notices of Fungi," p. 8, pl. 5, figs. 10-12; *Grevillea* (1891), vol. xix. p. 76.

species has been named.   It can scarcely be confounded with *Cordyceps Gunnii*, for the club is not nearly so thick or dark, and has a different form. The stem, besides being more slender, is irregular, contorted, and knotted, besides being woolly.   From *Cordyceps Robertsii*, again, it differs in the broader and shorter head, as well as in the character of the stem. A comparison of the figures of the two will show that there is no difficulty in distinguishing them.   To the entomologist an important difference from both the other species will be recognized, in the clubs springing from any part of the body of the insect.

This species has not been noticed in recent mycological works, partly on account of the memoir in which it was recorded having been privately printed, and hence comparatively unknown, and partly from the absence of any definite technical description. Although *Cordyceps Gunnii* appears now and then in different localities in Australia, the present species has not as yet been recognized outside of Tasmania.

We must, however, advert to the account which Mr. Gray[1] has given of this entomophyte from his own point of view, and his opinion of the host upon which it establishes itself.   "It bears," he says, "a great similarity to those of New Zealand, and, from its manner of growth, one is induced to suppose that

---

[1] Gray, "Notices," p. 8.

the external plant also forces its way at once through
the sandy soil, wherever the insect may happen to
be situated in its burrow when overtaken by the
effect of the internal development of the thallus.
Judging from the various lengths of the plant, this
takes place at different depths from the surface; and
it is sometimes evident that the two ends of the
caterpillar, when so affected by parasites, are buried
at unequal depths. Thus the plant emerging at the
anal portion in one example was apparently buried
for three and a half inches, while that originating at
the anterior part was not buried for more than two
and a half inches, showing a difference of one inch
between the two ends, and at the same time proving
the justice of the opinion previously expressed in
reference to the New Zealand entomophytes, that
the plant takes its rise from the caterpillar while
in a horizontal or nearly horizontal position. The
specimens in general show that the stem above the
surface (*i.e.* between the earth and the fructification)
did not exceed a half or a quarter of an inch in
length ; and the buried portion of the stem, it may
be remarked, especially that nearest the surface, is
covered with a quantity of fulvous woolly matter,
which matter sometimes extends itself to the body
of the caterpillar.

"The most curious feature, however, of this parasite
is that it grows from various portions of the body of

the caterpillar, and in this respect offers a great difference from that of the New Zealand kind. Various examples of this distinction are among the specimens sent by Mr. Hawkes to the British Museum. One exhibits two fungoid tubercles forcing their way through the head, two fungi growing from the same base on the side of the abdominal segments, and a short fungus proceeding from the anal segment posteriorly. Another specimen was apparently in the act of progressing head upwards, but which had been checked in its progress, and the fungus had thus grown from both its ends; yet the two plants had appeared above the surface of the earth near to each other. That from the head is about five and a quarter inches, while the one from the anal portion is eight and a quarter inches in length; the latter, however, proceeded from a short stem which had first apparently grown downwards before the plant turned towards the surface. The stem is irregular in its length, and in places is very woolly, especially the part near the surface, and is more so on the one from the head. Some of these caterpillars bear a fungus composed of a short stem at the base, which has evidently been broken, and has then given origin to several branches; these branches are more slender than where the plant consists only of a single stem throughout. The discovery of this species of parasite has dispelled the idea which had been entertained up to the present time, that *Cordyceps Gunnii* was the only one to be found in Tasmania. A similar one, or perhaps the same species, is also found in Victoria.

" The caterpillar may be that of a species of *Pielus*, or of some closely allied genus ; but the perfect insect is unknown at present. The fungus was found in a sandy district, but the exact locality was not mentioned, and from its appearance it is not improbable that the mode of life, and food of the caterpillar, are extremely like those of the New Zealand entomophytes. It is, however, of a peculiar deep reddish purple colour, about three 'or four inches in length, partaking of the same form as the others ; but the shields on the thorax differ. The prothorax is almost entirely covered ; the mesothorax has a narrow shield forming a cresent towards the anterior margin ; the metathorax is only furnished with a very narrow crescent-shaped shield, and a sub-quadrate spot on the side."

MURRUMBIDGEE VEGETABLE CATERPILLAR.

Cordyceps Taylori. Berk.[1]

The largest and finest of all entomophytes is that which was brought originally from the banks of the

---

[1] Berkeley, Hooker's *Journ. Bot.* (1842), ii. p. 210, pl. 7; Saccardo, "Sylloge," ii. No. 5041.

Murrumbidgee, in Australia, and thus described by
the Rev. M. J. Berkeley: "Springing from the head
of an extremely large caterpillar. About six stems
grow from the same point, forming a compact cylindrical mass two and a half inches long, three quarters
of an inch thick, connate, slightly branched and anastomosing; expanding slightly upwards, and giving
off a branch of short, much-compressed, forked, and
palmate branches, which are dotted above with the
perithecia. The apices are somewhat pointed. The
colour of the whole is a deep red brown, inclining to
tawny when dry. The whole of the branches are
clothed with a very thin coat of extremely short
forked irregular flocci, which give the surface a dull
appearance when dry. They are at first solid, but at
length become hollow. A portion of the caterpillar
is filled with a white corky substance, for the root is
more or less coated with a spongy mass, consisting of
very slightly branched wavy threads.

"The only specimen I have seen was not mature,
but probably arrived nearly at its full growth, as the
incipient perithecia were evident towards the tops of
the branches."

The following notes are from a letter of Dr. Joseph
Hooker. The information, he states, was received from
the Rev. Mr. Taylor, of Waimate. "This caterpillar
fungus was picked up on the banks of the Murrumbidgee river, ten miles from the township of Yap (in

New Holland), in a rich thick alluvial soil, with many others of the same kinds. When fresh it was eight inches long, and three inches of the fungus from the nape of the neck were buried underground, on the surface of which is the oval or circular flower-like bunch of branches of a brown velvety appearance when fresh. The caterpillar has a great resemblance to the green wattle caterpillar, which produces a large brown moth. The discoverer, Mr. John Allan, the only person who has heard of it, found many empty holes near, as if the chrysalis had been hatched, and he saw many empty shells of these grubs scattered about the same place, and at night the brown moths were so numerous as to be quite troublesome. The body of the insect was solid and pithy; the outer skin attached to the substance of the centre, which has no roots in it; and, moreover, the pith is of the same substance as the stem, which is as thick as, if not thicker than, the body of the caterpillar. Both the pith and stem when burnt have a strong animal smell. Mr. Allan saw nearly thirty about March, 1837."

Another specimen, sent over a year or two since, was in excellent fruit, being fully mature, and with this the technical description was completed (fig. 31).

Mr. Gray has some observations on this species which may be added to the above, although not containing much additional information, still leaving the grub undetermined. "The remarkable large caterpillar found in the neighbourhood of the river Murrumbidgee, New South Wales (probably also found at Murray River, Port Macquarie), may ultimately prove to be a species of the same family ; but it is to be regretted that no opportunity has occurred for carefully examining an example."

The caterpillars of these entomophytes, each of which measures some six inches in length, were found in a rich black alluvial soil ; and nearly thirty examples were secured by Mr. Allan in 1837.[1] Attention was directed to them in consequence of the ground being perforated in many places. From some of the tubes were seen emerging numerous pupa-cases, and from others these entomophytes, partly projecting above the surface of the earth. Many of the pupa-cases were open, as if the insects had performed the last act of their transitional life, *i.e.* throwing off the pupa-case, or last skin, before appearing in their aërial condition. The perfect insects afterwards showed themselves as night approached, and became extremely troublesome to travellers by flitting about their lights. On obtaining one it proved to be a large 'brown moth,' which may turn out to be an undescribed, though known, species of *Pielus*, or of an allied genus. The female measures, in expanse of wings, nearly ten inches, while the male is rather less.

---

[1] Taylor, *Tasmanian Journal* (1842), p. 308, fig. 2 ; Thompson, *Medical Times* (1844), p. 200.

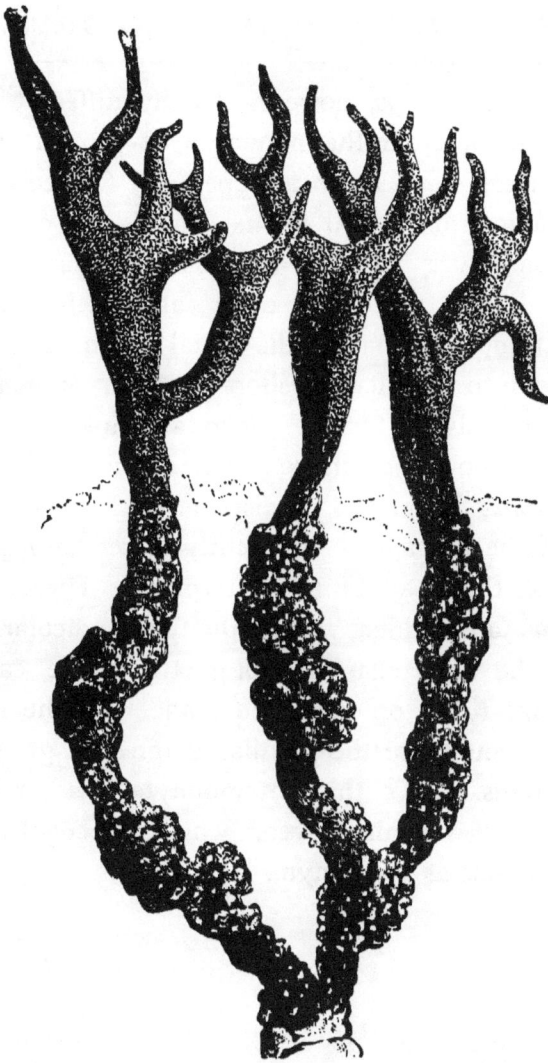

FIG. 31.—*Cordyceps Taylori* (from *Gardener's Chronicle*).

"The parasite is, however, totally different from any of the others in the manner of its growth; it has a very thick stem, which is apparently formed by the close union of several stalks (this is its condition when immature, but when fully matured the separate stalks divide from each other, and each becomes distinct and free), having the apical portion distinctly divided into a series of short irregular branches of a brown velvety texture. The anterior portion is just seen above the surface at the orifice of the tube, and affords the means of discovering it. The basal part of the parasite is apparently forced through the front of the head of the caterpillar. These latter portions are hidden within the perpendicular tube which the caterpillar had originally made, causing the plant to be on the same plane with the insect, which accounts for the peculiar manner of growth of the fungus."[1] To this entomophyte a second and later name was also given,[2] which, of course, now only reckons as a synonym.

GOAT-MOTH FUNGUS.

To this family, Mr. Gray[3] remarks, belongs the

---

[1] Gray's "Notices," p. 9.

[2] *Sphæria innominata*, Taylor, *Tasmanian Journal* (1842), p. 308, fig. 2; *Medical Times* (1844), p. 200.

[3] Gray's "Notices," p. 9.

goat-moth (*Cossus ligniperda*), "the caterpillar of which was found by Mr. Bond in England, in a burrow that it had formed in a tree, wherein it was attached by one side of the body to the surface of the tube by means of a mass of white cottony mould. The mould also extended partly round each segment, and appeared through the spiracles of the unattached side of its body, and also through the false feet, showing that the interior of the body was completely filled with it ; but the body was somewhat contracted." It would be futile to make any suggestion as to the parasite on the basis of such meagre information.

"The caterpillar of this insect always resides in the trunks of trees, such as willows, oaks, and elms, feeding on the wood, and at the same time perforating it in all directions. The number of burrows which these insects make during the period of three or four years that they are stated to live, greatly weakens the trees, so that they are sometimes blown down by the wind, or they even fall by the weight of the top part of the tree. When the caterpillar is about to pass into a chrysalis, it seeks the entrance of its burrow, where it is surrounded with a cocoon, composed of pieces of rotten wood glued together, a portion of which always remains apparent from the entrance, so that the perfect insect, after a time, may easily make its escape."

It is possible that the fungus alluded to in the

M

following note may be the same, or allied to, that of the *Cossus*, and is thus cited by Mr. Gray : "A wood-boring caterpillar has been mentioned by Mr. Hawkes in a letter in the following terms: 'The grub so destructive to the wattle trees in Tasmania has also been found converted into a fungus, the growth of which has been two or three feet, filling the channel the grub had made through the heart of the tree in the process of boring.' This may be the grub of which Mr. Milligan[1] mentions having picked up the skin, distended with the fungus-like substance characteristic of the .parasite, in a grove of young wattle trees on the eastern side of the Windmill Hill, near Launceston. The writer has since been informed by Mr. Bakewell that the caterpillar which is so destructive to the wattle trees is that of *Zeuzera liturata*. It is extremely common in many parts of Australia, where it is much sought after by the natives, who devour an immense quantity of them, as a favourite article of food." We have seen such borings in trees, filled with a kind of imperfect fungus, entirely mycelium, of the kind known as *Xylostroma*, but wholly unconnected with the insect. Examples are occasionally sent over from the Australian colonies.

---

[1] *Proc. Royal Soc. Van Diemen's Land* (1852), p. 149.

GOAT-MOTH MOULD.

Rotæa flava. Cesati.[1]

This mould appears in the form of minute superficial tufts, united and compacted at the base, so as to form little globose protuberances held together by a kind of gluten. These clumps are not more than half a millimetre in diameter, with a roughened surface. The conidia or spores are club-shaped, with from five to seven septa or divisions, lengthened downwards into a kind of stem, such stems being compacted into a sort of stroma. The spores are rounded at the apex, yellowish; involved in a glutinous mucus from thirty-five to forty micromillimetres long, and five or six broad.

This entomophyte is stated to occur on the *Cossus*, but whether on caterpillar or imago is not recorded. It is a very peculiar kind of mould, which we have never met with; but it would appear, superficially, to be somewhat related to the species of *Microcera*. Yet Saccardo has placed it in quite a different section; hence we presume that he had doubts of its relationship to the *Tubercularieæ*.

---

[1] Cesati, *Botan. Zeitung* (1851), p. 180; Bonorden, *Botan. Zeitung* (1853), p. 283, pl. 7, fig. 3; Saccardo, "Sylloge," iv. No. 1085.

COMMON CATERPILLAR CLUB.

Cordyceps entomorrhiza. Dicks.[1]

This British species of entomophyte was described by Dickson in 1785, and figured, although in a peculiar slender form, with a globose head, in which it differs from the examples seen in more recent times. Mr. Gray says that the larva represented by Dickson may probably belong to the *Silphidæ,* the typical example of the *Sphæria* springing from the pectoral portion of the thoracic segments. "Many of these insects," he adds, "frequent decomposed animal and vegetable substances, both in their larva and perfect states. Others reside under the bark of trees and in fungi." The original figure by Dickson suggests a distinct variety much more than the *gracilis* of Greville, which some continue to retain as a distinct species.

FIG. 32.—Common Caterpillar Club. *Cordyceps entomorrhiza,* on larvæ.

---

[1] Dickson, "Plant Crypt. Britt.," p. 22, t. 3, f. 3; Kirby and Spence, "Introd. to Entom.," iv. 208; Berkeley, "Outlines," p. 382, pl. 23, fig. 5; Persoon, "Syn. Fungi," p. 3; Tulasne, "Selecta Fung. Carp.," iii. p. 14, pl. 45, fig. 6; Saccardo, "Sylloge," ii. No. 5012; Currey, *Linn. Trans.,* xxii. pl. 45, fig. 6.

On one occasion we collected one hundred specimens in a brickfield at Hitchin, in Bedfordshire, in
the space of two or three hours, and yet it is not
generally common. In most instances only a single
fungus is seen on one larva, but occasionally two.
It consists of a white, branched mycelium, spreading
externally over the insect, and internally absorbing
the natural structure, converting it into a kind of
pulverulent sclerotium. From near the head of the
larva, as we observed, generally from the second
joint, and at the back of the head, arose a stem of
from three quarters of an inch to two inches in length,
bearing at its summit a small ovate, or egg-shaped
head, in which the fructifying organs are imbedded,
the length and direction of the stem being influenced
by the position of the insect (fig. 32). When, as is
often the case, the larva was imbedded at right angles
to the soil, head uppermost, and near the surface, the
stem was short, and in a line with the body; but if
more deeply imbedded the stem was lengthened, so
that the head was elevated about a quarter of an inch
above the surface. If the insect lay in any other
position the stem was contorted, or arose at right
angles to the larva, always striving to appear above
the surface, and there produce its rounded head.
The stem was externally of a dirty yellowish colour,
and the head of a brick-red, or livid brown. The
whole substance is fleshy and fragile when fresh, so

as to snap readily when roughly handled. Our figure (fig. 33) represents two specimens, natural size, and in the position in which they were found, the upper portion only, to the length of about half an inch, appearing above the surface.

If the head of this parasitic fungus be cut either vertically or horizontally, there will be observed near the margin a number of small cells which contain the perithecia, or flask-shaped vessels, within which the fruit is generated (fig. 33). These perithecia puncture the surface of the head with their ostiola, or necks, through an orifice of which the sporidia are ultimately excluded. Within the perithecia are a number of long cylindrical asci, or transparent membranaceous vessels, at first attached at the base, and closed at the summit, in each of which are produced eight long thread-like sporidia (fig. 33 *a*, top of ascus, the lower portion being removed to show the sporidia). Each sporidium ultimately breaks up into a number of small joints (fig. 33 *b*). A similar structure prevails in all the species of the genus *Cordyceps*, to which this fungus belongs.

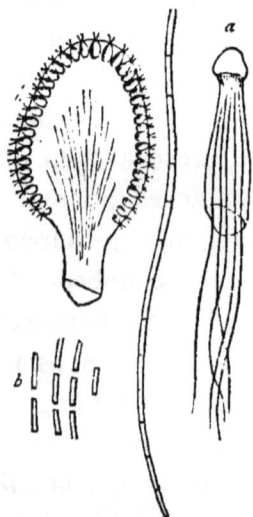

FIG. 33.—Section of the head of *Cordyceps* with sporidia, variously magnified.

A curious notion prevails in the district where these parasites were found, that they, and the insect, are somewhat mysteriously associated with the colts-foot (*Tussilago farfara*), that plant being common in the same locality ; and, certainly when breaking through the ground, the buds bear some resemblance to the *Cordyceps*. One individual transplanted into his own garden some larvæ with their parasites, confident that he should obtain from them as many plants of "coltsfoot." By the present time he is probably convinced, by failure, of his error.

var. *gracilis*. Grev.[1]

The form found in Shetland and in Scotland, and figured by Greville under the name of *Sphæria gracilis*, differs only in its rather more graceful habit and in a rather more yellowish tinge. It really does not merit to be considered even as a variety, although Saccardo[2] has thought fit to maintain it as a distinct species. It has also been found in Algiers,[3] and in the neighbourhood of Paris. The specimen figured by Mr. Gray as *C. entomorrhiza*[4] appears to be this slender form. He says of it, "From the appearances

---

[1] Greville, "Scot. Crypt. Flora," pl. 86 ; Berkeley, in "Eng. Flora," v. pt. ii. p. 232.

[2] Saccardo, "Sylloge," vol. ii. No. 5011.

[3] Durieu and Montagne, "Flore Algerie," 449, pl. 25, fig. 2.

[4] Gray's "Notices," p. 12, pl. 3, fig. 10.

exhibited by the caterpillar it is supposed to belong
to the *Lithosiidæ*. It was found at Bulstrode, in
Buckinghamshire, and had probably, while feeding
on the low-growing plants, come in contact with the
germ of the parasite. The caterpillar would seem
afterwards to have buried itself among the damp
vegetable *débris*, apparently to the depth of an inch
and a half. While thus located it germinates, and
the parasite grows from it, having the basal half of
the lengthened stem furnished with short slender
roots, proceeding from various parts within that
length, while the apical portion is smooth and without any such appendages, which shows that it was
exposed above the surface of the earth. The apex
terminates in a small (nearly) globular head. The
parasite grows from the thorax, which is completely
covered by the mycelium. The body of the insect
has minute roots springing from it."

The description given by Greville [1] of this variety
is as follows : " Root composed of a few stout divisions,
each throwing out fibres, but not freely. Stem one
to two inches long, erect, a line or more in diameter ;
form somewhat flexuous, equal, ochraceous-brown, of
a coriaceous texture. Receptacle roundish ovate, one-
fourth to one-third of an inch long, smooth, between
carnose and coriaceous, and of a darkish brown

---

[1] Greville, "Scot. Crypt. Flora," ii. pl. 86.

colour. Sphærules (perithecia) very pale, occupying the whole exterior of the receptacle ; oblong, with a short narrow neck, which is seen only on dissection, as the mouth does not project from the surface of the receptacle. I have not detected anything like regular sporules, but the sphærules (perithecia) contain a mass of filaments, which are very fragile towards their extremities, where I observed a few dissepiments. These, by separating, may perform the office of sporules." Of course, Greville was not acquainted at that time with the peculiarity of the sporidia, which are long and thread-like, separating into short joints.

var. *menesteridis.* Müll.[1]

In 1878 Baron von Mueller, and the Rev. M. J. Berkeley, described in conjunction, under the name of *Cordyceps menesteridis*, a form which is hardly even a variety of this species from Australia. We fail to detect any divergence from the type, and only retain the name here for the sake of recording it, and out of respect for our friends, who in this instance were evidently misguided. It is said

FIG. 34.—Common Caterpillar Club, Australian form. *Cordyceps entomorrhiza,*var. *menesteridis* (after Berkeley).

---

[1] *Gardener's Chronicle* (1878), p. 791, fig. 130.

of it that "the stem is slender, and attenuated upwards at first, with the elliptical rufous head dotted with the orifices of the perithecia. The stem is three quarters of an inch in length, becoming of a sienna brown, sometimes sending down a long root." It was found on the larva of *Menesteris laticollis*, in the neighbourhood of Melbourne, Australia (fig. 34).

American Caterpillar Club.

Cordyceps insignis.   Cooke and Rav.[1]

This claims to be the largest of the North American species of *Cordyceps*, and appears to have grown upon buried Lepidopterous larvæ. It was collected on the seaboard of South Carolina, by the late Mr. Ravenel, and has somewhat the habit and appearance of *Cordyceps entomorrhiza*, but much larger and more robust. The stem almost straight, from three to four centimetres long, thick and longitudinally sulcate, of a dirty white or pale ochre colour. The head, or capitulum, nearly globose, or oval, or pear-shaped, one centimetre and a half long, and one centimetre broad at the broadest part, livid purple, dotted and rough with the mouths of the imbedded perithecia, reminding one, in size, form, and colour, of *Cordyceps capitata*, which, however, does not grow on insects.

---

[1] *Grevillea* (1884), vol. xii. p. 38.

The asci are very long, and the thread-like sporidia nearly half a millimetre long, breaking up into frustules, about twelve micromillimetres in length. One of the specimens, which was attached, sprang from the back of the head of the larva (pl. 1, fig. 9). The shortness of the stem seems to indicate that the larvæ were not buried at any great depth, certainly not more than an inch, beneath the surface, and possibly not so much. When living and moist, the whole fungus was probably larger than the dimensions we have given from the dried fungus.

INDIAN CATERPILLAR CLUB.

Cordyceps falcata. Berk.[1]

Of the species of Entomogenous fungi brought home from India by Dr. Hooker, this is one of the most characteristic. It was found growing upon dead caterpillars at Myrong, but the species, or even the genus, of the host cannot readily be determined. The fertile stems are about an inch and a quarter in height, and a line thick, two or three growing together, with a quantity of sterile, thread-like, acute, abortive processes at the base. The fertile clubs are cylindrical, swelling gradually upwards into an

---

[1] Berkeley, in Hooker's *Journ. Bot.* (1854), p. 211, pl. 8, fig. 2; Saccardo, "Sylloge," ii. No. 5040.

oblique sickle-shaped head, or capitulum, the surface of which is rough with the projecting mouths, or ostiola, of the imbedded perithecia. The long asci and imperfect sporidia within them seem to be of the usual type of the genus (pl. 2, fig. 14). Botanically this species differs from all others known in the cæspitose falcate heads, which are naked at the base on the convex side. From dried specimens it is almost impossible to say what was the colour of the living fungus.

All that can be said on the entomological side of the question is contained in the following note by Mr. Gray:[1] "The Indian caterpillars are represented as having parasitical fungi growing from their heads. It must be remarked that the figures of the caterpillar are not sufficiently characteristic to make out exactly whether they belong to this family (*Hepialidæ*) or not; the manner of growth of the plants, however, induces the supposition that their habits, especially those of the caterpillar, which bears the *Cordyceps falcata*, most probably accord with those that have been previously given, and therefore they may also be species of the same family."

---

[1] Gray's "Notices," p. 10.

Knob-Headed Club.

Cordyceps racemosa.   Berk.[1]

Another of the Indian species of entomophytes brought by Dr. Hooker from Myrong is the above named, on a dead caterpillar, which Mr. Gray evidently thinks may belong to the *Hepialidæ*. In this species the stem is nearly two inches high, soiled below with fragments of earth, above very dark, smooth, and swollen at the top into a little ovate head, which is covered with short processes each tipped with an ovate knob. The fructification is immature, but otherwise it agrees so well with the general character of the genus that there is no room for doubt (pl. 1, fig. 9). It grows from a smaller caterpillar than *Cordyceps falcata*, and the stem is very different, so that it cannot be any form of that species. Except for its place of growth it might easily be passed over as an imperfect *Balanophora.*

Red Caterpillar Club.

Cordyceps militaris.   Linn.[2]

The well-known red *Cordyceps militaris* is a familiar

---

[1] Berkeley, in Hooker's *Journ. Bot.* (1854), p. 211, pl. 8, fig. 3; Saccardo, "Sylloge," ii. No. 5049.

[2] Linnæus, "Sp. Plant." (1562) ; Tulasne, "Selecta Fung. Carp."

object to most field naturalists in this country, and its bright colour prevents its being often overlooked.

The clubs are either solitary or in clusters, fleshy and red or orange, sometimes purplish, about one and a half or two inches high; the club is ovoid or club-shaped, but variable in form, and rough from the projecting perithecia; the stem is equal and comparatively short. Internal structure as in other species, with elongated asci, containing thread-like sporidia, which break up into short joints.

FIG. 35.—*Cordyceps militaris.*

Mr. Gray refers several of his figures to this species, but of some of these we entertain doubts, but from mere figures a decided opinion is scarcely possible. The chrysalis represented on one of his figures,[1] he says, "no doubt belongs to the family *Notodontidæ*, and is remarkable for being armed with hooks on the anal projection, each of which is bifid near the end, which character points it out as belonging to *Phalera bucephala*. The caterpillar of this insect undergoes its metamorphosis into the chrysalis state during the month of September, when it buries itself, without

---

(1865), iii. p. 6, pl. 1, figs. 19, 20; Berkeley's "Outlines," 382, pl. 23, fig. 2; Gray's "Notices," pl. 3, fig. 4; Saccardo, "Sylloge," ii. No. 5031.

[1] Gray, pl. 3, fig. 6.

any cocoon, near the surface amongst the decayed
leaves and moss in damp woods, where it awaits
the period for its transition into the perfect state.
While thus buried, some of the chrysalides, during wet
seasons, form the bases of this parasite, the germ
of which had probably been conveyed into the
interior of the caterpillar previous to its undergoing
its metamorphosis. The plant does not make any
external appearance until after the interior of the
chrysalis-case has become completely filled with
the mycelium ; it usually bursts forth in the form of
a club-shaped fungus, and takes its rise from the
sutures between the various cases that separately
cover the wings and antennæ; these together compose
the anterior part of the chrysalis.

" Another figure [1] represents a great variation in
the manner of growth, viz. the anterior portion of
the chrysalis is covered with a mass of mycelium,
from which proceeds a series of slender roots spreading
in various directions, while anteriorly it has two fungi,
with club-shaped heads, growing from the apex of
the thallus. Such examples are stated to be found
in the autumnal months. It is supposed ·that the
caterpillars represented in another figure [2] may belong
to the same species. Though in a great measure
filled with the mycelium, yet they present a wrinkled

---

[1] Gray, pl. 3, fig. 5.   [2] Ibid., pl. 3, figs. 8, 9.

appearance, while the parasite afterwards makes its way through the joint between the head and pro-thorax (pl. 2, fig. 15). They had probably buried themselves among decayed leaves or moss, with the intention of undergoing their metamorphosis into the chrysalis ; but this transition was hindered by the internal development of the parasite having pro-ceeded too far to allow of the change taking place."

It is to these figures of parasites upon caterpillars that we take exception, as doubtfully belonging to *Cordyceps militaris,* of which we have seen a large number of examples, but never a one that we remember on the caterpillar, but always on the pupa. So again the very interesting cæspitose specimens on caterpillars, of which the following are the details : "Two figures[1] represent the parasite growing on the surface of each segment ; this peculiar mode of growth is especially shown in one of the figures, where numerous fungi are proceeding from the different segments of the caterpillar under the same circumstances. Such an example has not been met with in any collection."

The bright attractive colour of this species makes it a marked object, when growing amongst moss or short grass, and hence it is extremely popular with the young mycologist. It is not unusual to find it,

[1] Gray, pl. 3, figs. 1, 2 ; Holm, "Acta Hafn " (1781), 289, figs. 8, 9.

with the base buried in the ground at the foot of a
wooden fence, and occasionally in a tuft of moss,
into which the larva had crept to undergo its change.
Only a single specimen, or at most two or three,
are commonly found at the same time, or even on
the same day, and some seasons have passed without
our having met with a single example. It must be
conceded that it is not a common fungus, for, with
its bright colouring, it could scarcely escape notice,
and possibly nearly every specimen is collected, out
of curiosity or otherwise, yet even amongst the
numerous botanists and entomologists who go to
make up the excursion party of a local Natural
History Society it is always regarded as a special
prize.

var. polycephala. Pers.[1]

Of the recorded varieties of this entomophyte one
is rather of small size, but the clubs are divided.
The whole plant is said to be about an inch high,
with from three to five clubs, and is mostly found
in cracks of tree-trunks, presumably upon some
hidden pupa.

var. sphærocephala. Schm.[2]

In this variety the stem is very long and flexuous,
consequently thinner than usual. The head, or
capitulum, is nearly globose. On pupæ of insects

---

[1] Persoon, "Synopsis."   [2] Schmidt, *Mycol. Heft*, i. 106.

in Saxony. We have seen nothing corresponding to this in Britain, and it is unknown whether any particular species of Lepidopterous insect is its host.

var. *Wallaysii.* West.[1]

This peculiar little variety was found in Belgium in 1859, on minute dead larvæ in the culms of grasses. The stem is short and twisted, a little more than a millimetre long, saffron-yellow, terminated by an oval head, which is rugose ; about two millimetres long and a millimetre and a half broad, of a red colour. The internal structure, sporidia, etc., correspond with the type. It is very probable that this is only a form of the variety *sphærocephala* with a very short stem.

MEALY ISARIA.

Isaria farinosa. Fries.

The conidial forms, or what are assumed to be the conidial forms, of *Cordyceps militaris* are numerous and variable, of which perhaps the best known is *Isaria farinosa*,[2] which was the *Clavaria farinosa* of Sowerby's "Fungi."[3] Three or four of the so-called species were considered by Fries as merely varieties

---

[1] Westendorp, *Bull. d'Acad. Roy. Bot. de Belgique* (1859), vii. 365 ; Tulasne, "Sel. Fung. Carp.," iii. p. 8.

[2] Fries, "Syst. Myc.," iii. 271 ; Holm, "Ot. Bot.," i. 94, pl. 7 ; Saccardo, "Sylloge," iv. 2772 ; Gray, "Notices," pl. 3, fig. 7.

[3] Sowerby's "Fungi" (1803), pl. 308.

of this species. It is tufted in habit, and white, one to two inches high, with a distinct simple unbranched smooth stem, proliferously branched above into thickened clubs, which are mealy from the profuse spores, the latter being globose, about two micro-millimetres in diameter. When young there is a profuse white mycelium over-running the pupa. It is found on the dead pupæ of various *Lepidoptera*, princi-pally amongst dead leaves, from which it "grows in a palmate manner. The para-site proceeds from the chrysalis through the surface of the cocoon."

Fig. 36.—Mealy Isaria. *Isaria farinosa*, on pupa.

Tulasne has deliberately recorded his opinion that this, and two or three other forms of *Isaria*, must be regarded as conidial states of *Cordyceps militaris*, but it seems difficult to obtain the evidence which would substantiate this as a fact. It is generally accepted as matter of belief, but rather as a question of faith than of demonstration.

VELVET-STEMMED ISARIA.

Isaria velutipes. Link.[1]

Fries considered this also as a variety of *Isaria*

---

[1] Link, "Obs. Diss." (1809), i. p. 20, pl. I, fig. 32; Ditmar, in *Sturm. Flora* (1817), iii. fasc. iv. pl. 54; Nees, "Syst. Pilze," p. 86, pl. 7, fig. 85; Saccardo, "Sylloge," iv. No. 2776.

farinosa, with a floccose stem and entire club; gregarious in habit, white, the stem-like base white and velvety. The pupæ are mostly overspread with a coating of mycelium, from which arise several stems, four or five or more, which are slender, and from half to three quarters of an inch in length, expanding at the apex into a pear-shaped or egg-shaped club, white and powdery with the profuse spores. The stems are not smooth, and almost shining, as in some species, but pubescent with a short velvety down (fig. 37).

FIG. 37.—Velvet-stemmed Isaria. *Isaria velutipes* (after Ditmar).

There is a marked difference between this and the usual form of *Isaria farinosa* in general appearance.

THICK CLUB ISARIA.

Isaria crassa.   Pers.[1]

One of the varieties of *Isaria farinosa*, according to Fries. The clubs are simple and thick, rather conical, with a distinct smooth stem. The stems are seated upon a white crust, and although simple are variable in form and breadth, sometimes compressed,

---

[1] Persoon, "Synopis," p. 637; "Comm. de Fungis Clav.," 231; Holmsk., "Coryph.," fig. *a*; Saccardo, "Sylloge," iv. No. 2774.

and sulcate or striate, covered above with the very mealy conidia. The smooth stem tinged with yellow. As already stated, M. Tulasne regards this, as well as *Isaria farinosa* and *Isaria truncata*, as conidial forms of *Cordyceps militaris*. It is desirable that more certain evidence should be obtained of this dimorphism, and the relation of other species of *Isaria* with *Cordyceps* established.

The only occasion on which we have met with this species in Britain occurred on a much larger pupa than those on which we find *Isaria farinosa*. In general appearance it resembles a large form of *Isaria velutipes*, but with a smooth stem. Three or four clubs arise from the same pupa.

Truncate Isaria.

Isaria truncata. Pers.[1]

Another of the varieties of *Iscaria farinosa* of some authors, and presumably of the conidia of *Cordyceps militaris*. It is white, growing in tufts, at length very much branched, branches truncate and crenulate, everywhere floccose and covered with the spores.

---

[1] Persoon, "Comm. de Fungis Clav." (1797), p. 231 ; Holmsk., "Nova Acta Dan.," p. 279, fig. 6 ; Schweinitz, "Syn. Fung. Car.," p. 99, No. 1296; Saccardo, "Sylloge," iv. No. 2773; Kirby and Spence, "Introd. to Entom.," iv. p. 207.

As far as description goes, this approximates much more closely to *Isaria farinosa* than either of the two immediately preceding species, but it must be rare, as it is seldom found in collections. It is said to occur in Northern Europe, and the United States. In the genus *Isaria* very much must depend on the form and dimensions of the spores in the discrimination of species ; yet there are so many of the presumed species of which the character of the spores is unknown, so that the names must only be accepted as provisional.

The caterpillar of *Lasiocampa rubi* has been found in France subject to parasitism. The insects, says Mr. Gray,[1] usually appear towards the end of summer and beginning of autumn, in woody plains and extensive heaths, feeding on the bramble. They conceal themselves throughout the winter among the large plants (under the leaves of which they are protected from the severity of the winter), where they await the arrival of spring, when they undergo the change into the chrysalis, and it is not until the end of May or beginning of June that they assume the perfect state. It is found to be very difficult to rear these caterpillars through their different stages of existence while in confinement, as most of them die, and become the bases of fungi. Others, in the middle

---

[1] Gray's " Notices," p. 10.

of March, are discovered more or less enveloped by a whitish down or mould[1] (resembling *Botrytis*), which fungoid mould is even found on some caterpillars while in a living state, when it generally appears on several of their segments, and on the anal segment particularly. These caterpillars after a short time become immovable, and eventually die, either straight or slightly curved. The body, however, keeps its usual bulk, and attains a singular firmness, while at the same time the fungoid mould makes rapid progress, completely covering the body, and scarcely leaving the long hairs visible.

DINGY PUPA CLUB.

Cordyceps fuliginosa. Ces.[2]

In its botanical aspect this is rather a peculiar species, since it has the appearance of *Xylaria scopiformis*, with the soft flesh and incipient structure of *Cordyceps*, but unfortunately was in a young and imperfect condition, and it has not been found since. Moreover, none of the species of *Xylaria* have been found growing on insects or animal substances, so that this is only a case of analogy and not of affinity.

---

[1] Tulasne, *Ann. des Sci. Nat.* (1857), p. 36.

[2] Cesati, *Giorn. dell' Inst. Lomb. Milan* (1848), p. 31 ; "Linnæa" (1848), xxi. p. 27 ; *Atti. Soc. Critt. Ital.*, i. p. 67, pl. 6, fig. 1 ; Tulasne, "Selecta Fung. Carp.," iii.; Saccardo, "Sylloge," ii. No. 5042.

The clubs are cylindrical, with an attenuated but rather obtuse apex, from fourteen to sixteen millimetres long, and one millimetre thick (pl. 1, fig. 5). The stem thinner, and greyish downwards, but in the club darker, and sooty. It was found on the pupæ of *Bombyx (Orgyia) antiqua* in Italy.

As far as can be judged from the figure, the head was not formed, and it cannot even be guessed what its form would have been. That it would ultimately have been small there is no doubt, and its colour and habit indicate the probability of its being distinct, as a species, from anything before recorded; but until perfect specimens are found it must be held to be a doubtful species.

Latterly M. Giard has decribed an Entomophthorus parasite on the larva of the brown-tailed moth *Liparis chrysorhœa*, which he has called *Chromostylium chrysorheœ.*

"ERIE" MOULD.

Sterigmatocystis ferruginea.   Cooke.

It was in 1878 that this mould first came under notice, on the pupa of the Erie silk-moth from Cachar. The greater part of its exterior was covered with a bright rust-coloured mould, to which the above name was applied. The woolly effused patches had just such an appearance as that of the common

Aspergillus glaucus, except for its bright rusty colour. The long slender septate threads, or stems, were about one-hundredth of a millimetre in thickness, terminated by a globose head of rusty spores, the stem itself being transparent, and almost colourless. The base of the threads was effused in a matted intricate mycelium, penetrating through the joints into the pupa. The most interesting part of the structure, however, was the capitulum, or head, of spores. By careful manipulation it soon became evident that the supporting threads were expanded at the apex into a globose knob, nearly three times the diameter of the thread. This was surrounded on all sides by a compact stratum of wedge-shaped bodies, four times as long as broad, and each of these bearing on its summit three or four elliptical cells, which cells were individually crowned by three or four short papillæ. To each one of these papillæ belonged a rough globose spore, nearly one-hundredth of a millimetre in diameter, or about the thickness of the primary thread, or stem. It was impossible to demonstrate with certainty whether the spores were produced solitary, at the tips of the papillæ, or in chains (plate 2, fig. 23). No evidence could be found that the spores were ever concatenate. Hitherto this interesting mould has only been found on the dead pupæ of *Lepidoptera*.

MUSCARDINE.

Botrytis Bassiana. Bals.[1]

Enough to fill volumes has been written about the silkworm disease, or Muscardine, which it is by no means our intention to reproduce here, and it is but a passing reference that we shall make to it, since all who are thoroughly interested in the subject will seek more detailed information in the treatises devoted to this subject. It is enough to say that through many years it produced great havoc amongst the silkworms on the Continent, and no effort was spared in search of some means to counteract its baneful influence. The chief agent was a white mould, under the above name, which is effused in a woolly stratum over the surface of the larvæ. The fertile threads are erect, and either simple or forked, with numerous short branchlets, scattered over the threads. The spores, or conidia, globose, collected together in rather globose heads, at the ends of the branchlets. This is the external character and appearance of the mould, the mycelium of which fills, absorbs, and destroys the interior of the larvæ.

The silkworm is liable, at any period of its growth,

---

[1] Robin, "Veg. Par.," p. 560, pl. 6, figs. 3—8 ; Saccardo, "Sylloge," iv. No. 608.

to become attacked by this destroyer. The caterpillars, when they come in contact with the infinitely
minute diffused spores of the mould, are infected by
them, and soon become torpid and stationary. It is
recorded of them that "the spores are so minute and
numerous that they are only visible when aggregated
in masses of thousands together, although they exist
everywhere suspended in the air." It is believed that
they adhere readily to leaves and other objects, and
thus find their way with the food into the interior
of the caterpillar, "where, during some humid seasons,
which occasionally happen in spring and autumn, the
germination of the parasite takes place with great
rapidity, filling the interior, and thus eventually the
vital organs are clogged up by it, and the caterpillar
becomes still. While in this state, the mould soon
shows itself on the external surface, as a white
efflorescence, which is the fructification." The
conidia, or spores, being developed in clusters at
the apex, and at the tips of all the lateral branches
of the filaments. "Before the outer skin is completely covered the insect dies, when the body, being
filled internally, and coated externally, becomes so
hard that it easily breaks into two pieces when bent,
In some seasons, which from their humidity are
favourable for the development of the mould, the
entire crop of domesticated silkworms is rapidly
destroyed, as if by contagion, occasioning a heavy

loss to the rearers of the caterpillars for the purpose of collecting the silk."[1]

By way of supplementary note, it may be added here that, of other silkworm diseases, the one termed "la flacherie," which is of a contagious character, is caused by one of the *Schizomycetes;* very minute, and somewhat aberrant fungi, the particular species being *Micrococcus bombycis,*[2] composed of minute oval cells, produced either singly or in chains. And also it is supposed that the epidemic disease called "pebrine" or "gattine" is produced by the oval cells of another species known as *Micrococcus ovatus;*[3] but this is not so certain. It is assumed to be this entomophyte that Mr. Gray alludes to when he writes of "another kind of fungoid parasite which first made its appearance in France, and became common in 1845, after which it appeared in Italy and Spain in 1854, and then extended itself into Switzerland and Germany. The caterpillars are not affected by it until after the second casting of the skin, and many perish without any external appearance, to the naked eye, of being so attacked. On the caterpillar assuming the third or fourth skin,

---

[1] F. E. Guérin-Méneville, "Muscardine" (Paris, 1847); "Etudes sur les Maladies des Vers-à-Soir" (1849); C. Montagne, Rapport sur un Memoire, "De la Muscardine," etc. (1857).

[2] Grove's "Synopsis of Bacteria and Yeast Fungi," p. 12.

[3] Grove, ibid., p. 14.

it becomes weak, and of a greyish colour, after which
the insect gradually dies by the progress of the
fungus; and the caterpillar then assumes a dusky
yellow colour, which pervades the whole system,
with some brown or black spots, which are formed
by the concentration of a series of fungoid tubercles.
Some caterpillars, however, live sufficiently long to
form their cocoons; after which a part die, while
others live long enough to transform into the
chrysalis, and a few even undergo their metamorphosis into the perfect state. Should they, however,
attain this last state, they always appear with their
wings crippled; these organs, with the antennæ,
legs, and body, show signs of black spots, around and
in which is found the parasite.[1] It is further thought
that after they have reached the perfect state they
are capable of propagation, and thus the disease
becomes hereditary. In this state it has been termed
"pattes noires," or "maladie de la tache."

FLOCCOSE ISARIA.

Isaria floccosa. Fries.[2]

One of the conidial or *Isaria* forms, which is but
little known, is the above; it is reported to have been

---

[1] Lebert, *Berl. Entomol. Zeit.* (1858), p. 149.
[2] Fries, "Syst. Myc.," iii. p. 274; Saccardo, "Sylloge," iv. No. 2778.

found in Britain and Germany. It is a minute species, and might be a dwarfed variety of the very variable *Isaria farinosa*, but the fruit seems to be unknown. It is described as of a cæspitose habit, with short awl-shaped processes, not more than from two to four millimetres long, presenting the appearance of a resupinate *Hydnum*, white, and everywhere powdered with the conidia. Referring to this, Mr. Gray says,[1] "To the family *Lithosiidæ* belong the *Callimorpha Jacobeæ*, the caterpillars of which are clothed with short hairs, and are of solitary habits, feeding on the flowers of the Ragwort, and while thus engaged are subject, during very humid weather, to become the bases of *Isaria floccosa*. This parasitical mould no doubt commences internally, and afterwards progresses externally, like that which grows on the *Sphingides*, etc. The chrysalis is only enveloped in a slight kind of cocoon, and has been recorded to have been found covered by the same kind of mould, which had probably come in contact with the caterpillar when on the point of undergoing its metamorphosis."

It must be remembered that this species is credited with attacking both larvæ and pupæ.

---

[1] Gray's "Notices," p. 11.

ENCRUSTING ISARIA.

Isaria leprosa. Fries.[1]

This parasite is normally flesh-coloured, the short clubs, or processes, being gregarious, short, thickened, and obtuse, covered everywhere with the profuse powdery spores, or conidia. In one form the clubs are nodding, thickened upwards, and simple and regular; in another form the clubs are irregular, compressed and incised, or tubercle-like and sessile; in a third form it is reduced to a crust, which is equally effused over the matrix, in which condition it is mostly sterile, consisting entirely of mycelium. The chrysalis of *Tæniocampa instabilis* is reported to be subject to the attacks of this species.

Fries has a variety of this which he calls *corallina*,[2] still regarded by Saccardo as a distinct species, which infests the pupa of *Noctua instabilis* in Germany, and the larvæ of other Lepidoptera in Italy. The colour of the whole fungus is said to be vinous, with the stems paler. The processes are very much branched, fasciculate, long and slender, with many pendulous clavules at the tips. The conidia are said to be

---

[1] Fries, "Syst. Myc.," iii. p. 272; Robin, "Var. Par.," p. 608; Saccardo, "Sylloge," iv. No. 2784.

[2] *Isaria corallina*, Saccardo, "Sylloge," v. No. 2775; Fries, "Syst. Myc.," iii. p. 273.

rounded or elliptic. Nevertheless, it must be admitted to be a very rare and uncertain species.

Spiny Isaria.

Isaria strigosa. Fries.[1]

This is reputed to be altogether different from *Isaria floccosa*, like which it is, white. The mycelium forms somewhat determinate spots, from which arise spine-like processes which are mostly fasciculate, slender and simple, or, when coalescing, becoming branched ; from two to three lines long, sprinkled as if with flour with the conidia, but becoming at length naked and smooth, with a tinge of straw-colour. It is the pupa of *Hama upsilon* which has been recorded as subject to the attacks of this parasite. The spine-like habit marks it as distinct in external appearance from other allied species, but, in the absence of any indication as to the form and size of the conidia, it must be considered problematical. It would seem to be analogous, on a small scale, to the *Isaria sphingum* of the *Sphinxes*.

---

[1] Fries, "Syst. Myc.," iii. p. 274; Robin, "Veg. Par.," p. 607; Saccardo, " Sylloge," iv. No. 2777.

Tawny Isaria.

Isaria exoleta. Fries.[1]

The species under this name is an obscure one, which is said to attack the larvæ of *Noctua exoleta.* It consists of a fibrous mycelium, which is effused and leprous, consisting of fragile compressed threads of a pale tawny colour, everywhere powdery with the conidia. There are no distinct stems, but the surface is unequal, and the flocci are scarcely visible. It seems to be a low and degraded form of *Isaria,* approaching to a *Sporotrichum;* the description, indeed, as far as it goes, calls to mind the latter genus rather than *Isaria.* It is a misfortune that so many names are kept up in connection with imperfect descriptions, the types of which are nowhere, so that the identity could scarcely be established were the true species to be found again. It would be different, even, if the character and measurements of the fructification were known, because that would be a comparatively stable test ; but modifications in external form are so liable to occur, almost inevitable, in these complex moulds, that characters based upon external features *alone* are not to be trusted.

---

[1] Fries, "Syst. Myc.," iii. p. 275 ; Saccardo, "Sylloge," iv. No. 2779.

O

BLACK-STEMMED ISARIA.

Isaria nigripes.   Schwein.[1]

Of North American species of *Isaria* two or three were described by Schweinitz, and amongst them the above. The stroma is simple, from one to two centimetres high; the stems are thin, tapering, black and smooth up to the middle, then passing into a simple obtuse club, which is greyish-white, and powdery with the conidia. Sometimes the clubs are curved. It occurs upon buried chrysalides, but of what species is unknown.

FORKED ISARIA.

Isaria furcata.   Schwein.[2]

Another of Schweinitz's species, on unknown chrysalides, covered by dead leaves. It is very large and conspicuous, being from six to seven centimetres high. The stroma pallid, rather thick and twisted, smooth at the base, divided upwards into a forked white club, which is powdery with the spores or conidia, interspersed with the tips of the flocci. We can add nothing to this description.

---

[1] Schweinitz, "Syn. Amer. Bor.," No. 3068; Saccardo, "Sylloge," ii. No. 2782.

[2] Schweinitz, "Syn. Amer. Bor.," No. 3067; Saccardo, "Sylloge," ii. No. 2783.

THIN-STEMMED ISARIA.

Isaria tenuipes. Peck.[1]

Another North American species is equally deficient of information concerning the host. Like *Isaria furcata*, it is reported to occur on pupæ hidden under fallen leaves. The stroma is lemon-yellow, smooth, and elongated to from two to four centimetres in length, divided in the upper portion into a few unequal branches, which are mealy with the oblong-ellipsoid conidia, or spores, which measure from four to five micromillimetres in length.

There are more hopes of this species being recognized again than many which we have felt compelled to enumerate. The fruitful portion is rather large, and the presence of a lemon-yellow colour is important, in connection with a decided indication of the form and size of the conidia. It approaches somewhat to the Australian species, *Isaria suffruticosa*, but is more decidedly coloured, and less intricately branched.

Numerous instances have been recorded of the attacks of some species of *Isaria* upon the *Noctuidæ*. "The caterpillar of *Eurois tincta*[2] was found in some

---

[1] Peck, "Report of State Museum, New York;" Saccardo, "Sylloge," iv. No. 2786.

[2] Gray's "Notices," p. 12.

part of Kent, perfectly free from any appearance of having a parasite upon it, and was conveyed to a breeding-cage in London to undergo its metamorphosis, but was discovered some time afterwards completely filled with a fungoid substance, and at the same time exhibited two long very slender parasites, which grew from the back of the thoracic segments.

" Another caterpillar of this family was obtained in the autumn of 1843 from off palings, to which it had apparently been attached by a spider's web, and thus it was kept exposed to the influence of the weather. Its body was entirely coated by a white creamy mould, like that which attacks silkworms, and is termed Muscardine ; the insect is so completely filled, that even the feet, especially the false ones, are fully stretched out by the internal thallus."

Perfect insects are also equally infested with mould, both at home and abroad. Mr. Gray mentions *Erebus odora* from Ega ; a variety of the same insect from St. Domingo, *Plaxia macarea* from Surinam, and *Cerastis vaccinii* in Europe. Also undetermined species of *Noctuæ ;* one found in Devonshire, attached to a leaf ;[1] another in St. Mary's Isle, Kirkcudbright, attached to a branch of a tree ;[2] and a third from the New Forest, attached to a branch of heath. These

---

[1] Gray, pl. 3, fig. 14.   [2] Ibid., pl. 3, fig. 15.

imago insects are all apparently infested by some species of *Isaria*.

The caterpillar from the East Indies, figured by Robin in his "Vegetable Parasites,"[1] and Mr. Gray,[2] "is apparently furnished with slender hairs all over the body, and with short fascicles of hairs along each side, as well as with four fascicles of long strong hairs placed two anteriorly and two posteriorly, leading to the supposition that it may belong to the family *Liparidæ;* but further information cannot be given, as the parasite so completely covers the caterpillar as to obliterate all those minute specific characters which might assist in determining its name.

"The caterpillars of this family, it may be observed, are usually hatched in April, and consequently they remain in that state until the month of June, when they change to the pupa; from this latter state they do not change to a moth until towards the end of July.

"The parasitical mould had no doubt commenced as usual in the interior of the caterpillar and then covered the exterior, after which a series of lengthened filaments grew from the upper surface of the body. It is probably a species of *Isaria*, though M. Robin considers the structure of the plant to be like that of *S. entomorrhiza*."

---

[1] Robin, "Veg. Par.," t. ix. fig. 6.
[2] Gray's "Notices," p. 12, pl. 3, fig. 3.

SHRUBBY ISARIA.

Isaria suffruticosa.   Cooke and Massee.[1]

Parasitic upon a hairy caterpillar from Australia, we have found a distinct species of *Isaria* of notable appearance.   It was in tufts about three centimetres high, and white.   The stem quite distinct and smooth, or mealy, divided in the upper portion into very slender interwoven branches, bearing lateral branchlets up to the acute tips ; the whole compacted of delicate threads, the extremities of which were free, and bore the minute ellipsoid conidia (four to five by one and a half micromillimetres).   It will be seen from this that it differs much from the ordinary *Isaria farinosa*, and other British species, in the very slender and attenuated branchlets, and altogether more delicate habit, but resembles, except in colour, the North American *Isaria tenuipes*.   As the type specimen is still in existence, and in a public herbarium, it may be identified again.   There is a strong resemblance in appearance to some such species of *Clavaria* as *C. Kunzei*, but in structure and fructification a true species of *Isaria*.

"A species of the family of *Arctiidæ* has been recorded by Professor Lebert[2] as affected by a fun-

---

[1] Cooke and Massee, in *Grevillea*, vol. xviii.

[2] *Berl. Ent. Zeit.* (1858), p. 178.

goid mould. He collected in the neighbourhood of Berlin, during the summer of 1826, a great many caterpillars of *Arctia villica* for the purpose of watching their growth. These insects, on arriving at their full size, became quite soft, and then suddenly died; soon after they became hard, and if bent, would easily break into two pieces. Their bodies were covered with a beautiful shining white mould. If some of the caterpillars affected with the parasitic mould were placed on the same tree with those apparently free from its attack, the latter soon exhibited signs that they also were attacked in the same manner, in consequence of the two series only coming in contact with each other."[1]

Aulica Endophyte.

Empusa aulicæ. Reichardt.[2]

This species, found on the larvæ and pupæ of *Euprepia aulica, Euprepia villica,* and *Trachea piniperda,* in Germany, as well as on Lepidoptera in the United States, is considered by Roland Thaxter to be identical with *Empusa grylli.* This point, however, of specific identity does not concern us much here,

---

[1] Gray's "Notices," Addenda, p. 22.

[2] Reichardt, in "Bail Uber Pilzepiz," in *Schrift. Nat. Ges. zu Dantzig* (1869), p. 3; Saccardo, "Sylloge," vii. 971.

as we have included both. The fertile threads are erumpent after the death of the insect, forming tufts of about a millimetre in height. The conidia are ovate, and obtusely apiculate at the apex, from twenty-seven to thirty-eight, by twenty to twenty-seven micro-millimetres in size.

CHINESE PLANT WORM.

Cordyceps sinensis. Berk.[1]

As early as 1726 Reaumur[2] seems to have seen and mentioned this curious production, which at that time was a mystery. Nearly ten years later, and it is spoken of by Du Halde[3] in his " History of China." In March, 1841, Professor Westwood[4] exhibited specimens at a meeting of the Entomological Society, and made some observations to the following effect : " It is a Chinese larva, from the back of the neck of each of which a slender fungus, twice as long as the body of the insect, had been produced (pl. 2, fig. 18). This insect, when thus attacked, is esteemed of great efficacy as a drug in China, where, from its very great rarity, it is only used by the emperor's physicians; and

---

[1] Berkeley, Hooker's *Journ. Bot.* (1843), ii. p. 207.

[2] Reaumur, *Mem. de l'Acad. Sci.* (1726), p. 302, pl. 16.

[3] Du Halde, "Gen. Hist. of China " (1736), vol. iv. p. 41.

[4] Westwood, in *Ann. Nat. Hist.* (1842), viii. p. 217 ; *Journ. Proc. Ent. Soc.* (1838), p. vi. ; and 1841, pl. 6, fig. 5.

an extract was read from Du Halde's 'History of
China,' in which its virtues are elaborately detailed,
being especially serviceable in cases of bodily debility,
particularly when a small portion of it is boiled in the
body of a duck. The Chinese philosophers consider
it as a herb during the summer season, but as soon
as winter appears it changes into a worm. It is
named by Du Halde 'Hia Tsao Tchong,' the first
two names meaning 'summer herb,' and the last
two 'winter worm.' Mr. Reeves had stated that its
proper name was 'Hea Tsaon Taong Chung.' It is
brought to Canton, tied up in small bundles, each
containing about a dozen individuals. The parasitic
plant is analogous to that which infests the larvæ
sent from New Zealand."

In 1842 Dr. Pereira transmitted an account of it
to the *Pharmaceutical Journal*,[1] afterwards embodied
in his "Materia Medica,"[2] and he calls it "summer
plant, winter worm." Reproducing some of the remarks already quoted, he adds that it is known in
Japan, and there called "Totsu Kaso."[3] "Each individual is about three inches (a little more or less)
long. About half of it is a caterpillar of the usual
cylindrical form, and having a light yellowish-brown
colour. The head, neck, segments of the body, and

---

[1] Pereira, in *Pharmaceutical Journal* (1843), ii. p. 590.

[2] Ibid., "Materia Medica," vol. ii. p. 51 (4th edit.), 1855.

[3] Thunberg's "Travels in Japan," vol. iii. p. 68.

legs (thoracic, ventral, and anal) are all distinctly recognizable. Projecting from the back part of the neck is a slender club-shaped body. This is the fungus. It is, I think, a species of *Sphæria*, and is closely allied to *Sphæria entomorrhiza.*

"The Lepidopterous insect, on whose larva this fungus grows, has not at present been determined. Mr. Doubleday, who has carefully examined a very perfect larva, is of opinion that the insect is a species of *Agrotis.*

"Du Halde says that the insect fungus is scarce, and that at Pekin it is considered to be a foreign production. It grows, he adds, in Thibet; but it is found also, though in small quantities, on the frontiers of the province of Se-tchuen, which borders on Thibet or Laza.

"I now proceed to notice the opinions of the Chinese regarding its medical properties and uses. Thunberg states that it is reputed to possess cordial virtues. According to Du Halde, its properties are considered to be similar to those of *ging sing.* It strengthens and renovates the powers of the system, which have been reduced either by over-exertion or long sickness. The physicians of the Emperor of China stated that they used it only at the palace on account of its scarcity. Black, old, and rotten specimens cost four times their weight of silver.

"The mode of employing it is very curious. The

belly of a duck is to be stuffed with five drachms of
the insect fungus, and the bird roasted by a slow fire.
When done take out the insect fungus, the virtue of
which will have passed into the duck's flesh. The
latter is to be eaten twice a day for eight or ten
days."

There is a little addition to the romantic aspect
of the subject given in the "History of Insects,"[1]
where, after briefly describing the object, it proceeds :
" Father Parenin, who sent it to France, observes, in
his account of it, that it was a scarce plant ; being
found only at the palace of Pekin there, where also it
was not a native, but brought from the mountains of
Thibet, and some other places on the confines of the
Chinese dominions. This father had never seen the
leaves or flowers of the plant, but only its roots,
which were in high esteem there, not only because
of their miraculous changes, but from their possessing
the virtues of the ginseng (*ging sing*). This plant, we
are informed, is still in great estimation by the Chinese
nobles. The roots had nothing particular in their
figure or appearance ; but, with these, the father sent
home those which were supposed to be changed into
a worm. The Chinese suppose that this is a plant
during the summer season, but that in winter its stalk

---

[1] "History of Insects" (Murray's Family Library), vol. ii. p. 300
(1838).

dies, and the root becomes a worm; concerning which the father observed, that nothing could more exactly express a worm or caterpillar; the head, the eyes, the feet, and the mouth, being all plainly distinguishable, as well as the several folds and cuttings in of the body. This account was found to be perfectly true, but the mistake was owing to the want of proper accuracy in the observation; for the body, which was supposed to be the root transformed, had in reality never been any part of the plant, but was found to be really and truly a caterpillar. Some fanciful persons have supposed that when the time of its change approached, it always selected the roots of this plant as of a proper size and dimensions for its purpose, and, gnawing off the end, hollowed away the stump, so as to introduce its tail into the cavity, where it remained covered with the bark of the root, which so nicely joins to it, that those who observe it in a slight way cannot but mistake it to be a part of the root, or the remainder of the root a continuation of the body. On opening the body of larvæ, however, we find that the root of the fungus entirely occupies the whole interior portion, from the head to the opposite end."

It was at first, and for a long time, considered doubtful whether the plant was not collected for the Chinese in an immature state, since the Rev. M. J. Berkeley, and others who had examined it, had never succeeded in finding sporidia; but an examination made by ourselves was more successful, for we obtained quite mature sporidia, breaking up as usual into truncate joints.[1]

Fougeroux de Bonderoy has, in his "Memoir," [2] made reference to the Chinese worm. He says, "The plant-worm of which M. de Reaumur has spoken [3] is found upon a larva, and not upon a chrysalis; but the plant, in the specimens which M. de Reaumur has examined, was situated upon the last ring of the larva, near the anus. It seems that the plant presses and takes hold of the extremity of the insect's body. This position of the plant, with regard to the insect, is very different to that presented by those of the Caribbeans, and caused M. de Reaumur to think that the insect was thus attached to the plant, because it had chosen it in order to adhere to it, there to undergo the second metamorphosis, and to become a chrysalis, this position being common to many other species of insects when they change into nymphs.

"Indeed, it should cause no surprise (in the opinion of M. de Reaumur) to find the insect always attached to the same plant, since it would select it, as do

---

[1] *Grevillea,* vol. xii. p. 78; Saccardo, "Sylloge," ii. No. 5051.

[2] Fougeroux de Bonderoy, "Memoires de l'Academie des Sciences." Paris.

[3] M. de Reaumur, in "Memoires de l'Academie des Sciences," année 1726, p. 302. Paris.

many other species of insects, which, born upon a plant, there undergo all their metamorphoses.

"The plant-worm of the Chinese would prefer the extremity of the root in order to remain adherent to it, as is the case with other insects which continue always attached to the fibres of a leaf, and constantly upon the same part of the plant. In short, a plant, the proportions of which are so conformable to those of the insect, the animal which in its native place was perhaps living, and still moved about when the plant had attached itself to it, have induced the Chinese to maintain the change of an animal into a plant, whilst they did not affirm the same wonder in other circumstances, when the insect had attached itself to any other parts of the same plant, to undergo its metamorphosis ; and it never occurred to them, in this latter case, which did not favour the idea as did the first, to assert that the branches of these vegetables, to which insects were attached, transformed themselves into animals, or bore insects, as they produce fruits and seeds.

"Although there may be analogous facts which might lead M. de Reaumur to establish his way of regarding the plant-worm of the Chinese, we nevertheless admit that here it is the plant which seems to attach itself to the insect, and not the insect to the plant, and that the vegetative insects of the Caribbeans embarrass greatly M. de Reaumur's explanation. We confess also, with Mr. Needham, that the opinion of M. de Reaumur by no means explains how any of the specimens which we have just described come to be produced. We will add that the few carefully examined circumstances of the country do not yet put us in a position to speak with certainty upon these mysterious facts, and consequently I shall refrain from hazarding any conjectures."

Having given the history and mystery of this notable production, little more remains to be said except what relates to the identification of the insect, and for these entomological notes we must be indebted, as usual, to Mr. Gray.[1]

"In the great family of *Noctuidæ* must be placed the caterpillar of the far-famed Chinese 'summer plant, winter insect,' which exhibits, amongst other characters, that of having the prothorax entirely protected by a shield, and, from its general appearance, seems to form part of the genus *Gortyna*. The caterpillar, which is of a light yellowish-brown colour, probably bores into and feeds on the roots of aquatic plants, that grow abundantly in the marshy ground, on the sides of the numerous rivers and canals of China,[2] and they are also stated to be brought from

---

[1] Gray's "Notices," p. 12, pl. 3, fig. 31.
[2] Pereira, "Mat. Med.," ii. p. 52, figs. 43, 44.

Japan[1] and Thibet. The insect can only be discovered by the appearance of the plant, which, soon
after it is attacked, begins to droop and look sickly.
After the parasite comes in contact with the caterpillar, the latter buries itself in the earth; it first
turns with its head upwards; and then, being apparently checked by the presence of the parasite
internally, it remains in that position, and the outer
plant naturally grows upwards, and breaks its way
out, probably through the suture of the labium. As
it increases in size, it splits the head into two parts,
as is shown in the figure. Like the others that grow
in the same manner, the stem is thick throughout,
with the apex somewhat flattened, and rather broad,
so much so as to be palmated in some specimens.

" Reaumur, who in 1726 first published a notice of
this curious fungoid insect, stated that the parasite
was attached to the anal portion of the caterpillar,
and he represented that when the parasite was detached from the insect, the end gave the appearance
of lengthened roots, as if they had surrounded the
last segment of the body of the insect. The parasite,
however, springs from the head, and the Rev. M. J.
Berkeley says that it is attached by simple or very
sparingly branched, very slender flexuous threads,
which spread more or less over the surface of the

---

[1] Where it is known as " Totsu Kaso " (Thunb., " Trav.," iii. p. 68).

caterpillar. The substance of the caterpillar is replaced by a rough mass of very fine-branched threads, which are far more compact than those in the substance of the fungus, mixed with colourless oil-globules."

BLACK MUSCARDINE.

Tarichium megaspermum. Cohn.[1]

"This species is known only from its resting-spores, which have been thoroughly described and figured by Cohn, and is parasitic upon the larvæ of *Agrotis segetum*, which are turned black by the disease." The resting-spores are zygospores, produced by conjugation, with a dark brown outer coat, or epispore, marked by sinuous furrows (average 50μ diameter). It has thus been described: "Mycelium at first sacciform (5—25μ broad), hyaline or a little blackish, not at all, or sparingly, septate, with unicellular branches, resting-spores solitary, or two to three together, globose or pear-shaped (36—55μ diameter), covered with a dark brown epispore."

It will be seen that nothing whatever is known of the conidia, and consequently of the conidia-bearers. There is some probability of its being quite a distinct

---

[1] Cohn, *Beitrage der Pflanzen* (1875), p. 58; Thaxter, ibid., p. 189; Saccardo, "Sylloge," vii. No. 982.

P

species, when properly known, as indicated by the blackening of the caterpillars, which possibly originated the name of "Black muscardine."

GREENISH ENDOPHYTE.

Entomophthora virescens.   Thaxter.[1]

The following report will serve as introduction to the entomophyte above named : "In the spring of 1884, from the middle of May until the end of the first week in June, all the gardens and fields in the neighbourhood of Ottawa were severely attacked by the larvæ of *Agrotis fennica.* The disease pervading these larvæ was first observed in May, and was extremely virulent. Dead larvæ were to be found in all directions, on stone walls, on fences, and particularly on the tops of stems of grasses. The Entomophthora, however, was undoubtedly *the* influence which brought this insect down again to its normal rare occurrence at Ottawa." The specimens received were black and shrivelled, the fungus appearing as a greenish-yellow coating, emerging in small tufts, which, in the more mature specimens, appear to have coalesced over the body (plate 4, fig. 41).

The conidia are oval or oblong, of irregular shape, with a bluntly rounded base and apex, the former

---

[1] Thaxter, "Entomophthoræ U.S.," p. 178, pl. 18, figs. 251-261.

often hardly papillate, and not well distinguished from the apex; colour greenish yellow in dried material, containing numerous small irregular, often rod-like fat bodies (average size 14 × 30μ). Conidia-bearing threads digitately branched, arising individually from spherical hyphal bodies, which germinate in all directions, giving rise to very numerous threads, which subsequently become conidia-bearers. Secondary conidia like the primary. Resting-spores unknown.

GEOMETRIDÆ.

Several species of European *Geometridæ* have been found with some species of *Isaria* growing upon them; some have called it *Isaria arachnophila*, but this we venture to doubt. The species quoted are *Speranzia brunneata, Erannis defoliaria, Nyssia zonaria, Biston betularia,* and *Oporabia dilutoria*, while *Bupalus piniaria* has been found covered with a parasitic mould.

In addition to these, Mr. Roland Thaxter has made known two species of *Entomophthoræ* which attack the imagines of *Geometridæ* in North America.

GLOBOSE ENDOPHYTE.

Empusa apiculata. Thaxter.[1]

Of this species Mr. Thaxter observes that this is

---

[1] Thaxter, "Entomophthoræ U.S.," p. 163, pl. 15, figs. 63–70, 74, 75.

the first recorded instance of an *Empusa* growing upon a Lepidopterous imago as its host, although this is not a unique case. The geometrid moth, mentioned as one of its hosts, was taken on the wing, flying slowly with an unnatural fluttering motion, and being placed in a collecting box, it was soon fastened to a leaf by five or six long and powerful rhizoids terminating in a disc. The typical form is recorded on the larva of *Hyphantria textor*, imagines of a species of *Tortrix* and *Petrophora*, and on numerous genera of small flies or gnats in Maine and South Carolina.

The conidia are nearly spherical, with a prominent papillate base, terminating in a short sharp and abrupt point (28—30 × 30—37μ). The conidia-bearing threads sometimes with a tendency to become digitate, originating directly or indirectly from nearly spherical hyphal bodies (plate 4, fig. 43). Secondary conidia like the primary. Resting-spores (azygospores) formed from the hyphæ, spherical and hyaline.

GEOMETRID ENDOPHYTE.

Entomophthora geometralis. Thaxter.[1]

Geometrid moths of the genera *Petrophora, Eupi-*

---

[1] Thaxter, "Entomophthoræ U.S.," p. 170, pl. 17, figs. 173–178.

thecia, Thera, etc., have been attacked by this entomophyte in pine woods, in North America. "It is
usually the habit of these insects to rest with the
abdomen curved upwards, and, at one point of the
under surface, resting on whatever object the moth
may have lighted upon—usually a pine needle. At
this point of contact, as far as observed, nowhere else,
the rhizoids (rooting-fibres) are produced in a tuft
which thus fastens the insect by its abdomen. The
rhizoids appear before death, and I have found," says
Mr. Thaxter, "a small *Eupithecia* fluttering violently
in its efforts to free itself from a pine needle to which
the rhizoids had already become firmly attached."

In this species the conidia are short, elliptical or
ovoid (15—22×10—12μ), with contents finely
granular, and a hyaline nuclear body. The conidia-
bearers digitate, or branching like fingers, and
coalescing. Secondary conidia are like those of the
first generation, or long almond-shaped, and borne
obliquely on thread-like spore-bearers. Resting-
spores lateral or terminal on short hyphæ, spherical,
and colourless (average thirty micromillimetres
diameter).

The conidia are peculiar, and may be at once recognized by their short thick form.

SLENDER CATERPILLAR CLUB.

Cordyceps acicularis. Rav.[1]

A South Carolina entomophyte was described by Berkeley from specimens communicated by Mr. Ravenel, but the insect is difficult of determination, and Mr. Gray could not say to what family of the *Lepidoptera* the larvæ belonged. In this species the stems were three inches or more high, not half a line thick, brown below and tomentose, smooth above and tawny, grooved when dry. The heads about three quarters of an inch long, cylindrical, brown, studded with the perithecia, barren above and acuminate. Asci and sporidia as in the genus, the latter breaking into very small frustules, not more than five micromillimetres long.

There is something characteristic about this graceful species of *Cordyceps*, which terminates above in a short sterile beak, a peculiarity which has only been observed in a few species (plate 2, fig. 17). It cannot be very uncommon in South Carolina, since Mr. Ravenel himself collected upwards of a hundred specimens.

---

[1] Berkeley, in *Linn. Journ.* (1856), i. p. 158, pl. 1, fig. 2 ; Saccardo, "Sylloge," ii. No. 5037 ; *Cordyceps Carolinensis,* Ravenel, "Fung. Car.," iv. No. 29.

LITTLE RED CLUB.

Cordyceps typhulæformis. Berk. and Cooke.[1]

Amongst the fungi collected in Java, in the Berkeley Herbarium, we discovered a minute *Cordyceps* which appeared to have originally been parasitic, but no trace of the insect could be found. The clubs were veritably club-shaped and red, resembling in miniature *Cordyceps militaris,* but not larger than some species of *Typhula* or *Pistillaria;* that is to say, not more than half an inch in total height. The clubs attenuated downwards into a very slender stem. The perithecia were rather prominent, so as to render the clubs rough when dry, and the fructification was fully developed and of the usual type, save that the sporidia showed no evidence of breaking up into joints. Failing to discover any notes or the least indication of its host, we can only assume it to have been parasitic. It was collected by Kurz in Java.

FRENCH INSECT CLUB.

Cordyceps Doassansii. Pat.[2]

Another parasite on Lepidoptera, but without any

---

[1] Cooke, in *Grevillea* (1884), vol. xii. p. 78.
[2] Patouillard, "Tab. Analyt. Fungorum," fasc. v. p. 213, fig. 494; Saccardo, "Sylloge," vol. suppl., No. 7511.

clue to the name of the insects on the pupæ of which it is accustomed to make its home.   The head, or capitulum, is from five to eight millimetres thick, ovoid, short, villose, and white, dotted with the prominent yellow ostiola of the contained perithecia (fig. 38).

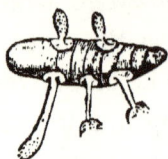

The stem very short, or as much as one centimetre long, also tomentose and white, girt at the base with a white downy mycelium.   Internal structure corresponding to other species, save that the thread-like sporidia, which are very thin and continuous, do not separate into frustules.   On the same mycelium

FIG. 38.—French Insect Club. *Cordyceps Doassansii* (after Patouillard).

conidia are produced on a floccose globule with a slender brown stem, from five to eight millimetres long.   The conidia, although called "sphæroid," are said to measure four and a half by two micromillimetres.   It is presumed that this species was collected in France.

SLENDER RED CLUB.

Cordyceps caloceroides.   Berk. and Curt.[1]

The description of this species is remarkably short

---

[1] Berkeley and Curtis, "Cuban Fungi" (1868), No. 749; Saccardo, "Sylloge," No. 5050.

and unsatisfactory, but on looking at the specimen
one becomes convinced that it is really an entomophyte, without being able to suggest the order of
insects to which it belongs; but as it is so characteristic in itself, there can be no difficulty in its
identification should it ever occur again (plate 2, fig.
16). Altogether, it is nearly five inches in height, but
with a stem as slender as a darning-needle, and a very
long cylindrical head, two inches long, about double
the thickness of the stem, or rather more. The stem,
in the type specimen, is forked about halfway up, of a
bright reddish colour, and quite smooth, each branch
with a capitulum. These clubs are rather pointed at
the apex, and the surface is very finely dotted with
the minute perithecia. The base is rather abrupt,
with a rooting thread or two, as if torn away from
some buried larva. The fructification is immature.
It was stated to have been gathered from the ground
in the island of Cuba, but it could scarcely have been
developed on the naked soil, since all the species are
parasitic either on insects or subterranean fungi.

Two-headed Club.

Cordyceps bicephala. Berk.[1]

It is by no means a good specific name for any of

---

[1] Berkeley, in Hooker's *Journ. Bot.* (1856), p. 278; Saccardo, "Sylloge," ii. No. 5029.

the species of *Cordyceps* that its distinguishing feature
should be the production of one or two heads upon
a single stem.   Several species could be referred to,
although normally with a single head, occasionally
producing two, and even the present may be mono-
cephalous, for aught we know to the contrary, since
only a single specimen has hitherto been seen.

In this species the stem is slender and erect, about
two inches long, smooth, and brownish,
dividing near the top in a forked manner,
producing a small globose head at the apex
of each branch (fig. 39). The heads are described as elliptic, but in the dried specimen
they are as nearly as possible globose and
powdery. The internal structure and fructification partake of the character of the
genus. The base of the stem is abrupt,
and there is every probability of its being
a true entomophyte.   Berkeley says it is
almost intermediate between *Cordyceps* and
Xylaria, approaching the latter in substance,
but being truly *fleshy*, and not corky, to say
nothing of colour, it is proved to be a
genuine *Cordyceps* with characteristic fruit.

FIG. 39.—Two-
headed Club.
*Cordyceps bi-
cephala* (from
specimen in
Berkeley
Herb.

The locality from whence it came was Rio Negro,
in South America.

American Swamp Club.

Cordyceps palustris. Berk. and Br.[1]

Another of the South Carolina entomophytes, found attached to larvæ in moist putrid logs, cannot be referred to any place, since no larvæ are preserved with the fungi. The whole plant is from one to two inches high when fresh, much shorter when dry, of a dull brownish purple, or flesh-colour. The stem is cylindrical and powdery, divided above into two or three clavate heads, the stem about as long as the head, but not so thick. The heads rough with the mouths of the perithecia. Asci and sporidia as in other species, the ultimate frustules of the sporidia being very small, not more than two micromillimetres long.

The commonest form assumed by these species of *Cordyceps* is that of a simple club, either with a globose, or more or less elongated head, but in this instance the club is divided or branched, each division being somewhat club-shaped (plate 2, fig. 20). The figures given in this work will illustrate the different modes of branching in the few species in which the head is divided, the most notable example being the large Australian species *Cordyceps Taylori.*

[1] Berkeley and Broome, *Linnæan Journal* (1856), vol. i. p. 159, pl. 1, fig. 5 ; Saccardo, " Sylloge," ii. 5018.

New York Club.

Cordyceps superficialis.   Peck.[1]

As far as its entomological aspect is concerned, this is another of the uncertain American species, which was described by Peck in 1877.   It is slender, and about one inch in total height, the stem and club being of about equal length.   Clubs cylindrical, gradually tapering to a point at the apex, which is sterile.   The perithecia are crowded together and superficial, more loosely placed at the extremities of the club, which imparts to it a somewhat fusiform shape.   The elongated asci and the thread-like sporidia are in accord with the genus.   The specimens found are stated to have occurred on buried larvæ beneath hemlock trees.   It may be intimated that the species in which the perithecia are free and superficial, and not immersed in the substance of the club, are remarkably few.   In three species only do they appear to be entirely free, and in three others the upper portion of the perithecia become free and exposed, but do not appear to have been so in the early stage of development.   Of the three species in which the perithecia appear to be always free, this is one,

---

[1] Peck, in " Twenty-eighth Report of New York State Museum " (1877), p. 70 ; Saccardo, " Sylloge," ii. No. 5036.

the others being *Cordyceps memorabilis* and *Cordyceps sphingum.*

WEST INDIAN CLUB.

Cordyceps sp.

Mr. Gray has figured an interesting minute species of *Cordyceps*,[1] which may possibly be different from any hitherto described. It was growing upon a small caterpillar from St. Vincent, and the fungi upon it were elongated slender club-shaped spines, little more than half an inch in length, growing from the upper surface of the thoracic segments, while from beneath the abdomen sprouted various short fungi of different lengths and forms. The characters of the insect were so obliterated, by the fungoid matter, that it was impossible to give any idea of its position in the system.

With such a meagre description, and only on the faith of a figure, it would be imprudent to attach any name to this entomophyte, but it is alluded to in the hope that it may be found again, and then better characterized.

---

[1] Gray's "Notices," p. 13, pl. 3, fig. 11.

DIPTERA.

TWO-WINGED FLIES.

THIS order is notable for the very large number of species of destructive *Entomophthoreæ* with which its members are visited. It is probable that the four very minute species of *Cordyceps* referred to this order are not all of them really distinct ; but, at any rate, all of them are rare. The three species of external parasites, belonging to the *Laboulbeniaceæ*, are of interest, but cannot be considered destructive ; whereas eighteen species allied to the very common mould of the house-fly make up for the absence of other entomophytes. And, whatever their relation, if any, the *Empusa* is supplemented by a variety of the salmon disease (*Saprolegnia*), which establishes itself upon dead flies in water. Mr. Gray gives the following insects as subject to *Empusa muscæ*, namely, *Dexia canina, Musca domestica, Musca vomitoria, Anthomyia pluvialis*, and *Scatophaga stercoraria ;* these are probably but a few of its hosts. Some persons have denied the fungous nature of this disease, which is now established beyond any reasonable doubt, and attributed it to the result of plethoric disease. The Rev. M. J. Berkeley [1] combated this view at the time it was advocated in the pages of the *Athenæum*, and firmly asserted that it was a fungus mould.

After enumerating the different species known to him as subject to attack, Mr. Gray proceeds to say, "All these insects may occasionally be seen, after autumnal rains, dead on the bark of trees, on portions of various plants, on the windows and ceilings of houses, etc., adhering by means of a whitish fungoid matter or mould,[2] which seems to have emerged from between the last segments of the abdomen beneath, and the joints of the legs. The body and wings also become entirely covered by the same parasite, which, under a highly magnifying power, 'appears to consist of elongated filaments in close contact.' When separated from the mass, some are found simple, and others terminated by a minute globule; those upon the wings appear merely globules.[3]

"These flies, which are in the perfect state, become while in activity suddenly overtaken by the effect of the parasite internally, which causes the insect to settle on any object that may be in its way. Death soon after ensues; and the rapid growth of the parasite

---

[1] *Trans. Ent. Soc. Lond.* (1841–43), iii. p. v.

[2] *Sporendonema muscæ*, Fries, "Syst. Mic."

[3] Westwood, *Journ. Proc. Ent. Soc.* (1837), ii. p. lxiii. pl. 20, fig. 2.

having first affixed them by the abdomen and legs to
the object on which they had rested, it then develops
itself entirely on the outer surface of the insect, and
even spreads itself for some distance around it, as
may easily be noticed in those seen on windows, etc."

DUNG-FLY CLUB.

Cordyceps Forquignoni.   Quel.[1]

The only perfect *Cordyceps* yet recorded on *Diptera*
in Europe is one which has occurred in France on a
dung-fly—*Musca rufa*, or *Dasyphora pratorum*.   The
stem is not more than half an inch
long, slender and thread-like, cream-
coloured, with a white floccose
base.   The head, or capitulum, is
cylindrical, half to three quarters of
a millimetre long, torn at the base,
so as to be free at the edge round the top of the stem,
and a little yellower than the stem, punctate with
the ostioles of the perithecia.   The asci and sporidia
are elongated and minute.   Small conidia were also
found, which were ovoid, and about eight micromillimetres long.   The only locality yet recorded
was in the Vosges (fig. 40).

It will be observed that this species is primarily

FIG. 40.—Dung-fly Club.
Cordyceps Forquignoni
(after Quelet).

---

[1] Quelet, *Association Française* (1887), pl. 21, fig. 18.

distinguished from *Cordyceps dipterigena* in having a cylindrical instead of a globose capitulum. The fruit in these minute species is very difficult to discriminate in respect to size, and reliance has to be placed almost exclusively on external characters. The difference between a cylindrical and globose capitulum is an appreciable one ; but when there are two or three claiming specific distinction with such a character in common, discrimination is scarcely possible.

AMERICAN FLY CLUB.

Cordyceps armeniaca. Berk. and Curt.[1]

This little obscure parasite was found in South Carolina, on the excrement of birds, apparently, but really, it is suspected, upon the minute larvæ of some unknown insect imbedded therein. This, however, must remain a mystery until the species is found again. The whole plant is apricot-coloured, and consists of a flexuous or twisted stem, one-third of an inch long, and paler than the head. The capitulum nearly hemispherical, and rough with the ostiola (plate 1, fig. 7). Internal structure, asci and sporidia the same, except in size, as in other species. In Berkeley's

---

[1] Berkeley and Curtis, *Linnæan Journal* (1856), vol. i. p. 158, pl. 1, fig. 1 ; Saccardo, "Sylloge," ii. No. 5016.

Q

"Herbarium," on the same sheet, and under the same name, there are specimens of a *Cordyceps* from Rangoon on a fly, and another from Ceylon, also upon a Dipterous insect. Berkeley evidently considered them all to be identical, and therefore the entomophyte belongs to *Diptera*. Further than this, it is impossible to detect any difference between the specimens named *Cordyceps armeniaca* and those called *Cordyceps dipterigena;* hence we are strongly of opinion that both are the same species, if not also *Cordyceps flavella.*

CEYLON FLY CLUB.

Cordyceps dipterigena.   Berk. and Br.[1]

There is but a very short description, and very scant information about this parasite on *Diptera* in Ceylon. It was described from specimens sent over to this country for determination about 1870, and was stated to be of the total height of an inch and a half, pallid in colour, with a slender stem and a globose head. Whether occurring on pupa or perfect insect is not intimated.

Very similar to this is a specimen figured by Mr. Gray,[2] of which he writes, "A minute pupa of a

---

[1] Berkeley and Broome, "Ceylon Fungi," No. 980; Saccardo, "Sylloge," ii. No. 5653.

[2] Gray's "Notices," p. 17, pl. 4, fig. 16.

Dipterous insect, which was found buried in moss, having a long, slender, smooth stem, that rises from the middle of one side, and a globose head at its apex. It is referred to a species of *Claviceps* of Wallroth's by Gray, but this is most improbable, as that grows only upon an ergot. Its appearance certainly is that of a *Cordyceps*, and we cannot detect any difference between this figure and the description of *Cordyceps dipterigena.* It is not stated in what locality it was found, or if it was British."

Again, Mr. Gray alludes to another parasite which he has also figured [1] on a Dipterous insect (*Tabanus ?*), having a long fungus, which springs from one end of the pupa ; it gradually enlarges to the apex, where it is somewhat truncated. It is difficult to form an opinion of this, which may only be a simple *Isaria.*

WEST INDIAN FLY CLUB.

Cordyceps flavella.   Berk. and Curt.[2]

A small species was found in Cuba amongst dead leaves in a wood, growing, as it was stated, upon some small *Sclerotium.* The above name was given to it on account of its yellow colour, and although

---

[1] Pl. 4, fig. 17.
[2] Berkeley and Curtis, "Cuban Fungi" (1868), No. 748; Saccardo, "Sylloge," ii. No. 5022.

the slender thread-like stem was stated to be an inch in length, it is hardly more than half an inch in the dried specimen. The head is globose, and not more than a line in diameter. Two or three may be found growing together from the same matrix, and a barren specimen, in which no heads have been produced; the stems are more elongated and flexuous, and ten or twelve together, with the appearance of an *Isaria*. The whole plant is yellow, and the fruit, as far as it is perfected, accords with the genus (plate 1, fig. 10). As to the *Sclerotium*, we imagine it to have been an error, as it is not so hard, or possessed of the internal character of a Sclerotium; it resembles rather the abdomen of some fly, or other insect, filled with mycelium, and the *Cordyceps* itself has a strong resemblance—a close affinity, at least—with *Cordyceps dipterigena*. Mr. Sprague remarked of a fly in the Boston Museum, many years ago,[1] that "from its back grow two little fungi, undeveloped, looking like two black pins; I doubt not that they are some species of *Cordyceps*. But in the absence of perithecia it is futile to attempt to name it; it may be a *Stilbum*, but that is now thought to be immature Sphæria."

---

[1] *Proc. Boston Soc. Nat. Hist.* (1867), vol. xi. p. 124.

FLY STILBUM.

Stilbum Kervillei.   Quelet.[1]

The species of *Stilbum* have a superficial resemblance to minute forms of *Cordyceps*, but of course differ in internal structure and fructification.   Dr. Quelet has described one on *Leria cæsia*, from two or three localities in France.   The head, from a fifth to more than a half a millimetre in diameter, is hemispherical, or lens-shaped, smooth, and of a bright yellow colour. The stem slender, thread-like, two to five millimetres long, often branched or proliferous, fibrillose and woolly, or frosted and quite white, arising from a thin yellow tomentose mycelium.   Conidia ellipsoid, about two and a half micromillimetres long, scattered over the head, borne on the tips of the central septate radiating threads, at first enveloped in mucus.   *Stilbum Buquetii*, also mentioned in this volume, has a rather woolly stem, whilst that in another species, *Stilbum formicarum*, has a smooth black stem.   The woolliness of the stem in *Stilbum*, or its absolute smoothness, have always been regarded as important characters, and almost of generic value.   Specifically the colours of the stem and head, combined with the form and size of the spores, are sufficient to delimitate species.

---

[1] Quelet, in "Gadeau de Kerville Champ. Entom.," p. 4, with fig. ; Saccardo, "Sylloge," iv. No. 2679.

HOUSE-FLY ENDOPHYTE.

Empusa muscæ.   Cohn.[1]

We commence this notice with a popular narrative, which did its duty twenty years ago,[2] and will accomplish that purpose even now.

"In the month of September last, the weather having being exceedingly humid and oppressive for several days, we observed, as the dusk of evening approached, that an unusual number of unhappy flies had come to an untimely end in various parts of the house, not on the windows only, but, as a closer examination showed, they were tightly fixed to the wainscoted walls and other smooth and polished surfaces. Varnished and glass-like objects had been generally selected, although rarely rougher surfaces had sufficed, the smoother being evidently preferred as being probably better adapted for adhesion. We could remember the time when we had seen dead flies sticking to the windows, surrounded by a little cloud, which in our ignorance we then thought was only dust; but the time arrived when we learnt that the so-called dust was a vegetable growth, and we were now aware that these flies had died in consequence of the over-powering attack of a fungus, to which they had

---

[1] Cohn, "Nova Acta Ces Leop." (1855), p. 301.
[2] W. M. B., in *Science Gossip*, January, 1865.

succumbed. The curiosity which at times had possessed us so strongly as to make us look with longing eyes at the victims on our neighbour's windows, and wish we might be allowed to cut out a small piece of his glass, say 'three inches by one,' induced us now to investigate a little more closely than hitherto the humble subjects of our remarks.

"A diligent search rewarded our endeavours, for after some time had been spent in watching our small friends, we perceived one which was not so lively as its companions, but rather in a semi-torpid condition, which had extended its proboscis and by aid of its two fore feet appeared to be clutching the glass with a spasmodic effort. Here then, at last, was an opportunity of obtaining a good specimen for further examination. One minute sufficed to fetch a slip of glass, and then, carefully placing the fly on the centre of it, we were gratified at beholding the victim again extend its proboscis, and, with the assistance of all its legs, resume the position in which we first saw it. For security we placed a large bell-glass over it and resumed our hunt. Another 'incurable' quickly met our fond gaze, and in its turn was placed on another glass slide. It proved as docile and tractable as its fellow, and readily adhered to the glass. Feeling we were now sufficiently supplied, we proceeded to watch with some attention, but were not enlightened by any movement on the part of the patients. Unlike the

Davenport Brothers, they were evidently unable to release themselves from the bonds which restrained them, so we left them quietly for an hour, and at the end of this period observed a dulness on the glass, though it was so slight as not to be easily discernible. At the end of two hours, another peep revealed the fact that what had appeared as only a dulness before had now developed to a distinct white cloudiness, which extended for a short space from each side of the abdomen, and gave evidence of forthcoming work for the microscope, as soon as the slides might be safely moved, without risking the somewhat fearful calamity of disturbing the innocent subjects of our notice. We therefore left them for the night, full of hope that the returning day would reveal a further development of this interesting parasitic plant.

"With the 'cock's shrill clarion' we awoke on the following morning, and no follower of the chase ever left his bedchamber more eager for the sport than we were to ascertain the state of our prisoners; nor were we disappointed in our hopes as to the result of the last eight hours. The flies were dead, but we did not grieve; on the contrary, we rather preferred it, for it promoted the object of our inquiry, by rendering the vegetation of the plants more complete, as was proved by the first glance we took at the glasses. The white dust now extended to the edges, although not at all in a regular and even film, but seemed radiated in waves more or less opaque, while the flies had maintained their original position and consequently had all the appearance of life.

" Desirous to see the end of this parasitic growth, we refrained from disturbing it until more than a week had elapsed, when we submitted one of the slips to examination under the microscope. We then perceived that what appeared to be a white dust, consisted of innumerable small disc-like spores or seeds, which were flat and circular, each having a nucleus and a few markings or rays extending from the centre to the edge, so that they might be familiarly compared to cart-wheels in appearance. The fly itself also proved an interesting subject for examination, as the hairs which covered it in all directions were beautifully decorated with snow-white globules, like bunches of grapes. The wings, legs, and proboscis were likewise dotted with similar spores, while they were abundant at the less horny parts, between the plates of the abdomen."

This fly-mould is now known by the name of *Empusa muscæ,*[1] and is found upon house-flies, and other species, in Europe and North and South America. The mycelium pervades the body of the

---

[1] Cohn, "Nova Actæ Nat. Cur." (1855); Fresenius, "Insekten Pilze," p. 883; "Entomophthora," p. 202, figs. 1-23; Thaxter, "Entomophthoreæ U.S." (1888), p. 155, pl. 14, figs. 1-9; Saccardo, "Sylloge," vii. No. 968.

insect, thrusting out conidia-bearing threads through the joints of the host, and producing the conidia on the surface ; these, again, have the power of producing secondary conidia direct from themselves. The mycelium within the insect has the power of producing resting-spores internally, so as efficiently to provide for the reproduction of the mould. In this species the conidia are nearly spherical, with a rather truncate base, and minutely pointed, or apiculate, apex (18 by 20, or 25 by 30μ), containing a large oil-globule, surrounded after discharge by a mass of protoplasm. The fertile threads simple, broad, and stout, tapering gradually downwards to a narrow base ; emerging in white rings between the segments of the fly, without coalescing over the body (plate 4, fig. 39). Secondary conidia like the first, or rather ovoid, smaller, rounded at the apex, and formed by budding direct from the primary form. Resting-spores produced from hyphæ within the host, spherical, colourless (30—50μ diameter).

Clustered Fly Endophyte.

Empusa conglomerata. Sorokin.[1]

To this species Mr. Roland Thaxter has assigned

---

[1] Sorokin, "Ueber zwei Entomophthora," p. 388, pl. 13, figs. 1-11 ; Thaxter, "Entomophthoreæ U.S.," p. 162, pl. 15, figs. 56-62.

the entomophyte found on larvæ, and imagines of *Tipula*, in North America, and, if the determination is correct, it occurs also on gnats in Europe. The larvæ were met with amongst moss over which water was running. These larvæ were dead, having a milky colour, and after being placed upon slightly damp moss, which absorbed the excess of moisture from them, produced conidia with great rapidity, but not in very considerable quantities. The conidia are broadly ovoid, usually with a single large oil-globule (22×25 to $25 \times 40\mu$) on simple fertile threads, or conidia-bearers. Secondary conidia like the primary. Resting-spores (azygospores) produced from spherical hyphal bodies, and borne on a neck-like process of variable length.

The large number of species of *Empusa*, and *Entomophthora*, now recognized as growing upon *Diptera* affords a strong contrast to only a few years ago, when *Empusa muscæ* was the only known species, and had been so for almost half a century.

GNAT ENDOPHYTE.

Empusa culicis. Braun.[1]

There is some feeling of personal gratification that

---

[1] A. Braun, "Unicellular Algæ," p. 105; Thaxter, "Entomophthoreæ U.S.," p. 157, pl. 14, figs. 10–16; Saccardo, "Sylloge," vii. No. 969;

the gnat, which has no compunction in its refined
tortures of the human subject, should at last be
compelled to succumb to a pervading mould, similar
to that which fixes the house-fly on the window-
pane.   It is a minute entomophyte common to
Europe and the United States, having been found
also in Britain.   Sometimes the infected insect
attaches itself to die on the under side of leaves, and
sometimes to the sides of tanks, or to stones and
rocks by water-courses, being fixed by rooting-
threads, which proceed from the mycelium in the
under portion of the body, and attach themselves by
a glutinous surface ;   these threads of attachment
being called rhizoids (plate 4, fig. 40).

In the present instance the conidia are nearly
spherical, with a rather truncate base, and sharply
pointed or acuminate apex, as in the fly-mould, of
an average dimension of eleven by twelve micromillimetres, being one-third smaller, at least, than
those of the house-fly, usually with a large oil-
globule, surrounded by a mass of protoplasm after
discharge.   Fertile threads simple, or with a tendency
to become compound, broad at the apex and
attenuated downwards to a narrow base, producing
white or greenish masses, which may or may not

Entomophthora rimosa, Sorokin, p. 393, pl. 13, figs. 12–19 ; Saccardo,
" Sylloge," vii. No. 979.

overrun the body of the gnat. Secondary conidia like the first, or ovoid, with a rounded apex, budding direct from the primary spore. Resting-spores produced internally from the hyphæ, spherical and uncoloured.

Little Gnat Endophyte.

Empusa papillata. Thaxter.[1]

Mr. Thaxter first noticed this species on the wet *Sphagnum* surrounding a spring, in the United States. He also found a number of examples upon minute gnats in the beds of mountain-brooks, on moist logs. The conidia are of a very large size, and are even visible to the naked eye; they are broadly ovoid, evenly rounded, with a very large tongue-like, slightly truncate papilla, clearly defined from the spore body (35 × 50μ). The conidia-bearing threads are stout and unbranched. Secondary conidia the same as in the first series. Resting-spores, produced without conjugation apparently, spherical, and slightly brownish. The gnats were attached to the objects on which they were found by means of a few rooting-fibres, or rhizoids, with a sucker-like expansion at the extremity.

Hitherto it seems to be confined to Diptera, having

---

[1] Thaxter, "Entomophthoreæ U.S.," p. 166, pl. 15, figs. 82-90.

only been found on minute gnats, and is, so far, an entirely North American species.

Carolina Tipula Endophyte.

Empusa caroliniana.   Thaxter.[1]

This parasite on Diptera is considered by Mr. R. Thaxter to be decidedly different from any form known to him, and easily recognized by its shapeless conidia, borne upon threads which are rarely branched, within the body of the host, and perfectly simple at their extremities. The insects affected were a brown *Tipula*, with mottled brown wings, and were found in a small group of hemlocks, among deciduous woods, and occurred invariably hanging from the lower dead twigs, about which the extremities of their long legs were knotted in such a manner that it was impossible to disengage them.

The conidia are ovoid, oblong, or elongated elliptical, with rounded extremities, the base hardly separable from the apex, without large oil-globules (10×26 to $15 \times 45\mu$). The conidia-bearing threads unbranched, barely projecting beyond the body of the host between the segments of the body and from the thorax, originating directly from rounded hyphal bodies. Secondary conidia like those of the first

---

[1] Thaxter, "Entomophthoreæ U.S.," p. 167, pl. 16, figs. 91-105.

generation.   Resting-spores, without conjugation, spherical and hyaline, averaging forty-five micro-millimetres diameter.   The insects attached by their legs.   Only found hitherto in North Carolina.

ROOTING FLY ENDOPHYTE.

Entomophthora muscivora.   Schroeter.[1]

This entomophyte occurs on large flies, which are attached by numerous rooting-fibres.   The same species appears to have acquired two names—that given above, and *Entomophthora calliphoræ* (Giard). The resting-spores are of a deep chestnut-brown ($24-28\mu$ diameter).   The conidia are ovoid, with a blunt papilla ($20-24 \times 11-13\mu$).

Mycelium formed of branched threads (24μ broad). Conidia-bearing threads branched, expanding outside the host, yellow or whitish ; conidia ovate, obtusely papillate.   Resting-spores evolved from the hyphæ of the mycelium, globose with a thick chestnut-brown epispore.

---

[1] Schroeter, "Entomophthorei in Flora von Schlesien " (1886), p. 223; Thaxter, p. 188 ; Saccardo, "Sylloge," vii. No. 978.

EGG-SPORED FLY ENDOPHYTE.

Entomophthora ovispora.   Nowakowski.[1]

This European species occurs also on flies, as on *Lonchæa vaginalis*, *Syrphidæ*, *Sapromyza*, etc., in wet situations, on damp ground, planks, etc. The conidia are described as being somewhat long-ovoid, with a papillate base and rounded apex, containing numerous small oil-globules, and also with very large cystidia. The conidia measure 22 to 28 by 14 micromillimetres, and the resting-spores are zygospores, produced by conjugation (31μ diameter).

ANTHOMYIA ENDOPHYTE.

Entomophthora pelliculosa.   Sorokin.[2]

Another imperfectly described species, said to have occurred in Europe on *Anthomyia pagana*. It is said to "resemble the ordinary *Empusa muscæ*, but the discharged conidia have the strange peculiarity of being covered with several layers concentrically distributed, as if a drop of protoplasm discharged simultaneously with the conidia had dried at several

---

[1] Nowakowski, "Entomophthoreæ" (1883), p. 160, figs. 33-58; Thaxter, ibid., p. 188; Saccardo, "Sylloge," vii. No. 981.

[2] Sorokin, "Entomophthora" (1883), p. 240, fig. 629; Thaxter, ibid., p. 189.

different intervals, forming each time something in the shape of an envelope. This characteristic is so constant that all the conidia scattered along the substratum were surrounded by sharply defined concentric lines."

Curved Spored Fly Endophyte.

Entomophthora curvispora. Nowakowski.[1]

Parasitic upon a small fly, *Simulia latipes*, in Europe, this species is little known. The conidia are strongly curved, elongated, rounded at both ends (10—15 × 25—40μ). The secondary conidia are said to be perfectly spherical. The resting-spores are true zygospores, produced by conjugation. "Tufts whitish, soft, conidia thickened at the base, zygospores formed by scalariform conjugation, globose, even, guttulate."

Variable Fly Endophyte.

Entomophthora variabilis. Thaxter.[2]

This minute parasite on Diptera has been found on minute gnats of various genera in North Carolina. It seldom occurs in any abundance in one locality,

---

[1] Nowakowski, "Entomophthoreæ" (1883), p. 163, figs. 68–70; Thaxter, ibid., p. 189; Saccardo, "Sylloge," vii. No. 980.
[2] Thaxter, "Entomophthoreæ U.S.," p. 183, pl. 20, figs. 327–343.

R

and is very difficult to find from the minute size of the insects which it attacks, yet it is almost always recognizable by the olive colour of the conidia-bearers, which, though not invariable, usually affords a ready means of separating it from other species with which it may be associated.

The conidia usually vary according to the period of their discharge, those first formed being ovoid, short and stout, with a papillate base and broadly rounded apex (about $15 \times 11\mu$). Those formed later are much more elongate, either shaped like a short straight club or strongly curved (18—30×7—9μ). Conidia-bearers having in the mass, as a rule, a distinctly olive tint. Cystidia in small numbers, slightly tapering, larger than the conidia-bearers. Secondary conidia, like the primary, of two general types. Host attached by rhizoids.

LARGE TIPULA ENDOPHYTE.

Entomophthora sepulchralis. Thaxter.[1]

This species has been found commonly on the largest *Tipulæ*, which occurred in considerable numbers, adhering to wet logs, or similar objects, along small brooks, in the Carolina Mountains. Although the abdomen of the insect is usually

---

[1] Thaxter, "Entomophthoreæ U.S.," p. 181, pl. 19, figs. 306-326.

narrow, and not more than a few millimetres broad, the conidia-bearers, after bursting through the integument about the thorax and between the segments, become confluent, and spread to some distance on either side of the body, forming a clear white mass of considerable dimensions.

The conidia are long-ovoid to long-elliptical, or rather spindle-shaped, rounded at the apex, and with a papillate base, commonly bent to one side, hyaline, with numerous large oil-globules (35—48×10—15μ in size). Conidia-bearers digitate, arising from large spherical hyphal bodies, and coalescing over the body of the host in a clear white mass. Cystidia very large, slightly expanded, or commonly becoming branched at their apices. Secondary conidia like the primary, or short-ovoid. Resting-spores (zygospores) spherical, hyaline (35—50μ diameter), formed as the result of conjugation between two hyphæ, and arising by budding from the connections.

SLENDER GNAT ENDOPHYTE.

Entomophthora gracilis. Thaxter.[1]

This species attacks the most minute gnats, and has only been known in South Carolina. The conidia are slender, and somewhat spindle-shaped,

[1] Thaxter, "Entomophthoreæ U.S.," p. 185, pl. 21, figs. 379-391.

with a neck-like papillate basal portion, and attenuated apex, strongly curved, rarely straight, containing large oil-globules (average size, 40 × 8μ). The conidia-bearers are digitate, coalescing over the host in a white mass (plate 4, fig. 46). Secondary conidia like the primary, or nearly spherical and papillate. Insects attached by rooting-fibres, or rhizoids.

Of no particular interest except from the peculiar type of the conidia. Resting-spores are unknown.

CONICAL FLY ENDOPHYTE.

Entomophthora conica.   Nowakowski.[1]

This European, and North American, species is found on Diptera, on the imagines of *Chironomus*, and other small gnats. It occurred on moss along the borders of small brooks.

The conidia are long, slender, conical, often strongly curved, with a rounded papillate base, tapering to the usually blunt extremity (25—80 × 10—14μ). Conidia-bearers digitate, arising, as a rule, directly from nearly spherical hyphal bodies, and coalescing over the body of the host in a clear white mass. The cystidia are larger than the conidia-bearers,

---

[1] Nowakowski, "Entomophthoreæ," p. 155, pls. 8, 9, figs. 1–32; Thaxter, "Entomophthoreæ U.S.," p. 186, pl. 21, figs. 392–410; Saccardo, "Sylloge," vii. No. 982.

rounded at the apex. Secondary conidia like the primary, or broadly ovoid, rarely pointed at the apex. Resting-spores (zygospores) produced by conjugation, usually budding from one of the connections, spherical, colourless (30—50μ diameter). · Insects attached by numerous rooting-threads.

EUROPEAN TIPULA ENDOPHYTE.

Entomophthora tipulæ. Fresenius.[1]

This species was found on a large *Tipula,* which was wingless and adhering to a rush. The mass of spores and threads had a greenish-brown colour. The conidia are ovoid, with a short, broad, rounded projecting base (33—40μ long).

M. Giard has also described an endophyte on the larva of some Dipterous insect, and he names it *Halisaria gracilis.* It is formed of slender slightly branched filaments, bearing greatly elongated, cylindrical spores.

SPINY-SPORED FLY ENDOPHYTE.

Entomophthora echinospora. Thaxter.[2]

The imago of the Dipterous insect *Sapromyxa*

---

[1] Fresenius, "Ueber der Pilzgattung Entomophthora," p. 206, figs. 46-50; Thaxter, "Entomophthoreæ U.S.," p. 188; Saccardo, "Sylloge," vii. No. 976.

[2] Thaxter, "Entomophthoreæ U.S.," p. 180, pl. 19, figs. 286-305.

longipennis, and other small *Diptera*, were found first in 1886, attacked by an *Entomophthora*, with the peculiarity indicated by the specific name.

The conidia in this species are ovoid, tapering to a papillate base, usually nearly symmetrical (20—25 ×.10—14μ), containing one or more large oil-globules. The conidia-bearers digitate, coalescing into a mat-like covering, which turns rust-coloured on exposure. The secondary conidia are like the primary, or varying very slightly. Resting-spores (zygospores) spherical (30—40μ diameter), the outer coat, or exospore, spinose; commonly produced externally as well as internally, and in the former case held slightly, after maturity, by a delicate mesh of hyphæ (plate 4, fig. 45). The host-insects are attached by rooting-fibres (rhizoids), coalescent around the abdomen in the conidial form.

MOUNTAIN GNAT ENDOPHYTE.

Entomophthora montana. Thaxter.[1]

Another mould on *Diptera*, found in abundance in 1886, on small gnats common about a brook, and some hundreds of the diseased insects were found amongst the *Sphagnum*, on the borders of the brook. "The species presents no peculiarities of interest

---

[1] Thaxter, "Entomophthoreæ U.S.," p. 180, pl. 18, figs. 274-285.

beyond the shape and size of the conidia, which are readily distinguished by their usually pointed base and broad apex, which give them the appearance of a long top."

Conidia from ovoid to top shape, usually tapering from a broadly rounded apex to a somewhat attenuated, slightly pointed base, containing numerous large oil-globules (11×18 to $15 \times 25\mu$). Conidia-bearers digitate, coalescing over the host in a livid white mass, and arising directly from rounded hyphal bodies. Cystidia tapering, or rounded at the apex, larger than the conidia-bearers. Secondary conidia like the primary, or shortly ovoid. Host attached by numerous rhizoids.

AMERICAN FLY ENDOPHYTE.

Entomophthora americana. Thaxter.[1]

The *Diptera* are furnished with a rather numerous company of mouldy foes, of which the above is common in parts of North America. It is frequently met with from June to October on the borders of woods near brooks, or in shrubberies about houses. The host is generally found fixed to the under, rarely on the upper, side of the leaves, or on bare twigs, a few feet from the ground. The rooting-threads (rhizoids),

---

[1] Thaxter, "Entomophthoreæ U.S.," p. 179, pl. 18, figs. 262-273.

instead of growing out in the form of numerous scattered threads, are developed in an even layer around the host's body, forming, with the conidia-bearers, a continuous mat-like covering, which becomes often dark rust-coloured on exposure to the weather.

The conidia are elongated ovoid, with a broad, evenly rounded apex, tapering for some distance to a papillate base, often slightly bent on one side. Within the spore are usually numerous fatty bodies, often very regular in size and shape (average size 28—30 × 14μ). Conidia-bearers regularly digitate, arising from large irregular, roundish, hyphal bodies, and coalescing over the host in a mat-like covering, which becomes slightly rust-coloured on exposure. Secondary conidia like the first. Resting spores colourless, hyaline, spherical (average size, 38—45μ). The host is attached by numerous filamentous threads, without terminal root-like expansions, forming an even mat-like attachment continuous around the abdomen of the host.

Found on *Musca domestica*, *Musca vomitoria*, *Lucilia Cæsar*, and numerous other large flies in New England and North Carolina.

THAXTER'S FLY ENDOPHYTE.

Entomophthora dipterigena. Thaxter.[1]

A somewhat remarkable mould on *Diptera*, especially on small *Tipulæ*, and other small flies or gnats,
has been found in the United States. The species is
not uncommon, occurring only on the under side of
leaves, in woods or thickets, in several States. The
conidia are variable in shape, ovoid or oblong, or
rather fusiform, with a papillate base, often bent to
one side, and containing numerous large oil-globules
(average size, $11 \times 22\mu$). The conidia-bearing threads
digitate, coalescing over the body of the insect in
a clear white, very rarely bright pea-green, mass.
Cystidia slender, tapering towards the apex. Secondary conidia like the primary, or broadly ovoid.
Resting-spores produced externally in grape-like
clusters, spherical, hyaline ($20-40\mu$ diameter). The
host is attached, to whatever stratum it is affixed, by
means of a few rooting-fibres, or rhizoids, with a
discoid extremity (plate 4, fig. 47).

It will be observed that in this species the conidia
and resting-spores are produced simultaneously and
externally.

---

[1] Thaxter, "Entomophthoreæ U.S.," p. 177, pl. 18, figs. 241-250.

Russian Fly Hanger.

Stigmatomyces muscæ. Karst.[1]

This entomophyte is similar to *Laboulbenia*, to which it is sometimes referred, but differs in the perithecia being thickened in the middle, terminating in a thick neck, and in the pseudo-paraphyses being single and curved, with tooth-like projections on the convex side. The present, and only species, occurs on the bodies of flies in Russia and Austria.

Stem cylindrical, two-celled, with a nodule at the base ; perithecia elongated-conoid, thicker below the middle, attenuated about the apex ; brown, with a two-lobed mouth. Pseudo-paraphyses lateral, single, acuminate at the apex, curved on the convex side with five or six acute teeth. Asci and sporidia as in *Laboulbenia*.

American Fly Hanger.

Appendiculina entomophila. Peck.[2]

This entomophyte was found in North America on small flies, *Drosophila nigricornis*, in March. The

---

[1] Karsten, "Hedwigia" (1888), p. 141; Peyritsch, p. 250; Saccardo, "Sylloge," viii. No. 3615 ; *Laboulbenia muscæ*, Peyritsch, " Laboulbenia," p. 444, pl. 1 ; " Laboulbenia Baeri Knoch." (1867).

[2] Peck, "Thirty-eighth Report of New York State Museum," p. 96, pl. 3, figs. 1–4 ; Saccardo, "Sylloge," viii. No. 3617.

fungus grows upon almost any part of the body—
the head, thorax, abdominal rings, occasionally on
the costæ of the wings, but most frequently on the
legs. Attached to one leg were seven well-developed
specimens, and one or two imperfect ones. The
whole fungus is about one-fortieth of an inch long,
or less than one-third of a line; it would not then
be readily seen by the untrained naked eye of an
observer. The perithecium, which is of a beautiful
amber-brown colour, appears like an enlargement
of the central part of the fungus, its long rostrum
or beak extending above it, nearly as far as its
pedicle does below it. The pedicle has one septum
a little below the perithecium, and another a little
below the middle. At the apex it is slightly
thickened, which gives it a somewhat clavate shape;
and this enlargement is obscurely marked by short
transverse and longitudinal septa or wrinkles. On
one side, at the base of the perithecium, is the
singular erect appendage, the office of which is
involved in obscurity. It is even and glabrous on
the side next the perithecium, but elsewhere it is
roughened by short ascending projections or serra-
tions.

The above is the original account of this parasite,
which is allied to *Laboulbenia*, and is thus briefly
described—

Perithecia ovoid, brown, produced above into an

acute straight or curved pallid neck; stem two-celled below, upwards thickened and many-celled. Pseudo-paraphyses inserted laterally at the base of the perithecium, oblong, single, external edge serrate, or bearing tooth-like appendages (plate 3, fig. 28). Sporidia fusiform, acute, septate at the middle, expelled from the mouth of the ostiolum or beak of the perithecium (30—35 × 3—4μ).

Peck did not observe the asci, but in this group they are so delicate, and soon dissolved, that this is by no means surprising.

NYCTERIBIA HANGER.

Helminthophana nycteribiæ.   Peyritsch.[1]

On account of some technical difference this little parasite has been removed from *Laboulbenia*, to which it originally belonged; the principal difference being that the pseudo-paraphyses are produced at the base instead of the side. It occurs on the living insects of the genera *Nycteribia* and *Megistopoda*. The entire fungus is from three hundred to seven hundred and fifty micromillimetres long. The perithecia are cylindrical below, attenuated upwards in a neck of equal length, crowned by a many-lobed

[1] Peyritsch, "Mon. Laboulbenia," p. 250, p. 45, pl. 2, figs. 1–3; Saccardo, "Sylloge," viii. No. 3616.

mouth. The pseudo-paraphyses are many-celled, the lower cell forming a cylindrical stem, above which are three whorls of three to four spicular appendages; the pseudo-paraphyses being single, and seated at the base.

FLY MUSCARDINE.

Botrytis Bassiana, var. *tenella*. Sacc.[1]

A thin variety of the Muscardine, under the above name, has occurred on the larvæ and pupæ of Diptera, and Wasps, in Italy, and on cockchafers in the Austrian Tyrol. The minute globose spores are stated to be about a micromillimetre and a half in diameter. In habit and appearance it does not seem to differ from the typical form, with variations consistent with such differences as might be caused by a difference in the host.

---

[1] *Botrytis tenella*, Saccardo, "Fungi Italiei," pl. 692; Saccardo, "Sylloge," iv. No. 608.

AQUATIC INSECT MOULDS.

THESE differ so much from the ordinary moulds, are not in any sense parasitic on living insects, but truly saprophytic, that our remarks upon them had better come together, as it would serve no useful purpose to scatter the various species over the different orders to which their hosts are suspected to belong. Although there is no doubt of one of the included species being fearfully parasitic upon fish, yet it is not upon aquatic insects that it occurs, and hence only after death. The *Saprolegniaceæ* for some time hovered between fungi and algæ; but since they are now recognized as fungi, it would have been imprudent to have ignored them, whilst at the same time any extended notice or profuse illustration is unnecessary.

The order to which they are referable is that termed *Phycomycetes*, the leading feature of which is their sexual reproduction, as the result of a kind of conjugation, resembling that which prevails in the *Conjugatæ* of the fresh-water algæ. Systematically the entomophytes of the family *Entomophthoraceæ*

belong to the same order, as will be seen on reference
to the mycological synopsis at the end.

AQUATIC FLY MOULD.

Saprolegnia ferax. Nees.[1]

It has long been known that when the house-fly,
infested with *Empusa muscæ*, falls, or is thrown into
water, a more complex mould is developed, which
really is identical with the salmon disease. This
would seem to indicate that the *Empusa* is a conidial
form of the *Saprolegnia*, which view has been asserted,
even by mycologists, whilst we venture to doubt
whether there is really any genetic relationship between them.

These dead insects are soon surrounded by a mass
of long and intricate mouldy threads, which are
attached to the body of the insect by a creeping
mycelium. From these root-like threads the fertile
threads proceed in all directions, gradually increasing
in number, until the whole insect is enveloped. When
the growth has once commenced it is very rapid, and
the microscope must be used to trace the details of
its development. When these threads are fully
mature their outer extremities become more dense,

---

[1] Nees, in "Kutz. Phyc. Germ.," p. 157; Max Cornu, "Mono-
graphie des Saprolegniées" (1872: Paris).

and the contents undergo differentiation into a mass of nearly globose minute bodies, which at length are a little pointed at one extremity, so as to be almost egg-shaped, furnished at the thin end with a pair of delicate movable threads, not visible until these bodies make their escape from a pore at the apex, into the surrounding water (fig. 41), in which they move with great agility, and are recognized as *zoospores.* They are capable of coming to rest after a short period, germinating and reproducing the original plant by this simple method of asexual reproduction.

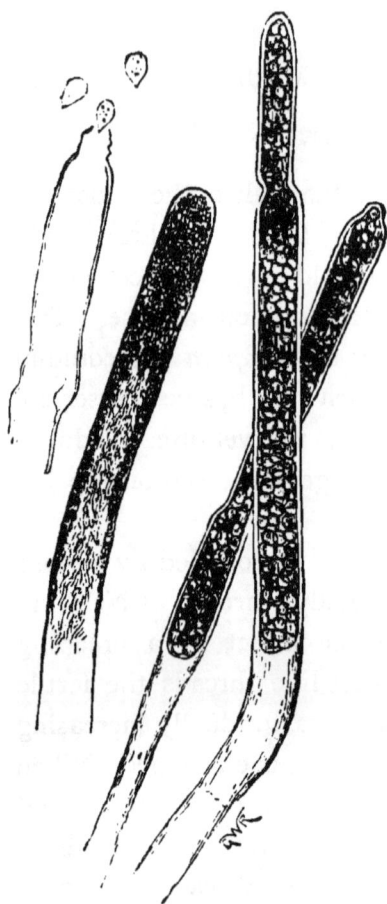

FIG. 41.—Aquatic Fly Mould. *Saprolegnia ferax.* Extremities of threads magnified, with zoospores.

But there is another and more complex mode by which a continuance of the species is assured, and this is by means of resting-spores, which provide against the vicissitudes which might befall the zoospores, and, after a period of rest, themselves reproduce the plant. The oogonia, or female cells, are sub-globose terminations, formed at the apex of short branches of the threads. These differ a little in the different species and genera into which the family is divided. Some ultimately contain *one* oospore, and others *many*. Beside these are lateral branches, the upper portion of which becomes an antheridium, or male receptacle, the lower portion, or stem, being of variable length. The antheridia are cut off by a septum from the lower portion of the branch, and may be either simple or branched. When the time arrives for fecundation, the oogonia contain usually several globose oospores; the extremities of the lateral branches approach the oogonium; sometimes one, and often more, delicate tubes are evolved from the antheridia, which penetrate the oogonium, and, seeking out the oospores, attach themselves to them, and the connection is complete. In some species the outer wall of the oogonium is perforated with pores, to facilitate the entrance of the tubes from the antheridia, and this is the case with *Saprolegnia ferax.* This is also a diœcious species, without lateral branches, so that there are separate male and female threads, the antheridia crowning the apices of the male filaments.

S

Monoicous Water-Mould.

Saprolegnia monoica.   Prings.[1]

There is also a monœcious species of *Saprolegnia*, which is developed on dead flies; hence there are diœcious species, in which the male and female elements are on different filaments, and monœcious, in which the same filament bears the oogonia and antheridia.   The present species is *Saprolegnia monoica*,[1] and has the oogonia either at the apices of the threads or lateral, the outer wall being perforated for facility of fecundation, the antheridia being formed from the apices of lateral branches (plate 4, fig. 51). . The oospores are one-third smaller than in *Saprolegnia ferax*, the oogonia containing each a number of oospores.

Star-spored Water-Mould.

Saprolegnia asterophora.   De Bary.[2]

A very characteristic monœcious species, as above, has occurred in Belgium and Germany on dead flies; the oogonia are stellate, or star-shaped, each containing from one to three oospores (plate 3, fig. 38). The antheridia are worm-shaped.

---

[1] Pringsheim, *Jahrb.*, i. 292, pls. 19, 20.
[2] De Bary, in Pringsh., *Jahrb.*, ii. p. 189, pl. 20, figs. 25-27.

Proliferous Water-mould.

Pythium proliferum. De Bary.[1]

The technical differences between *Pythium* and *Saprolegnia* will not, probably, be fully appreciated by other than mycological readers. The zoosporangia are formed from the protoplasm, then enclosed in a very delicate cuticle, like a soap-bubble, called the *vesicle*. In *Saprolegnia* the zoospores are perfected within the zoosporangium, but in *Pythium* they are not perfected, and furnished with cilia, until after escaping from the zoosporangium. The oogonia contain but one oospore, and the oospores are at length cristate. The species above named is found on dead insects in water in Britain, Belgium, and Germany, and has elongated, or sometimes lemon-shaped, papillate zoosporangia ; when mature the zoospores make their exit at the papilla by the breaking of the cuticle.

Of the present species it may be said that the mycelium is often profusely branched ; the zoospores are kidney-shaped, with two cilia, escaping through the teat-like projection at the apex of the zoosporangium. A second zoosporangium commonly is produced from the base, and within the empty one.

---

[1] De Bary, in Pringsh., *Jahrb.*, ii. p. 182, pl. 21, figs. 28–37 ; Ward, *Quarterly Journ. Micr. Sci.*, vol. xxiii. p. 497, figs. 11–21.

LEITGEB'S WATER-MOULD.

Diplanes saprolegnioides.   Leitg.[1]

It is supposed by M. Cornu that this is an unnecessary genus, which bears the name of *Diplanes*, and that it is no other than *Saprolegnia*. The minute difference suggested, that the zoospores are first covered with a membrane within the zoosporangium, and afterwards, when expelled, naked, whilst in *Saprolegnia* there is never a membrane, is even dubious. The threads are a little branched. The oogonia are produced at the apices of the branches, and are perforated, containing numerous oospores. Antheridia produced on lateral branches (plate 4, fig. 50). The zoospores are ovoid when coated, and trifoveolate, but when naked are bean-shaped and unifoveolate, with two cilia. Whatever may be said in favour of the numerous genera of *Saprolegniaceæ*, it must be confessed that the distinctions are infinitesimally minute, and difficult of discrimination.

It is recorded on dead insects, of various kinds, in water, in France and Germany, and is also stated to have occurred in Britain.

---

[1] Leitgeb, in Pringsh., *Jahrb.*, vli. p. 374, pl. 24, figs. 1–12.

PROLIFEROUS WATER MOULD.

Achlya prolifera. Nees.[1]

The species of *Achlya* have very much the habit of those in *Saprolegnia,* and are sometimes confounded with them.   One distinction insisted upon is that in *Saprolegnia* the zoospores are always destitute of a membrane, whilst in *Achlya* the zoospores are naked when in the zoosporangium, but covered with a membrane when outside.   The zoospores are of two kinds—the first agile, with two movable cilia ; and after a time these come to rest, and produce a second kind of zoospore, which is kidney-shaped and flattened. Some of the species of *Achlya* are also monœcious, and others diœcious.   The species to which the above name is applied is diœcious, in which no lateral branches are produced to carry the antheridia, which are borne on separate threads.   The oogonia contain numerous oospores, and the wall is perforated to assist in fertilization.   This is one of the oldest known species of Saprolegniaceæ, and occurs on putrescent insects, presumably of almost any order, and has occurred in Germany, and other parts of Europe.

[1] Nees, De Bary, *Botan. Zeit.* (1852), pl. 7, figs. 1-28

Achlya dioica.   Prings.[1]

If *Achlya dioica* is really a distinct species from *Achlya prolifera*, it is very much like it, occurring under the same conditions and in the same places; and some have ventured to doubt if there is any manifest distinction between them, which is not revealed by the description.

POLYANDROUS WATER-MOULD.

Achlya polyandra.   Hilde.[2]

Of the monœcious species of *Achlya*, we have an example here, which occurs on dead flies in water in Germany, and rarely in Britain. In this instance the oogonia are oblong, and not perforated, and the oospores are numerous in each oogonium, and brown (plate 4, fig. 48). Antheridia are lobed and very numerous, proceeding from lateral branches, and everywhere concealing the oogonium. The zoosporangia are apical, very long and solitary, never broader than the filament which bears them. The specific name is derived from the fact that from two to six antheridia will be seen attaching themselves to the same oogonium.

---

[1] Pringsh., *Jahrb.*, ii. p. 206, pl. 23, figs. 1–9.
[2] Hildebrand, in Pringsh., *Jahrb.*, vi. p. 258, pl. 16, figs. 7–11.

STELLATE WATER-MOULD

Aphanomyces stellatus. De Bary.[1]

Technically the species of *Aphanomyces* differ from those of *Saprolegnia,* and its more immediate associates, by the very long and narrow zoosporangia, in which the zoospores are arranged in a single row. The oogonia contain one, or rarely two, oospores. The species named above has been found on putrescent insects in water, in Germany and Belgium, and is also recorded as having occurred in Britain (plate 3, fig. 36). The erect fertile threads arise from the creeping mycelium, and the oogonia are large, and at length stellate, containing mostly a solitary oospore, but sometimes two. The rays of the oogonium are from four to five micromillimetres long.

SMOOTH WATER-MOULD.

Aphanomyces levis. De Bary.[2]

Another *Aphanomyces* has also occurred upon dead insects in water, in Germany and Belgium, which differs at once from the foregoing in the globose oogonia being quite even, and the oospore having

---

[1] De Bary, in Pringsh., *Jahrb.,* ii. p. 170, pl. 19, figs. 1–13.
[2] Ibid., p. 199, pl. 20, figs. 17, 18.

one large central oil-globule.   As far as we are aware, this has never been found in Britain (plate 4, fig. 49). It would be easily recognized by the even oogonia, which are deficient of the small projections found in the next species, or the larger and stellate processes of the former.

ROUGH WATER-MOULD.

Aphanomyces scaber.   De Bary.[1]

The third *Aphanomyces* differs from the other two, already enumerated, in that the oogonia have the outer cuticle rough with small projections (plate 3, fig. 37).   The mature oospores contain a large oil-globule.   This species is also found on decaying insects in water, amongst aquatic plants, in Belgium and Germany.

---

[1] De Bary, Pringsh., *Jahrb.*, ii. p. 178, pl. 20, figs. 14–16.

NEUROPTERA.

NERVE-WINGED FLIES.

THE Neuroptera are for the most part free from
Entomophytes ; the only two species at present
known to us belong to the *Entomophthoreæ*, that destructive group of parasites to which the well-known
disease of the house-fly belongs. They undoubtedly
attack their victims in the living state, and the internal mycelium is gradually developed, until at
length the whole internal structure is disintegrated,
and the fungus becomes supreme. As death approaches, the insect attaches itself to some object,
either by its proboscis or feet, or by the production
of rooting-threads from the body, which fix the insect,
as if it were glued down, to some near object, and
in this position it dies.

NEUROPTEROUS ENDOPHYTE.

Entomophthora rhizospora. Thaxter.[1]

There are but few entomophytes which attack

---

[1] Thaxter, in "Entomophthoreæ U.S.," p. 183, pl. 20, figs. 347, 348.

Neuroptera, and hence this one, which occurs on several species of *Phryganeidæ*, is of interest. The affected imagines were found concealed under saturated logs, or very commonly under stones, partially exposed in the bed of shallow wood streams, or in swampy places in woods, in Maine and North Carolina. No affected larvæ have been seen.

The conidia in form were like a straight short club, varying to almost crescent-shaped, very variable, tapering more or less at either extremity; the basal portion of the spore neck-like, bearing the rounded papilla of attachment, and containing large fat globules ($30—35 \times 8—10\mu$). Conidia-bearers digitate, coalescing in a livid white mass over the insect. Cystidia large and slightly tapering. Secondary conidia like the primary, or spherical, with an abrupt delicate papillate base. Resting-spores (zygospores) spherical, with a brownish epispore ($40—60\mu$) · budding from conjugating connections, and subsequently surrounded by rhizoid-like outgrowths, which are closely applied to the spore, and originate at its base. The hyphæ-producing zygospores are always external, and subsequently become thickened and horny, turning dark chocolate-brown, and holding the spores in a spongy mass. The insects are attached by rooting-fibres, or rhizoids.

PHRYGANEA ENDOPHYTE.

Entomophthora phryganeæ.   Sorokin.[1]

The above entomophyte was found on *Phryganea grandis* in 1881, in Europe, growing only on the lower surface, between the first and second pair of legs, being wholly superficial, and not appearing within the body of the host. The hyphæ consist of two portions, separated by a septum. The conidia are round (8×6—7μ). It seems doubtful whether this belongs to the Entomophthoreæ at all, and indeed it must be regarded as a doubtful species altogether, named from insufficient material. Thus, then, of the two entomophytes accredited to the *Neuroptera*, only one can be regarded as positively certain, and that a North American species.

Recently M. Giard has made known an entomophyte, to which he gives the name of *Epichlæa divisa*, found on the body of an Ephemeron. It is composed of short cylindrical cells, bearing one or two spores at each of their extremities.

---

[1] Sorokin, "Entomophthora" (1883), p. 239, figs. 578, 628 *a b*; Thaxter, ibid., p. 189.

ORTHOPTERA.

CRICKETS AND COCKROACHES.

IN Mr. Gray's time only one species had been noticed as attacked by a fungous parasite. A specimen of *Gryllotalpa americana* was found "in a wood near Newark, Delaware, upon turning over a log. The insect was seen standing very quietly at the mouth of its oval cell, which is formed in the earth, having a short curved tube to the surface. Upon taking it up it exhibited no signs of movement, though perfectly fresh and lifelike in appearance." On examining it next morning "it still presented no signs of life. Every part of the insect was perfect, not even the antennæ being broken. Upon feeling it, it was very hard and resistant; and on making an incision through the thorax it exhaled a fungoid odour. The insect had been invaded with a parasitic fungus, which everywhere filled the animal, occupying the position of all the soft tissue, and extending even into the tarsal joints. It formed a yellowish, or cream-coloured compact mass, and, in the abdomen, enclosed in its centre the stomachal teeth of the insect."[1] This fungus is thought by Dr. Leidy[2] to be the same as that which sometimes attacks the larvæ of lamellicorn insects. Evidently it was only in the early condition, in which only the mycelium was developed internally. The entomophytes since added belong to the *Entomophthoreæ*, which are analogous to the common mould of the house-fly.

Grasshopper Endophyte.

Empusa grylli. Fresenius.[3]

Roland Thaxter[4] says, " I have observed numerous epidemics of the grasshopper form at Kittery, in Maine, near Boston, and in North Carolina ; and the caterpillar form seems also very common, assuming an epidemic character among the *Hyphantria* larvæ, which have recently done considerable damage to the shade trees in Washington." He then argues that the mould on the larvæ of many genera of Lepidoptera, which has been called *Empusa aulicæ*, is only a form of the present species ; however we

---

[1] Leidy, *Proc. Acad. Nat. Sci. Phil.* (1851), pp. 204, 210 ; Smith's " Contrib. to Knowledge," v. p. 53.

[2] *Proc. Acad. Nat. Sci. Phil.* (1851), p. 235.

[3] Fresenius, "Entomophthoræ," p. 203, figs. 24-43 ; Saccardo, "Sylloge," vii. No. 970 ; Fresenius, *Bot. Zeit.* (1856), p. 883.

[4] Thaxter, "Entomophthoræ U.S.," p. 159, pl. 14, figs. 17-48.

have assumed it to be different by including it in the section devoted to the Lepidoptera. In the present species the larvæ seem to be attached to the object on which they are fixed by a contraction of the legs. The conidia are ovoid or pear-shaped, with a broad papillate base, and rounded apex ($30—40 \times 25—36\mu$), hyaline, and containing one or more large globules. The fertile threads are simple, coalescing externally when growing luxuriantly, and arising directly from rounded irregular hyphal bodies, either with or without branching. The secondary conidia are like those of the first series. Resting-spores spherical and colourless, produced from the internal hyphæ, directly within or by budding from hyphal bodies, or by a kind of pseudo-conjugation between two divisions of a single hyphal body. Adverting to this peculiar phenomenon of pseudo-conjugation in the present species, Roland Thaxter says, "In the first place we have, before reproduction of either type, a condition characterized by the presence of irregular rounded hyphal bodies of various size and shape. Instead of producing a resting-spore (azygospore) by any of the usual methods, one of these bodies may become septate by the formation of a median cross partition. An elevation of the cell wall presently appears around the hyphal body, between the cells thus formed, which develops into a two-lipped fold. The partition between these two cells is then apparently absorbed, for the contents of one gradually pass into the other to form a 'zygospore.'"[1] The process, he adds, is not uncommon, occurring chiefly in the femoræ; but in all cases the usual resting-spores (azygospores) are by far the most abundant form of resting-spores.

This entomophyte is found on the larvæ, pupæ, and imagines of many genera of Acridians in different States of North America.

EUROPEAN GRASSHOPPER ENDOPHYTE.

Entomophthora colorata. Sorokin.[2]

This species, which occurs in Europe on grasshoppers, is peculiar from its coloured conidia, which are described as reddish brown and spherical. In this species Sorokin observed peculiar amœboid bodies within the host, which produce resting-spores laterally or terminally.

It must be admitted that this species is very imperfectly known, resting entirely upon its first observation by Sorokin, which was also its last. It was ignored by Saccardo, in his "Sylloge," and if not characterized as doubtful, it must at any rate be

---

[1] Thaxter, " Entomophthoræ U.S.," p. 149.
[2] Sorokin, " Memoirs Imp. Acad. Sci. St. Petersburg" (1880), p. 62, pl. 13, figs. 5, 6, 19–27 ; pl. 4, fig. 28 ; Thaxter, p. 187.

considered at present as an obscure species, concerning which further information is desirable.

Under this order we may refer to the remarks of Piso, who, speaking of the Mantis, says, "Those little animals change into a green and tender plant, which is of two hands breadth. The feet are fixed into the ground first; from these, when necessary humidity is attracted, roots grow out, and strike into the ground; thus they change by degrees, and in a short time become a perfect plant. Sometimes only the lower part takes the nature and form of a plant, while the upper part remains as before living and movable; after some time the animal is gradually converted into a plant. In this nature seems to operate in a circle by a continual retrograde motion."[1] This little romance may receive some illustration from what has been written of "Vegetable Wasps," but it is difficult to separate fact from fiction. Donovan ("Insects of China") seems to think that Ovid's account of the transformation of Phaeton's sisters into trees had its origin in some such idea as this.

Locusts, which have contributed no little to the annoyance of mankind, by the destruction of crops, in their turn have to submit to parasitism. A white

---

[1] Cowan's "Curious Facts" (1865), p. 91.

mould, to which the name of *Botrytis acridiorum* has been given, is very destructive to locusts in North Africa ;[1] whilst another mould, *Oospora ovorum*, forms a white efflorescence upon *Acridium peregrinum*, producing clusters of from twenty to thirty long chaplets of spores. Two other fungi have been credited with attacking locusts, one of which belongs to the yeast-fungi, or *Saccharomycetes*, and will probably prove to be very destructive. This is some little consolation to those who have suffered from the devastations of the insect.

[1] Bonnier, " Rev. Gen. de Bot.," iii. 1891, p. 401.

HETEROPTERA. ·

D R. GRAY was unsuccessful in finding examples of the attacks of entomophytes upon insects of the order Heteroptera, and he quotes the observation of Dr. Leidy, that, as "they suck the juices only of plants and animals through a delicate proboscis, they were placed under circumstances the most favourable of all animals to avoid taking in, with their food, spores and plants of a parasitic character." The only two species cited would not appear to be true parasites, but only moulds which attach themselves to dead animal matter.

GARDEN-BUG MOULD.

Penicillium Fieberi.   Corda.

Corda described and figured (in 1846), in his splendid work, " Mucedines de l'Europe," a mould found upon a Hemipterous insect (*Pentatoma prasina*), under the name of *Penicillium Fieberi* of Corda, which was afterwards (in 1851) figured in part

by Bonordeu, and called by the same name. Professor Saccardo has, in his "Sylloge" (vol. iv. No.
388), ignored Corda, and given Bonorden as the
authority, contrary to all precedent and justice. It
is possible that this mould is not really entomogenous, but would develop on various dead animal
substances ; yet it is only recorded on insects. It
is effused over the insect, particularly the thorax and
legs, of an olive or brown colour, with the creeping
threads of mycelium branched, the fertile threads
erect and septate, uncoloured. The chains of spores
which are produced at the apex of these threads are
at first crowded together in an ovoid head, or capitulum ; but afterwards they separate, and become
divergent and nodding (plate 2, fig. 24). The spores
forming the apical chains are globose, with a warted
surface, and of an olive colour, the terminal spore
being the largest. Although there is no information
on this point, it is improbable that this mould attacked
the insect when living, but simply established itself
upon the dead body, in accordance with the general
habit of moulds of this genus.

The other parasite alluded to in this order rests
upon the exhibition by Professor Westwood,[1] at the
Entomological Society, of a large species of *Acan-
thocephalus* (so-called), but which we presume is the

---

[1] *Trans. Entom. Soc. Lond.* (1841-43), iii. pl. 6.

same as *Metapodius latipes.* From the scutellum of this a great number of filamentous fungi had been produced,

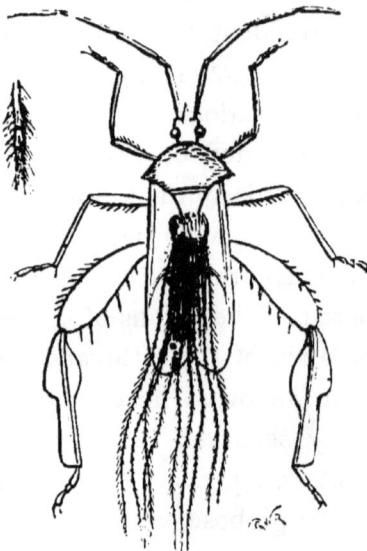

FIG. 42.—Parasite on Heteropteron (after Westwood).

each being as long as the entire body (fig. 42). The only interpretation we are able to suggest is that the entomophyte was some kind of *Isaria,* the long threads being woolly, or with projecting filaments throughout their length, which correspond to the ends of the delicate threads combined in each filament.

STILBOID ISARIA.

Isaria stilbiformis.   Speg.[1]

On a minute species of *Pentatoma,* in Italy, Spegazzini discovered a peculiar *Isaria,* which he named as above. It was either solitary or gre-

[1] Spegazzini, in "Michelia," vol. i. p. 476; Saccardo, "Sylloge," iv. No. 788.

garious. The compound yellowish stems, from three to seven millimetres high, formed of bundles of hyaline yellowish threads firmly agglutinated together, diverging at the apex, and forming a tomentose, almost spherical or pear-shaped head, like a *Stilbum*. The tips of the threads swollen in a club shape with an acute apex, and quite colourless, bearing a cylindrical spore or conidium, rather attenuated at each end, and from eight to eleven micromillimetres long, and two to two and a half broad. Technically, it only differs from a species of *Stilbum* in not having the conidia at first involved in a kind of mucus.

HOMOPTERA.

PLANT-SUCKERS.

THE order Homoptera contains the various species of *Cicada*, which are liable to attack from different species of entomogenous fungi. The New Zealand Cicadæ suffer from one species, and those of the West Indies from another; whilst in South America a new and distinct parasite is on the alert; and, so far as it can be guessed, the Cicada of the United States has to bear the infliction of an entomophyte differing from all the rest.

The *Aphidæ* are extremely subject to attack from species of *Entomophthoreæ*, which are so destructive and so readily communicated, that the proposition has been made to introduce some one or more of the most favourable kinds of moulds of this class amongst the *Aphides* in greenhouses, with a view to their destruction.

The *Coccidæ* also are the hosts especially of the Sphæriaceous kinds of Entomophytes, both in their perfect and conidial conditions.

For observations on the entomological aspects of this portion of our subject we must again be indebted to Mr. Gray's memoir.

" These insects (*Cicadæ*) reside, during the first two periods of their existence, in the earth, into which they descend immediately after being released from the eggs (which had previously been deposited by the female in slits in dead branches, by means of an ovipositor), seeking the roots of trees, ferns, and other plants, to which they cling, and extracting the sap by the insertion of their proboscis into the bark, thus causing even large trees and plants to wither and die, from the countless number of their assailants. They continue to reside in the earth even after they have undergone their metamorphosis into the pupa state, in which condition they are equally active and destructive to the roots of trees, etc.; indeed, the only difference between these two states is that the pupa possesses rudimental wings, visible on the sides of the body. They usually remain near the surface, but as winter approaches they descend into the earth, to the depth of two or three feet, which they are enabled to do by means of the great strength of the anterior legs of the larvæ and pupæ, which can even penetrate through the most solid and hard-trodden road; but the digging apparatus is transformed into legs resembling the other four, on the insect assuming the last or perfect stage of life. It is during the first two stages that these insects, especially in rainy seasons, become the bases of the parasite, which first commences in the interior of the insect; after a time the thallus bursts forth at that part of the outer case from which the insect would escape at the period of assuming the different states of pupa and imago; that is to say, at the longitudinal suture on the middle of the upper surface of the head, and on the dorsal portion of the prothorax and mesothorax. It is from this thallus that the fungoid parasite takes its rise, either from the head or from the prothorax, and even from the mesothorax; but this may depend upon the position of the insect at the commencement of the outer development of the fungus. In some specimens, however, the fungus springs from the joints of the upper and under surface of the abdomen, and sometimes also from the joints of the two fore legs. The examples all show that the insect was only imbedded just below the surface of the earth, or in vegetable matter, during the period of the growth of the fungus."[1]

NEW ZEALAND CICADA CLUBS.

Cordyceps Sinclairii. Berk.

Some of the small species of *Cicada* in New

---

[1] Gray's "Notices of Insect Fungi," p. 16.

Zealand are subject to the attacks of a species of *Cordyceps*, as above, which has been specifically involved in some confusion, caused in the first instance by Tulasne describing it as *Cordyceps cæspitosa*,[1] after it had already been described by Berkeley under the above name,[2] and apparently not only from the same locality, but from the same set of specimens. Saccardo has repeated the same error, by including both species, as if they were perfectly distinct, instead of being synonymous, in his late work.[3] Truly, however, there is but one species, figured by Berkeley in his "Cryptogamic Botany," and by Dr. Gray in his memoir (pl. 4, figs. 9, 10). It is described as "yellowish, from three quarters to an inch high. Stems cylindrical, slender, simple or forked, sometimes confluent, divided above into numerous more or less cylindrical, either simple, or slightly lobed heads, which are sometimes disposed into a flabelliform mass, clothed with innumerable oblong conidia." This was the only condition of the specimens examined by Berkeley, for he adds, "the specimens are unfortunately destitute of perithecia;" and Tulasne obtained no more than this, in which, as in other particulars, the two independent descriptions will be

---

[1] Tulasne, "Selecta Fungorum Carpologia," vol. iii. p. 11.
[2] Berkeley, in Hooker's "New Zealand Flora," vol. ii. p. 338; "Crypt. Bot." (1857), p. 73, fig. 17.
[3] Saccardo, "Sylloge," ii. Nos. 5043, 5054.

found to agree. The only variation being that the one describes its habitat as "on the larvæ of some Orthopterous insect," and the other "on buried Cicadæ." As if two names were insufficient, Taylor mentions what is probably the same thing under the name of "Locust, or Sphæria Basili."[1]   Berkeley

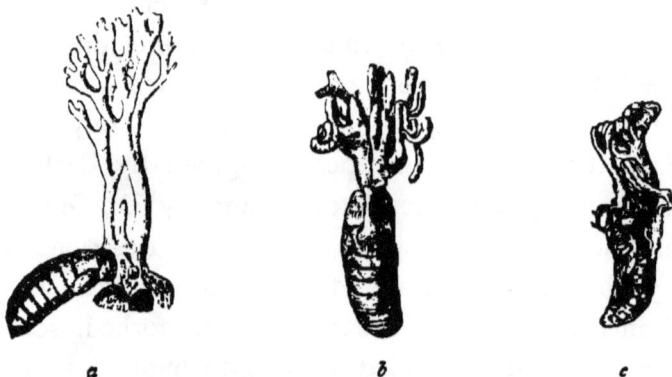

Figs. 43 45.—New Zealand Cicada Clubs. *Cordyceps Sinclairii (a* after Berkeley, *b* and *c* after Gray).

proceeds to state of this entomophyte that "the pale-yellowish tint, inclining to lemon-yellow, seems characteristic, and forbids, in the first instance, their union with *C. sobolifera,* a West Indian species, which also occurs on Orthopterous larva.   In that species, however, the normal form seems to be simply clavate, as in *C. entomorrhiza,* and the divisions are merely proliferous.   There does not seem, in the present case, to be any indications of such a primitive form,

---

[1] Taylor, " New Zealand," p. 424, fig. on p. 421.

and in consequence I suppose the head to be essentially divided, as in *C. Taylori.* I have, therefore, no hesitation in considering it as new, more especially as the West Indian species is a purely tropical form, and does not ascend as far as the southern United States, which produce some New Zealand species, but is represented by an allied form, still normally simple, on the larvæ of cockchafers."

As for the species of *Cicada* on which this fungus is found, we have the authority of Dr. Gray[1] for saying that it is difficult to determine, out of the ten species recorded for New Zealand. "As the insects thus infested are always in their larva and pupa states, it becomes impossible to correctly affix to them their proper specific names, but as the habits of all the species are similar in every respect, it is most likely that all those species which usually inhabit localities where the germs of these fungoid parasites exist are equally liable to become the basis of them."

The parasites usually grow from the head and thorax in a series of short stems, that are sometimes matted together, each ending in several tuberculated proliferous processes; sometimes the fungus also springs from the joints of the fore legs (figs. 43–45).

Specimens exhibited very recently, at one or two

---

[1] Gray, " Notices of Insect Fungi," p. 17.

of the meetings of the Entomological Society of London, do not appear to differ at all from the present species, and they also occurred on the larvæ of some species of *Cicada*. The clubs are branched, of the usual size and appearance of the original examples. By the courtesy of F. D. Godman, Esq., we have seen the specimens in his collection, and arrived at this conclusion concerning them.

BRAZILIAN CICADA CLUBS.

Isaria cicadæ. Miq.[1]

This is another instance in which we cannot think that Tulasne was justified in applying to an *Isaria*, with external dust-like spores, the generic appellation of *Torrubia* or *Cordyceps*, which assumes a more perfect fructification immersed in the substance, and enclosed in asci. Such speculations in advance are only an embarrassment of science by the introduction of unnecessary synonymy.

The present parasite is found on the larvæ of some species of Cicada in Brazil, and Miquel states distinctly that he considers it developed after the death of the insect, and not, as in some other instances,

---

[1] Miquel, " Bullet. des Sci. Phys. Neerl." (1838), p. 85, t. 1, fig. A ; Robin, " Veg. Par.," p. 665 ; Mulder, " Chim. Phys. Gen." (1851), i. p. 90.

on the living animal. It is described as having a harder and more compact stroma than in most species, consisting of a central resistant white tissue, and a floccose brown sporiferous bark. It is clongated, cylindrical, tough, branched in the upper portion, and produces cylindrical, obtuse conidia, the dimensions of which are not given. Whether, as suggested by Tulasne, the same species has occurred in North America on some lamellicorn beetle, we cannot affirm, but must take leave to doubt.[1]

WEST INDIAN CICADA CLUBS.

Cordyceps sobolifera. Hill.

This, which is one of the most notable of Insect fungi, is the celebrated "Vegetable Fly," of which remarkable stories have been told. Originally, it was considered to be peculiar to the West Indian species of *Cicada*, but some authors have of late attributed it also to certain beetles, possibly without much justification.

The Rev. M. J. Berkeley, in determining its scientific affinities in 1843, writes of it thus: "This species is extremely variable in form, but in its most perfect state has a subglobose head and proliferous stem.

---

[1] *Torrubia Miquelii*, Tulasne, "Selecta Fungi Carpologia," iii. p. 11 ; *Cordyceps Miquelii*, Saccardo, "Sylloge," ii. No. 5046.

Sometimes the terminal head is not developed, and
the stem is terminated by a number of little heads,
which form a cluster, as in a recorded variety of *C.
militaris;* sometimes the stem is branched above,
each branch being terminated by a little clavate
head ; sometimes a single head only is developed, but
tuberculated, and in this case there are no proliferous
processes on the stem ; and occasionally not only the
stem is even, without any proliferous processes, but
the head, instead of being subglobose, is absolutely
linear, as in *C. sinensis.* I have in vain examined
specimens, both dry and preserved in spirits, in the
hope of finding perfect asci; but the perithecia, though
tolerably well formed, contained merely a few threads,
which broke up into short cylindrical portions. These
are probably imperfect strings of sporidia, and, if so,
differ materially from those of *C. entomorrhiza* and
C. Robertsii."

It is undoubtedly true that this parasite varies much
in its mode of branching, but there is a general resemblance in habit in the majority of forms (figs. 46–48).
Mr. Gray attempts to particularize some of these
variations, thus : A lengthened stem with proliferous
processes at or near the middle, and a subglobose
head at the apex ;[1] a short stem with proliferous
processes, but without terminal head ;[2] several stems

[1] Gray's "Notices of Insects," pl. 4, fig. 11.
[2] Fougeroux de Bonderoy, "Memoires," pl. 4, fig. 4.

proceeding from one base,[1] terminating in subglobose heads; a lengthened and smooth stem ending in a clavate head;[2] a lengthened and smooth stem with short tuberculated heads;[3] a smooth stem with irre-

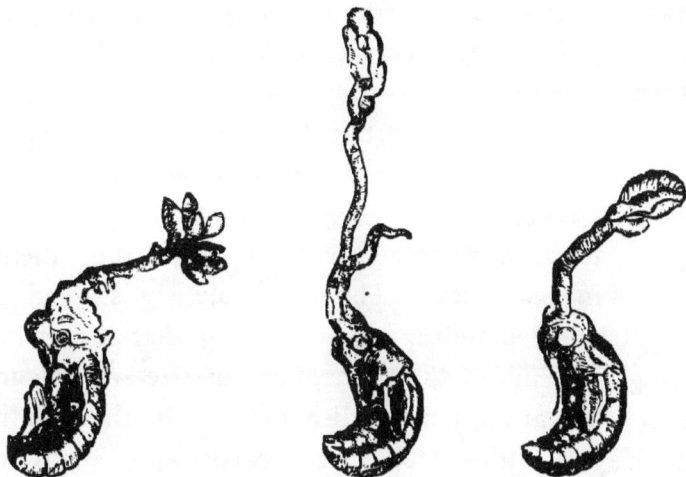

Figs. 45–47.—West Indian Cicada Clubs. *Cordyceps sobolifera* (after Fougeroux de Bonderoy).

gular formed heads;[4] a lengthened and smooth stem with a very long granulated head;[5] proliferous processes proceeding at once from the head or thorax;[6] and the fungus also appearing from the joints, either in the upper or under surface of the abdomen,[7] and

[1] Gray's "Notices of Insects," pl. 4, fig. 13.
[2] Ibid., pl. 4, fig. 12.
[3] Fougeroux de Bonderoy, pl. 4, fig. 4.
[4] Ibid., pl. 4, figs. 5, 6.
[5] Gray, pl. 4, fig. 14; Fougeroux de Bonderoy, pl. 4, fig. 7.
[6] Gray, pl. 5, figs. 1 3.   [7] Ibid., pl. 5, figs. 2, 3.

sometimes from the fore legs.   This is supposed to
include the principal forms under which the present
fungus appears, but under each form there will probably be some variation of detail.   Mature specimens
exhibit the linear sporidia breaking up into joints, as
seen by Berkeley, but smaller than in many other
species.

As far as we can ascertain, the first detailed account
of this entomophyte is contained in the communica-
tion by Watson to the Royal Society in 1763.[1]   In
order to save reference, we will quote the salient
points in this paper.   " The Vegetable Fly is found in
the Island Dominica, and (excepting that it has no
wings) resembles the drone, both in size and colour,
more than any other English insect.   In the month
of May it buries itself in the earth, and begins to
vegetate.   By the latter end of July the tree arrives
at its full growth, and resembles a coral branch, and
is about three inches high, and bears several little
pods, which, dropping off, become worms, and from
thence flies, like the English caterpillar."   This is
the account as communicated to Dr. Watson by his
friend Dr. Huxham, and in narrating it the former
remarks that the latter can by no means think the
above relation true in all its circumstances, yet he is

---

[1] " An Account of the Insect called the Vegetable Fly," by William
Watson, M.D., in *Philosophical Transactions* (1763), vol. liii. pp. 271–
274.

persuaded that there is something of reality in it, which perhaps further accounts and observations may set in a full and true light, though at present, as represented, it seems quite repugnant to the usual order of nature. Dr. Watson then states that he had never seen this production before, but had been informed that Dr. Hill had examined some of them; therefore he wrote to that gentleman, desiring to be informed of the result of his examination, to which he received the following reply: "There is in Martinique a fungus of the Clavaria kind, different in species from those hitherto known; it produces soboles from its sides—I called it, therefore, *Clavaria sobolifera* (fig. 49). It grows on putrid animal substances, as our fungus from the dead horse's hoof. The Cicada is common in Martinique, and in its nymph state, in which the old authors call it 'Tettigometra,' it buries itself under dead leaves to wait its change, and when the season is unfavourable, may perish. The seeds of the Clavaria find a proper bed on this dead insect, and grow. This, you may be assured, is the fact, and all the fact, though the untaught inhabitants suppose a fly to vegetate, and though there exists a Spanish drawing of the plant's growing into a trifoliate tree, and it has been figured with the creature flying with this tree upon its back.

> 'So wild are the imaginations of man,
> So chaste and uniform is Nature.'"

U

Dr. Watson then refers to Mr. Edwards, who, he says, in his "Gleanings of Natural History," has given a figure of this extraordinary production. He concludes with the intimation that he had carefully examined the specimen, and confirmed Dr. Hill's account.

As Edwards has been referred to, and as his account must have preceded 1763, and therefore been a prior allusion to the fungus, we quote a portion of his remarks. "The insect figured (pl. 335) has a kind of fungus growing out of the head. It was brought from Dominica, in the West Indies. Many of them were found together, buried in the earth, all having the like fungus shooting from their heads. The moisture of the earth, I suppose, causes these funguses to shoot. The imperfect insect, or nymph,

FIG. 49.—West Indian Cicada Club. *Cordyceps sobolifera* (after Dr. Watson).

on which they grow seems to be the Cicada in its infant state, as described by Reaumur. I suppose, before the Cicada arrives at its perfect state, the fungus dries, and falls off." [1]

Shortly afterwards, or in the early part of the year 1769, M. Fougeroux de Bonderoy submitted a memoir

---

[1] Edwards, "Gleanings of Natural History," pt. iii. p. 263, pl. 335; see also "History of Insects" (Murray's Family Library), ii. p. 298 (1838).

on this subject to the French Academy,[1] but as it is
not easily accessible, and has never been translated,
we venture to give such portion of it as refers to the
present species. After referring to Dr. Watson's com-
munication, and Mr. Needham's notes on his transla-
tion of Abbé Spalanzani, he says that the latter "sees
in these plant-animals a proof of the passage and
mutation of animal species into the vegetable, and
reciprocally from the vegetable to the animal. My
intention," he adds, "is not to examine whether this
mutation is proved in such a manner as to leave no
doubt, and whether the decomposition of one body
can produce, whilst developing itself, other living
beings. I shall here confine myself to adding observations to those which have already been given concerning the plants which vegetate upon insects. It
may be that, in multiplying the remarks which have
reference to these singular facts, we shall be led to
find their true explanation ; at all events, it is certain
that they will induce educated travellers to study
these plant-animals in the places where they are
common, and under circumstances which should give
a complete account of the manner in which they are
produced.

"I propose in this memoir to bring under notice

---

[1] "Mémoire sur des Insectes sur lesquels un trouve des Plantes,"
by M. Fougeroux de Bonderoy, in *Mémoires de l'Acad. Roy. des
Sciences* (Paris : 1769).

different species of insects upon which plants are found. I will describe a worm upon which is found the plant which is most usually found upon the larvæ of the *Cicada ;* and, after having described the states and sizes of these plants as I have been able to procure them, I will point out a plant of a kind different from that which I have just brought under notice but still like it—a kind of fungus, which I have had the opportunity of examining, upon a Cicada from Cayenne. Finally, I shall conclude this memoir by considering the opinions most likely to explain this reunion of the animal and the plant.

" Many of these plant-animals which I have seen in collections of Natural History present a plant which vegetates upon the chrysalis of a species of Cicada, and upon the (Tettigometra) larva, as described by Mr. Hill. We cannot doubt but that these insects are chrysalides of Cicadæ, because we can recognize upon many two characteristics which principally distinguish them—the proboscis or sucker, and the two large feet or claws.

" The plant grows upon the head of the insect upon its corselet, or upon the body of the animal ; the part of the insect upon which this plant is placed is not, therefore, always the same, since upon those which I describe the stems vary in their position, and there are found upon the insects one, two, or three stems, placed upon different parts of their bodies. Some

bear one or two stems upon their head ; others have
them upon the corselet, or upon the body of the
insect ; others, again, have even three separate ones,
the positions of which vary.

" It appears to me that the plant vegetates almost
always upon the upper part of the body of the animal,
and not underneath ; I say, nevertheless, almost
always, because 1 have seen a beginning of these
plants under the body of a chrysalis of a Cicada,
which carried another on its head.

" There are also remarkable differences in the plants
which are found upon these insects ; they vary much
in length. The highest which I have seen were two
inches in height, and were surmounted by a head, or
mass. There are, nevertheless, some which bear only
a simple fillet, of an almost equal thickness throughout the whole length of its stem. In the plants which
have only one stalk, it is terminated by a head more
or less inflated, or it carries at its extremity a mass ;
or, again, the head ramifies, and the branches are
terminated by little tubercles. The Tettigometra
bears upon its head a plant which terminates in two
pretty large tubercles, of which one is hollow.

" The examination of these plants leaves no doubt
as to what class they belong ; they must be placed in
that of *Clavaria*, described by Linnæus, because he
has included with them the genus which Micheli has
called *Lichen-agaricus*, with which our plant has still

more affinity than with the *Clavaria* described by
Vaillant (since separated from *Clavaria* under the
name of *Cordyceps*).

" The root of the plant only covers the body of the
insect upon which it vegetates.   When the insect and
the plant are preserved in spirits of wine, and have
not been dried, the plant may be raised and separated
from the animal without any injury to the latter.   We
then perceive, under the stipe of the plant, flutings
which may be produced by the rings of the insect's
body.   Thus the roots of the plant do not penetrate
the body of the animal at all.

" The plant, which has not yet put forth its capitulum, and which is not yet at its last stage of growth,
is filled ; it is as if composed of longitudinal fibres.
When they are dried, on the contrary, they are hollow,
and it often happens that the apices are pierced by an
opening, which appears to have served as an outlet to
an insect ; but we know how common it is to find fungi,
eaten by worms (maggots) which are metamorphosed
on leaving these plants."

Then follow some remarks on a filamentous fungus
found on the imago of Cicada in Cayenne, and descriptions of other entomophytes on larvæ.   These
are followed by the quotation of Dr. Watson's com-
munication, principally as regards the explanation
by Mr. Hill, and then he proceeds—

" There can no longer be any doubt as to the

principal facts, which numbers of specimens, contained in our cabinets, tend to confirm ; it is a plant of the order of fungi, and of the genus *Clavaria*, the root or stipe of which is implanted upon the body of an insect. Such are the principal facts. That deceptions practised in the native country change this peculiarity, by putting seeds in the stalk of the *Clavaria*, should not be the occasion of exciting the attention of the natural philosopher ; there remain, without that, plenty of difficulties to explain, how established and received facts take place, after having separated from the accounts of travellers circumstances wrongly interpreted, which should induce us not to seek for explanations all the more useless, in that they bear upon false and imperfectly observed details."

After referring in some detail to the Chinese plant-worm, he concludes thus : " We will add that the few carefully examined circumstances of the country do not yet put us in a position to speak with certainty upon these mysterious facts, and consequently I shall refrain from hazarding any conjectures ; I ask only to compare the opinion of Mr. Hill with the principal facts, which are certain, and it can be determined whether it is not the most simple and the most probable of those which have been advanced.

" It is known that there are fungi which live only upon one species of plant, or which derive their

nourishment from one particular substance ; thus one
kind is found solely upon the hoofs of dead horses ;
certain fungi come only upon such or such roots of
plants ; in short, parasitic plants or bulbs derive their
nurture only from the same kind of plant. We should
not, therefore, be more astonished to see the *Clavaria*
always attach itself to the larvæ, or nymphs, of
Cicada, and with insects that bury themselves, than
we are to find the same fungus upon the hoofs of a
dead horse ; a sponge and a species of *Alcyonium*
upon crabs ; mushrooms upon the root of the horn-
beam ; the tacon upon the saffron ; the hypocist upon
the cistus, etc.

"We have seen that the fungus is placed upon
every part of the insect's body ; these different
positions of the plant may depend, in Mr. Hill's
opinion, upon that which is the most usual to the
body of the insect when it is about to undergo its
metamorphosis, and when the plant begins to vegetate upon the animal.

"In short, the great number of these aurelias,
which continually, in the country of the Caribbeans
at certain seasons bear these plants, adds nothing to
the wonder that an isolated case would cause. When
there are many of these larvæ, or of these chrysalides,
the circumstances which produced one of these plants
will be repeated upon many others, and if the plant
grew in a country where we do not find it, when the

insect itself would be living there, we should never see the phenomenon happen of which we speak."

Mr. Gray gives the species of West Indian Cicadæ as *Cicada albiflos* and *Cicada mesochlora* for Jamaica, *Cicada chariclo* for Cuba, and *Cicada tomentosa* for St. Thomas.

Fougeroux de Bonderoy described and figured in

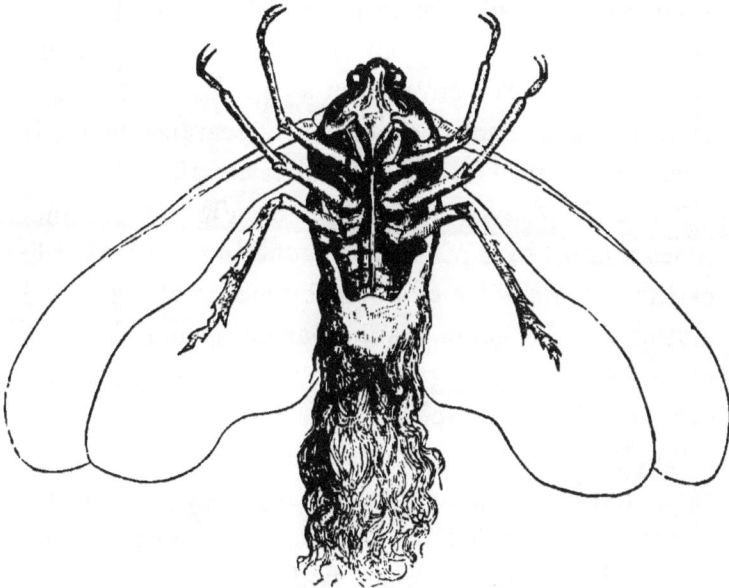

FIG. 50.—Exudation from body of *Cicada*, resembling a parasite (after Fougeroux de Bonderoy).

his memoir something which resembles an *Isaria* on the imago of *Cicada*. "This latter," he says, "is a native of Cayenne, and the plant is a species of fungus, but different from those we have described.

It is formed of long and silky filaments, which cover
the whole body of the insect, and project about seven
to eight lines above and below the belly of the animal"
(fig. 50). It is quite true that the figure has some
resemblance to an *Isaria*, but as a similar specimen
came into the hands of Mr. Gray, he consulted with
the Rev. M. J. Berkeley, and in consequence of their
examination they came to the conclusion that it was
not a fungus at all, but an exudation from the body
of the insect. We have given a copy of the figure in
question, which has certainly an appearance which is
misleading, but which is not a parasite after all.

"The *Delphax saccharivora* of St. Vincent is sometimes found," says Mr. Gray, "adhering to the midrib
of the under surface of a leaf by means of a fungoid
matter, in the same manner as flies, and from its
body also spring lengthened filaments having a sub-
ovate head at their apex.

"It is on the young and tender shoots of the sugar-
cane that these insects are usually seen in immense
quantities, sitting on the midrib or large sap-vessels
of the leaf, probing them with their proboscis to
obtain the saccharine juice on which they regale
themselves, and thus often causing, from their number,
the death of the plant, to the serious loss of the
growers. It is apparently while thus engaged that
the parasite shows itself on the perfect insect."[1]

---

[1] Gray, "Notices of Insects," p. 17, pl. 4, fig. 15.

The description of this entomophyte suggests at once some species of the *Entomophthoraceæ*, but this can only be a suggestion for lack of evidence.

KATYDID ENDOPHYTE.

Massospora cicadina. Peck.[1]

This entomophyte on the seventeen-year *Cicada* is peculiar to North America. It occurs on larvæ, pupæ, and imago of *Cicada septemdecem,* and its affinities are not yet quite certain. Conidia are produced from short hyphæ, or hyphal bodies, within the host, and are nearly spherical or ovoid, tapering towards a small basal papilla of attachment, smooth or papillately warted (10×18 to $18 \times 25\mu$), forming a yellowish mass in the abdominal cavity, exposed as a coherent mass by the falling away of the abdominal rings. The supposed resting-spores are spherical, roughly reticulated, slightly coloured (38—50μ). The host is not attached.

This description at once suggests an explanation of the observations made by Dr. Leidy, in 1851, on a parasite of the same insect. Mr. Roland Thaxter believes it to be related to *Empusa* and *Entomoph-*

---

[1] Peck, "Thirty-first Report of New York State Museum" (1879), p. 44; Thaxter, "Entomophthoreæ U.S.," p. 190.

thora, and is therefore included by him in the same family, although Professor Saccardo has given it a different position in his " Sylloge." [1]

The seventeen-year Cicada of the United States (*Cicada septemdecem*), according to Dr. Leidy,[2] is liable to suffer from a fungus parasite. The posterior part of the abdomen has been observed, in several instances, to be filled with a mass of oval spore-like bodies, embossed upon the surface, but becoming smooth from endosmosis when placed in water. Of course these details are insufficient to indicate what kind of fungus it may be.

In alluding to this parasite, Mr. Gray gives the following notes on the insect, which may interest our younger readers. "The specific name," he says, "indicates that the remarkable period of seventeen years recurs with perfect regularity, before each generation, numbering many millions of individuals, attains sufficient maturity to change into the imago, or perfect state. Their appearance varies in different districts, though this lengthened interval always passes before each series appears, and must occasion the insect to undergo many changes of temperature and weather. The same reason probably causes it to be liable to become the basis of the fungoid

---

[1] Saccardo, " Sylloge," iv. No. 19.
[2] Leidy, *Proc. Acad. Nat. Sci. Philadel.* (1851), p. 235.

parasite. It dwells chiefly in localities abounding in trees, and even on land which was free of them before, when trees, especially those bearing fruits, have been planted upon it, although it remains, in some localities, even after the trees have been removed, and then feeds on the roots of grasses, etc., still making its appearance regularly, after the allotted period of seventeen years is passed. Their metamorphosis usually takes place in the night ; but their reappearance is anticipated by the inhabitants of some localities, who register the year when they may be expected, so that they appear without creating much surprise.[1]

The manner in which this disease attacks the United States *Cicada* is given chiefly on the authority of Dr. Leidy, but the proper determination of its botanical affinities does not appear to have been made.

During the spring of 1851, some twelve or twenty specimens were found from amongst myriads of *Cicada septemdecem*, which, though living, had the posterior third of the abdominal contents converted into a dry powdery ochreous yellow compact mass of sporulioid bodies. The outer coverings of that portion of the insect were loose and easily detached, leaving the fungoid matter in the form of a cone, affixed by

---

[1] Gray's "Notices of Insect Fungi," p. 15.

its base to the unaffected part of the abdomen of the insect. The fungus may commence, says Dr. Leidy,[1] its attacks upon the larva, develop its mycelium, and produce a sporular mass within the active chrysalis (pupa). When in this condition many are probably destroyed ; but should some be only affected so far as not to destroy the organs immediately essential to life, they might undergo their metamorphosis into the imago, in which case they would be affected in the manner previously described. The reason he assigns of the fungoid production being always found in the last-mentioned situation, arises probably from the fact that the access of the sporules to the interior of the animal is much easier through the generative and anal apertures than through the more delicate passage of the proboscis.

CICADA MOULD.

Sporotrichum minutulum. Speg.[2]

This species of mould belongs to a genus not at all uncommon on decaying animal and vegetable substances, but not truly parasitic. The present was found in South America on putrescent larvæ

---

[1] "Smithsonian Contributions to Knowledge," v. p. 53.

[2] Spegazzini, "Fungi Argentini," ii. p. 42 ; Saccardo, "Sylloge," iv. No. 504.

of a *Cicada* (*Fidicina bonærensis*). The tufts are white and scattered, or gregarious and confluent, very small, scarcely reaching a millimetre in diameter. The threads are creeping, sparingly septate, and thin, with short branches, bearing at the tips from one to three elliptical conidia, the ends of which are rounded, not more than three to four micromillimetres long, and one to one and a half broad. Most of the species form rather thin velvety patches on dead leaves, rotting bark, and wood, plants, rags, leather, and all kinds of rotting materials. Some are white, others yellowish, brownish, greenish, or grey, very simple in structure, and with minute conidia or spores.

JASSUS ENDOPHYTE.

Empusa jassi. Cohn.[1]

This entomophyte of *Jassus sexnotatus* has been so imperfectly described that very little can be said about it, except the meagre account by Cohn, that the mycelium is evolved within the body of the insect, and appears on the surface in a velvety stroma. The conidia are simply stated to be globose, and twenty micromillimetres in diameter.

---

[1] Cohn, in *Jahres d. Schles. Ges. f. Vaterl. Cult.* (1877), p. 116; Saccardo, "Sylloge," vii. No. 972.

Universal Endophyte.

Entomophthora sphærosperma. Fresenius.[1]

One of the most universal of entomophytes is the present species, which has been observed on all orders of insects excepting Orthoptera, and it often produces epidemics of considerable proportions. Mr. Thaxter writes, "I have observed two epidemics caused by this species; one among certain small flies in a wood, near marshy ground, at Kittery, Maine, where the hosts occurred in considerable numbers, fixed by the fungus on the under side of the lower leaves, a few feet from the ground. The second instance occurred in two orchards in the same locality, where the hundreds of the previously mentioned epidemic were replaced by tens of thousands, the host in this instance being the leaf-hopper (*Typhlocyba mali* and *rosæ*), a pest only too well known to cultivators of roses. Having first observed it in some abundance on roses in a garden, I was led to make an examination of adjacent apple-orchards, and found the lower branches of the trees literally covered

---

[1] Fresenius, "Entomophthora," p. 207, pl. 9, fig. 68; Thaxter, "Entomophthoreæ U.S.," p. 172, pl. 17, figs. 200–219; Saccardo, "Sylloge," vii. No. 974; *Entomophthora radicans*, Brefeld, *Bot. Unt. Ent.* (1881), iv. p. 97; *Entomophthora phytonomi*, Arthur, *Bot. Gaz.*, xi. p. 14.

with the affected hosts, a dozen or more being often fastened to a single leaf.

"The whole mass of conidia-bearing threads coalesces over the body, often leaving only the middle of the thorax uncovered; but instead of presenting the rounded form usual in other Empusæ, the upper surface has a flattened appearance, and is the only portion from which conidia are discharged. This is due to an oblique tendency, observable in the growth of the main hyphæ. The basidia thus have a general tendency to point upwards, instead of in all directions, as is usually the case. The occurrence of specimens in which the mass of conidia-bearers is coloured green or greenish is not common, and the colour fades on drying; but in two cases, in the epidemic among leaf-hoppers just mentioned, I found specimens in which it was coloured a vivid pea-green—a circumstance that can hardly be due to any colouring matter from the host, which is of a pale-yellowish tint."

The conidia are long-elliptical to nearly cylindrical, papillate at the base, and tapering very slightly near the rounded apex (average about 20 by $5\tfrac{1}{2}\mu$), usually with a fine granular contents and a central oval nuclear body. The conidia-bearers are much-branched, digitate, and confluent over the body of the host, forming usually a mass, the upper surface of which is flattened. Colour of the fungus as a whole white, varying to a bright pea-green. Secondary

X

conidia like those of the first generation, or else elongated almond-shaped, and borne on a hair-like spore-bearer. Resting-spores borne lateral, or terminal, from the hyphæ ($20-35\mu$), spherical and hyaline, or very slightly yellowish.

Found in Europe as well as in the United States.

APHIDES.

PLANT-LICE.

These minute pests of the cultivator have at length been discovered by fungoid enemies, and suffered retribution. No less than five entomo-phytes of the *Empusa* kind have been recorded as destroying them, and this so effectually, that it has been proposed to utilize the fungus in order to reduce the number of insect pests in the conservatory. The three other parasites may possibly only be Sapro-phytes, but they find a place here, since they have never been found on any other substances. The *Isaria* is the only one which offers a probability of its being truly parasitic.

STAR-LIKE ISARIA.

Isaria stellata. Cooke.[1]

Some Mango-leaves from India came into our

---

[1] Cooke, in *Grevillea;* Saccardo, "Sylloge," iv. No. 2785.

hands some years since, and upon the under surface were found beautiful star-like, snow-white objects, almost like crystals of snow. Minute examination proved them to be minute insects, apparently *Aphides*, encrusted with an *Isaria*, about two millimetres in diameter, and sometimes confluent. The rays were numerous, radiating from a sort of discoid centre, regular, and not at all corresponding to any members, or projections, of the imbedded insects; the latter impossible to extricate for identification. The whole mass of fungus was composed of delicate agglutinated threads. As often is the case, a considerable number of Aphides were congregated on the leaves, so that when they were close together, the encrusting *Isaria* united, becoming confluent in an irregular crust; but in cases where the insects were isolated, the star-like shape of the parasite was maintained.

Planchon's Aphis Endophyte.

Empusa Planchoniana. Cornu.[1]

The above-named parasite, and that found by Thaxter, in the United States, on several genera of Aphides, appear to be identical; it occurred on numerous Aphides infesting the white birch, and

---

[1] Cornu, *Bull. Soc. Bot. de France* (1873), xx. p. 180; Thaxter, "Entomophthoreæ U.S.," p. 165, pl. 15, figs. 76-78.

other plants, in late summer and autumn. The conidia are nearly spherical, or broadly ovoid, with a papillate base, which is sometimes furnished with a short point (28—33 × 30—40μ). The fertile or conidia-bearing threads simple, partially coalescing over the host. Secondary conidia like the first series. Resting-spores (azygospores) produced internally on the hyphæ, and spherical. The attachment of the host to the matrix accomplished by the insertion of its proboscis.

Whether this is really the species of M. Cornu need not concern us much, as his description is rather too meagre for certainty. It differs from *E. apiculata* in the absence of rhizoids, as well as by the variability of the conidia, which are rarely pointed.

COMMON APHIS ENDOPHYTE.

Entomophthora aphidis. Hoffman.[1]

Under the above name is included a parasite which has been of considerable advantage to the culturist by facilitating the destruction of a grievous pest. The experience of Mr. Thaxter on this species in the United States commenced in a greenhouse,

---

[1] Hoffman, in Fresenius's "Entomophthoreæ," p. 208, figs. 59–67 ; Thaxter, "Entomophthoreæ U.S.," p. 175, pl. 18, figs. 220–240; Saccardo, "Sylloge," vii. No. 975.

where, he says, it acted as a decided check to the multiplication of the Aphides, yet did not spread with sufficient rapidity to render "smoking" in the greenhouse unnecessary. At Kittery he found it on numerous genera of *Aphides*, and especially destructive to the forms which injure the hop. In one case he observed a large hop-vine, some twenty feet high, completely covered with Aphides, which were killed off by this fungus in about two weeks, the affected hosts being fastened to the under side of the leaves and to the young shoots in vast numbers. The destruction of colonies of *Aphides*, by this species, seems to be the rule rather than the exception, and is at least of very common occurrence. He also mentions the case of a great quantity of *Aphides* dying of the disease on clover at Washington. It is a species common to Europe and North America.

The conidia are ovoid, or elliptical, or subfusiform, commonly unsymmetrical and very variable, with a papillate base, and containing numerous oil-globules (average size, $25 \times 12\mu$). The conidia-bearing threads digitately branched, sometimes simple. Hyphal bodies spherical, germinating in all directions, and giving rise to numerous contorted hyphæ, which grow into conidia-bearing threads. Cystidia rather slender and tapering at their extremities. Secondary conidia like the primary, or shortly ovoid, with a single large oil-globule. Resting-spores spherical, terminal, or lateral. Host attached by rhizoids ending in a disc-like expansion.

BIRCH APHIS ENDOPHYTE.

Entomophthora occidentalis. Thaxter.[1]

Another of the entomophytes which infest the *Aphis* of the American white birch is the above. It has nothing very peculiar in its structure or habits, and depends for its characteristics on microscopical features. Conidia elongated elliptical, sometimes slightly fusiform, often tapering strongly towards the apex, with a broad, rounded, papillate base (average $35 \times 10\mu$). The contents usually finely granular, sometimes with larger fatty bodies. The spore-bearers irregularly branched in a digitate manner, coalescing in a white or slightly yellowish mass. Secondary conidia like the first, or else long almond-shaped, borne obliquely on hair-like spore-bearers. Resting-spores borne laterally or terminal by budding from the hyphæ, colourless, spherical ($20—35\mu$ diameter). The insects are attached by rooting-fibres (rhizoids) to the objects (plate 4, fig. 44). Mr. Thaxter remarks that "the resting-spores often occur in specimens also producing conidia, and are commonly formed by lateral budding, from short

---

[1] Thaxter, "Entomophthoreæ U.S.," p. 171, pl. 17, figs. 179-199.

hyphæ, in an apparently non-sexual manner; but numerous instances also occur where the budding is associated with a partition, which may perhaps indicate a sexual process. In a few cases, spores developing from long hyphæ, growing in the legs, seemed to result from a process which may be considered a form of conjugation.

FLASK-SHAPED ENDOPHYTE.

Empusa lageniformis. Thaxter.[1]

An entomophyte on Birch Aphides has been found in North America, which is of systematic interest, since it is possible that, in conjunction with another similar species, they may constitute the types of a new genus, for which the name of *Triplosporium* has been suggested. This, however, is a technical question. The parasite itself possesses conidia which are slightly smoky, flask-shaped, with a truncate but scarcely papillate base, and rounded apex; the contents are granular (20 × 35μ). The conidia-bearing threads are simple, or when young sometimes fasciculate, or spreading like one's fingers, terminated by a weak tapering spore-bearer. The secondary conidia are like the first, or almond-shaped, and set obliquely on

---

[1] *Empusa* (*Triplosporium*) *lageniformis,* Thaxter, " Entomophthoreæ U.S.," p. 169, pl. 16, figs. 141–160.

hair-like spore-bearers.   Resting-spores at present
unknown.   The affected insect attaches itself by the
insertion of its proboscis.   This is a larger species
than the next (*Empusa Fresenii*), and it is probable
will be found to exhibit a true conjugation.   Numerous
examples were examined for resting-spores, but none
were found ; perhaps the favourable moment may be
discovered when the species is better known.   Mr.
Thaxter thinks that it has such an undoubted close
affinity to *E. Fresenii,* that he anticipates eventually
to discover similar fructification.

FRESENIUS'S APHIS ENDOPHYTE.

Empusa Fresenii.   Nows.[1]

Another Aphideous mould, common both to Europe
and the United States, found upon the *Aphis* of the
apple tree, and several other species.   The production
of the resting-spores, by means of a process of conjugation, demand special notice.   The conidia are
nearly spherical or shortly ovoid, often with a short,
truncate, or commonly slightly papillate base, with
granular contents, without large fat globules, and
slightly smoky in colour (either $15 \times 18\mu$ or $18
\times 20\mu$).   The conidia-bearing threads unbranched,

---

[1] *Empusa* (*Triplosporium*) *Fresenii,* Nowakowski, " Entomophthoreæ," p. 171, pl. 12, figs. 115-125 ; Thaxter, " Entomophthoreæ
U.S.," p. 167, pl. 16, figs. 106-140.

arising directly from small spherical hyphal bodies of a yellowish colour. Secondary conidia of two kinds ; the one like the first generation, the other almond-shaped, and borne obliquely on hair-like supports. The resting-spores, or zygospores, elliptical or sub-ovoid yellowish, often becoming smoky and opaque, formed by the conjugation of two small spherical hyphal bodies (fig. 51), by means of slender connections, above the point of junction of which the spore rises as a bud (30 × 19μ). The insects were attached to objects by the insertion of the proboscis.

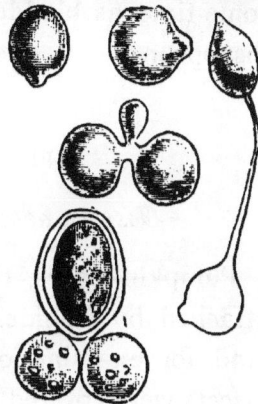

FIG. 51.—Secondary spores of *Entomophthora.*

The explanation of the sexual process in this species is thus given by Mr. Thaxter :

"The hyphal bodies, as they occur in the host just prior to the production of conidia, or zygospores, are almost perfectly spherical, and very uniform ; and are derived from large shapeless bodies which have the appearance of naked protoplasm. The spherical hyphal bodies, lying side by side within the host, proceed to conjugate in this manner. A slight projection first appears from the upper inner end of either hyphal body. These projections soon meet midway between the hyphal bodies, after which a bud begins to rise directly above their point of union. The contents of both bodies pass into this bud, forming the mother-cell of an elliptical zygospore, which, I believe, affords the only known exception to the usual spherical shape. After the spore is mature, the two hyphal bodies usually persist for some time, as bladder-like appendages, which slowly disappear."[1]

APHIS CHAIN MOULD.

Oospora aphidis. Cooke and Mass.[2]

Pumpkin-leaves, the under surface of which were attacked by Aphides, were sent to us from Queensland for examination, and we found that the dead insects were covered with a minute mould, having but very short and almost inconspicuous threads, but a profusion of spores, produced regularly in chains. In form they had resemblance to a lemon with an apiculus at each end, containing nuclei at first, but without colour, from seventeen to nineteen micromillimetres in length, and twelve in breadth. The same mould did not appear on the leaves, apart from the insects, so that it is evident it did not spread from the plant to the dead insects (plate 2, fig. 21).

---

[1] Thaxter, " Entomophthoreæ," p. 148.
[2] Cooke and Massee, in *Grevillea*, vol. xvi. p. 76.

At first there might seem a suspicion of this, since the species of *Oidium* and *Oospora* are common, and injurious to the foliage of living plants.

APHIS BLACK MOULD.

Cladosporium aphidis. Thum.[1]

Black moulds are common enough on putrescent substances, vegetable and animal; but such as these, even if confined to insects, only appear on them in decay, and then, however interesting they may be to the mycologist, have little charm for the entomologist. The present small species was found on dead *Aphis symphyti* in Austria. The fertile threads growing in tufts, branched a little, and very obscurely jointed, of a pale brown colour, bearing at the tips oblong spores, acute at each end, sometimes without a division, or longer, and divided in the centre, or occasionally with two divisions, six micromillimetres long when simple, ten to twelve when once divided, or eighteen to twenty when twice divided. These spores, or conidia, are very numerous, and almost of the same colour as the threads.

Species of this genus of moulds are exceedingly common on all kinds of decaying vegetable matter;

---

[1] Thumen, in *Œsterr. Bot. Zeit.* (1877), p. 12; Saccardo, "Sylloge," iv. No. 1772.

scarcely a dead leaf or stem which has lain upon the ground for a few days is without them. So common are they as to be almost a nuisance to the fungus-collector, and have produced much vexation of spirit, because indeterminable without the use of the microscope, and then one after another the leaves are discarded as only bearing a *Cladosporium.*

At p. 331 we have alluded to other *Cladosporiæ* which have been found on insects, but our own opinion is that they have not an established claim to be regarded as true parasites, although one or two authors have contended that they are destructive to insects, by closing the tracheæ. Hitherto we have doubted if they occur upon insect hosts until after death, and hence not destructive. We have contended rather from analogy than experience, inasmuch as the majority of the black moulds are not destructive to vegetable life, and only make their appearance subsequent to the early stages of decay. In two or three genera the moulds are destructive, such as *Cercospora* and *Fusicladium,* but these are exceptional.

COCCIDÆ.

SCALE-INSECTS.

The scale-insects affected by parasites are for the most part the attached females, which, from their position and habits, are especially liable. Two species of *Cordyceps*, of course of minute size, have been described, one of them British and North American, and the other from New Guinea. The only entomogenous *Nectria*, a species of *Sphæria* without a vertical stroma, has been found in Paraguay. Two compact moulds of the genus *Microcera*, allied to the common *Tubercularia*, have been found in Europe and Australia. It has long been supposed that, as far as the European species is concerned, it represents the conidia of some sphæriaceous fungus, but there is no direct and positive evidence. This completes the catalogue of coccigenous species hitherto known.

GREY COCCUS CLUB.

Cordyceps pistillariæformis. Berk. and Br.[1]

In 1861, Messrs. Berkeley and Broome described a little club-shaped fungus found on elm-twigs, but did

---

[1] Berkeley and Broome, *Ann. Nat. Hist.* (1861), No. 969, pl. 16, fig. 22 ; Saccardo, "Sylloge," ii. No. 5019.

not at the time give it so much attention as it deserved. The whole plant was about two lines high, with an oblong-ovate head, granulated from the perithecia, which were sunk in its substance, rather longer than the pallid cylindrical stem, which was slightly swollen at the base. They observed that it "grew upon a sclerotoid substance, but whether a part of it or not we cannot say." And they add, it "has not at present been gathered with perfect fruit."

Being very much interested in this curious production, we obtained the specimens from the Rev. M. J. Berkeley for re-examination, when we found that the sclerotoid substance at the base was a female *Coccus*, upon which the parasite had been developed. Its interior was filled with fungoid matter, so as somewhat to resemble a sclerotium ; but the shell of the *Coccus* was still present, and there was not the slightest ground for doubt (plate 2, fig. 19). Further, we examined the fungus itself, and the perithecia in the clubs contained true asci with long thread-like sporidia, as in other species of this genus.

In the United States, Peck published, in 1887, his "Twenty-eighth Report of the New York State Museum," in which he described, under the name of *Torrubia clavulata* (Schwein.), a species of which authentic specimens were distributed,[1] that proved to

---

[1] Thumen, "Myc. Universalis," No. 1258.

be identical with the fungus described by Berkeley
and Broome. The observations on this parasite were
to the following effect: " Schweinitz describes his
Sphæria clavulata as growing on a fibrillose membranaceous, shield-shaped subiculum, which adheres
closely to the bark of living branches of oak trees.
Our plant grows on the flattened, discoloured, or
blackened bodies of a scale-insect found on living
branches of *Fraxinus*. Notwithstanding this difference in habitat, and a slight discrepancy in the
arrangement of the perithecia, the species is so remarkable and so well characterized, that I cannot
believe our plant to be specifically distinct. It is
the smallest *Torrubia* known to me, and does not
well agree with the generic character. It occurs on
young and half-grown as well as on full-grown insects; but I have not been able to determine
whether it attacks the insect while living, or only
after death."[1] Examination of authentic specimens
resulted in their being identified with the British
pistillariæformis.

Subsequently Mr. J. B. Ellis, of New Jersey, distributed what proved to be the same species, under
the name of *Torrubia cinerea*, presuming that it was
the species so called by Tulasne.

These determinations show that the entomophyte

---

[1] Peck, "Twenty-eighth Report," p. 70.

on *Coccus* is the same in England and in the United States, and it is perhaps the smallest *Cordyceps* known, since the club is not more than four millimetres long, and the stem about the same length. Berkeley, in his Herbarium, has called the selfsame fungus *Cordyceps pachybasis*, apparently forgetting his previous name.

New Guinea Coccus Club.

Cordyceps coccigena.   Tul.[1]

This species is based upon specimens collected by Dumont d'Urville in New Guinea, parasitic upon a *Coccus.*   It is small, not exceeding from five to seven millimetres, with a rather stout, smooth, flexuous stem, and a globose head, about the size of a rapeseed.   The perithecia are immersed in the substance of the head, but are not prominent on the surface. Although perfect fruit has not been obtained, there is little room for doubt that it should find a place in this genus.   There is sufficient difference in appearance to enable any one at a glance to distinguish it from *C. pistillariæformis.*

The conidia-bearing condition is unknown, for it can scarcely be contended that there is any reason, or

---

[1] Tulasne, "Selecta Fungorum Carpologia," iii. p. 18, pl. 1, fig. 10; Saccardo, "Sylloge," ii. No. 5047.

analogy, in the supposition that another Coccophilous fungus, presently to be described as *Microcera*, has anything to do with this *Cordyceps*, although it is possible that it may have some relation to the European species (plate 1, fig. 11).

Coccus Nectria.

Nectria coccorum. Speg.[1]

It may be that the occurrence of a species of *Nectria* on dead *Cocci* is more accidental than parasitic, since the perithecia appear to occur sometimes on the bark as well as on the insect, but having been described under the above name, from Paraguay, it is included here. The perithecia are only like minute red dots to the naked eye, but under the microscope are seen to be globose and smooth, of an orange or orange-red colour, either solitary or from two to five together, with a minute brownish ostiolum, or mouth. In substance it is rather fleshy but membraneous, and not at all carbonaceous, as in *Sphæria* generally. The sporidia are cylindrically fusiform, or elongated elliptical, obtuse at the ends, and with a septum across the middle, each cell having nuclei, from twenty-two to twenty-five micromillimetres long, and five broad, and hyaline (plate 2, fig.

---

[1] Spegazzini, in "Fungi Guaranitici," i. 234; *Sacc. Syll. Supp.*, 7190.

26). The character of the sporidia is of the prevailing type in *Nectria*, and very different from those in *Cordyceps*.

COCCUS TUBERCLES.

Microcera coccophila.   Desm.[1]

This well-known parasite on dead *Coccus* is not uncommon in Europe, and has been found several times in Britain. They form little rosy knobs, with a short, whitish velvety stem-like base. Sometimes it is conical and sometimes club-shaped, and rather hard and horny when dry. The whole mass is composed of parallel hyaline delicate threads, densely compacted together, bearing at the apex very long curved conidia, or spores, which are acute at each extremity, and with three or five septa, or divisions (but sometimes evidently more), from seventy to one hundred micromillimetres long, and five thick. It is supposed to be the conidia stage of some more perfect fungus, but at present this is merely a supposition (plate 2, fig. 22). The bright-red spots on dead *cocci* are recognizable by the naked eye.

---

[1] Desmazieres, *Ann. Sci. Nat.* (1848), p. 359; Saccardo, "Sylloge," iv. No. 3473.

ORANGE COCCUS TUBERCLES.

Microcera rectispora.   Cooke and Mass.[1]

Corresponding to the European species of *Microcera*, we have found a similar one on the dead *Coccus* of the orange in Australia.   In appearance it differs so little from the European species, that apart from the fructification they would be regarded as the same. So much importance has of late years been given to minute differences in spores, that new species have become inevitable.   In this instance the spores are quite straight and spindle-shaped, acute at both ends, with about seven transverse divisions, and attaining a length of from one hundred and fifty to two hundred micromillimetres, and ten broad (plate 1, fig. 13).

---

[1] Cooke and Massee, in *Grevillea*, vol. xvi. p. 4.

HOSTS UNDETERMINED.

W E have been compelled to place at the end of the orders a few entomophytes of which the hosts are undetermined, without even a well-founded suspicion of the order to which such hosts might belong. Entomologically, it is a great disadvantage not to know even the order of insects attacked; but this, of course, has no influence upon the botanical character of the entomophyte, which so far is independent of its host. Some few species have been noticed at the end of the section devoted to *Lepidoptera;* but these are believed to be associated with that order, although the several families cannot be determined. The majority of records in which the parasite is accurately determined, or the information is sufficiently precise to attach a name, are mycological, and the mycologist is usually only interested, from his own point of view, in the parasite, and not in the host; hence the identification of the insect has not received that attention which satisfies the entomologist, and consequently there are a few species which to him are imperfectly described. On the other hand, many of the notices of entomophytes, in entomological works, and journals, are deficient in that precise detail of description which would enable the mycologist to determine, without doubt, the genus and species of the parasite, so that in turn the record is to him incomplete and unsatisfactory, and he can only leave such cases open for further inquiry.

MONTAGNE'S CLUB.

Cordyceps larvata. Mont.[1]

Montagne described, in 1855, under the above name, a fungus which so much resembled *C. militaris*, that in another place he called it by that name. Saccardo has,[2] as we think erroneously, placed it in another genus. It is characterized as fleshy, orange, with a cylindrical head, and an equal stem, continuous with the capitulum. The surface of the club dotted with the ostiola of the immersed perithecia. The asci are described as filiform, with numerous globose sporidia in rows. The query (16?) of Saccardo is gratuitous. The globose sporidia doubtless represent quadrate segments of thread-like sporidia breaking up into frustules. It is stated

---

[1] Montagne, *Ann. des Sci. Nat.* (1855), iii. 98, p. 341; Mont., "Syll.," p. 200.

[2] *Hypocrea larvata*, Saccardo, "Sylloge," ii. No. 4884.

that the specimens were found on bark, perhaps in the cracks of bark, or larvæ or pupæ, or amongst moss on bark.   It is hardly conceivable that M. Montagne would have mistaken it for *Cordyceps militaris* had there not been a close resemblance. And why call it *larvata* if there were no relations to larvæ?   On the whole, from the description, we determine in favour of Montagne, and against Saccardo, that it is an entomophyte, on some insect unknown, and closely allied to *Cordyceps militaris* derived from Guiana.

JURA PINE CLUB.

Cordyceps alutacea.   Quelet.[1]

Dr. Quelet has described a species, under the above name, found by M. Cornu in the Jura, amongst pine-leaves, but he has failed to give any information as to the insect on which it was growing.   It is scarcely probable that, in a genus like the present, there should be one exception to the general rule of the species being either found upon insects or subterranean fungi. That minute larvæ concealed amongst pine-leaves should bear a *Cordyceps* is probable, and that, in collecting the fungus, the stem should be separated

---

[1] Quelet, "Champ. Jura et Vosg.," p. 487 ; Saccardo, "Sylloge," ii. No. 5023.

from its host, and the host left behind, is also very
probable—far more so than that the species should
not be entomogenous. The stroma is described as
clavate, attenuated downwards into the stem, and
tan-coloured; but no intimation of dimensions are
recorded. The clubs are stated to be tuberculose,
which is supposed to mean that the perithecia were
prominent. The sporidia conform to the general
character of the genus, and therefore there can be no
doubt of its relationship.

BRANCHED STILBUM.

Stilbum ramosum. Peck.[1]

A species of *Stilbum* has been described, in the
United States, as occurring on dead larvæ of insects,
buried in rotten wood, without the least intimation
of the order to which the insects were believed to
belong. The head was nearly globose, and either
whitish or pale yellow, with a thick smooth branched
stem, whitish above, and pallid or brownish below,
sometimes creeping, and sending up branches at
intervals. The spores scattered over the surface of
the head were minute and oblong. There are a few
known instances in which the compound stem of a

---

[1] Peck, in "Twenty-sixth Report of New York State Museum," p.
78; Saccardo, "Sylloge," iv. No. 2696.

Stilbum divides into two or more branches, each
terminated by a capitulum; but this is the only
entomogenous species having that peculiarity. The
stem is composed of a number of parallel threads
agglutinated together, so that the division, after all,
is only a kind of pseudo-branching, caused by the
separation of the threads, at some portion of their
length, into two bundles instead of one. It is almost
a marvel that, in the rage for genera-making, some
enthusiast, aspiring to everlasting fame, has not con-
stituted a new genus for such species of *Stilbum* as
possess a divided stem.

LARVA TUBERCLE.

Fusarium larvarum.   Fuckel.[1]

This is a peculiar form of entomophyte on the
larva of insects, which appears in the form of little
red convex dots, not unlike a small red *Nectria* in
shape, but composed of closely compacted short
threads, firmly agglutinated together into a kind
of hemispherical cushion, bearing on the circum-
ference, at the tips of the component threads, curved
fusiform conidia, or spores, with from one to three
transverse septa, or divisions, twenty-four micromilli-

---

[1] Fuckel, "Symbolæ Fungorum," p. 369; Saccardo, "Sylloge,"
iv. No. 3355.

metres long and five micromillimetres broad. It
might be compared with a miniature form of *Microcera coccophila,* with much smaller spores. It will be
observed that the structure of the two has very much
in common, save that there is no indication of a stem.
There are a great number of species of *Fusarium*
known, and they occur on many kinds of animal
and vegetable substances, some of them being undoubtedly the incomplete, or conidia, stage of species
of *Nectria,* which in olden times would have been
called a *Sphæria* with bright coloured fleshy perithecia.
Although the above is recorded as a European species,
from the Rhine provinces, it is evidently very scarce.

INSECT WHITE MOULD.

Corethropsis pulchra. Sacc.[1]

A white mould of the genus *Corethropsis* has been
found in Italy on putrescent insects, of undetermined
order. The sterile threads are creeping and jointed ;
the fertile threads, rising at right angles from the
sterile hyphæ to the height of one hundred and ten
micromillimetres, with only one division nearly at
the base, and at the apex expanded into a spherical
head, from whence radiate in all directions the somewhat clavate basidia. Each of these basidia have at

---

[1] Saccardo, "Fungi Italici," pl. 46; "Sylloge," iv. No. 298.

their apex from three to five prominent points, or sterigmata, at the tips of which is produced a solitary minute spore, or conidium. The conidia are oblong, about three micromillimetres long, and one in diameter, and uncoloured. To the unaided eye, and even under a lens, this mould has the appearance of an *Aspergillus;* but examined more closely, and with a higher power, it is found that the spores are not produced in chains, as in that genus, but singly, at the tips of the radiating basidia, or conidia-bearers.

WHITE CHAIN MOULD.

Sterigmatocystis candida.   Sacc.[1]

This white mould, on the rotting larvæ of insects, has occurred in Italy, but the order of insects has not been stated.   It forms effused floccose white patches, with the fertile threads erect, and thread-like, without joints, inflated at the apex into a somewhat globose bladdery vesicle, about forty micromillimetres in diameter, rough, and bearing basidia all over the surface. These basidia are club-shaped and radiating, each one having at its apex three or four sterigmata, or projecting points, on which are seated the conidia, or spores; these latter are produced in chains, like a necklace of beads, the upper ones globose, and about

---

[1] Saccardo, "Fungi Italici," pl. 80; "Sylloge," iv. No. 345.

two and a half micromillimetres in diameter, the lower ones elongated, all of them being uncoloured. It will be observed that this mould differs from the preceding in having the conidia, or spores, produced in chains, and, like that, is also saprophytic.

WHORLED LARVÆ MOULD.

Verticillium minutissimum. Corda.[1]

A minute white mould on the surface of the larvæ of small insects, in a state of decay, can hardly be assumed to be a parasite, and yet it may not be quite out of place in a work of this kind. This one appears in small tufts, almost like little white points, consisting of erect threads, which are branched in whorls; that is to say, the short branches are given off at the same level, each branch being itself simple or forked, bearing at their tips the curved slender conidia, about four micromillimetres long. It is especially European, and, as far as we are aware, exclusively Bohemian.

M. Giard has enumerated a group of Entomophytic Fungi, which he terms Entomophytic Cladosporiæ, which kill the insects on which they grow, not by destruction of the tissues, but by closing up the tracheæ.

---

[1] Corda, " Icones Fungorum," vol. i. p. 20, fig. 274; Saccardo, "Sylloge," iv. No. 788.

We might have increased considerably the list of pseudo-parasites, or species which we deem to be saprophytic, by adding those which have sometimes occurred on insects, but also on other decaying substances. This would have served no useful purpose, and only proved a hindrance to those in search of information respecting veritable entomophytes. Beyond the redoubtable *Botrytis Bassiana*, there is scarcely a Mucedine known which is fatal to the health and life of the inhabitants of the insect-world.

ARACHNIDÆ.

SPIDERS.

SPIDERS, and their allies, do not appear to be so
liable to attack from fungal parasites as many
orders of insects ; nevertheless there are a few species
of entomophytes which are restricted to them,
particularly moulds of the genus *Isaria*. The dead
bodies of spiders, found in water, are commonly
attacked by a kind of aquatic mould, either identical
or closely allied to the well-known "salmon disease."
In this case, however, it is not parasitic and destructive,
as it only occurs upon the dead bodies in water, as
found also on the dead bodies of flies under similar
circumstances. Hence no very detailed account is
necessary beyond what is given previously, on *Diptera*.

In addition to the species alluded to here, it may
be added, on the authority of the Rev. M. J. Berkeley,
that "the eggs of spiders, which are usually found in
numbers together, carefully preserved in bags formed
of web, also form the basis of *Isaria farinosa*," and its
more perfect condition, *Cordyceps militaris*.[1]

---

[1] Berkeley, "Eng. Fl.," vol. ii. p. 232.

The reference to a species of *Verticillium*[1] on the pupa of *Bupalus piniaria* is too imperfect to determine whether it is the *Verticillium minutissimum*, Corda.

EUROPEAN SPIDER ISARIA.

Isaria arachnophila. Ditm.

The earliest reference to this parasite was by Ditmar, in Sturm's " Flora," where it was figured and described under the above name[2] in 1817. Dr. Gray copied this figure in his " Notices of Insect Fungi" (plate 4, fig. 18). It was, as he says, attached to a piece of rotten wood by means of the white fungoid threads which had emerged from the interior of the body, and had, after death, covered the upper part of the back, and then extended itself into several upright stems, enlarging towards their apex. The host was a species of *Ctinus*. According to Saccardo, it has been found in Germany, Italy, France, Holland, Belgium, Great Britain, and America. Professor Oudemanns recorded it from Leyden in 1874, and gave a new figure,[3] the colour in his specimen being somewhat flesh-colour, and he describes the conidia

---

[1] Lebert, *Berlin Entom. Zeit.* (1858), p. 179.

[2] Sturm, " Deutsch Flora," vol. i. p. iii. pl. 55 ; Pers., " Myc. Eur.," p. 45 ; Fries, " Syst. Myc.," iii. p. 274 ; Saccardo, " Sylloge," iv. No. 2791.

[3] Oudemanns, " Aanwinsten " (1874), pl. 4, fig. 4.

as oblong, or fusiform ($3\frac{1}{2}$ to $4\frac{1}{2} \times 1\frac{1}{2}\mu$). In other cases the whole fungus is said to be whitish.

It has been stated by Dr. Gray, on the authority of Robin,[1] that a small species of spider has been found in Europe attacked during the autumn months by *Isaria tartarea;* but as this is not an entomophyte, probably the name is an error, or the *Isaria* may have spread to the spider from the subjacent wood.

AMERICAN SPIDER ISARIA.

Isaria aranearum. Schwein.

The descriptions given by Schweinitz of the species of parasitic *Isaria*[2] found by him in North Carolina are very deficient in detail, but there is sufficient in them to show that the above-named species is very different from the ordinary European form. It forms an effused yellow crust, from which arise the un-branched clubs in divergent tufts, the basal portion of the clubs being of a bright lemon-yellow, and the upper part paler, and powdery with the conidia, or spores, with somewhat a flesh-coloured tint. It is said to be parasitic on some species of *Aranea* and *Phalangium;* that on the latter having borne at one

---

[1] Robin, "Veg. Par." (1853), p. 608.

[2] Schweinitz, "Syn. Car.," No. 1299; Fries, "Syst. Myc.," iii. 273; Saccardo, "Sylloge," No. iv. 2792.

time a special designation,[1] now merged as a synonym.
The colour of this species is significant, in a genus
where so many are white, that there should be no
difficulty in recognizing it should it be found again.
Unfortunately, most of the *Isariæ* are very erratic in
their appearance, and at all times rare, so that it is
not surprising when we hear of species, bearing marked
characters, not occurring a second time for half a
century, or not twice within the memory of any living
man. Curtis and Ravenel collected for many years
in North and South Carolina, and we are not sure
that they ever encountered this species.

CUBAN SPIDER ISARIA.

Isaria gigantea. Mont.

In the Island of Cuba, Ramon de la Sagra collected
the indigenous species of *Mygale*, the body and legs
of which were infested with the species of *Isaria*
which Montagne described under the name of *Isaria
gigantea*.[2] This has never been figured, but was
described as growing either solitary or in clusters,
thread-like, long and slender, attenuated upwards,
and either simple or branched, externally whitish and

---

[1] *Isaria phalangiophila*, Link, "Sp. Plant.," ii. p. 114; Schweinitz,
"Amer. Bor.," No. 3057.

[2] Montagne, "Cuba," p. 309; "Sylloge," p. 293; Saccardo, iv.
No. 2790.

powdery, but brownish within. The form and size of the conidia do not appear to have been determined, and there is no record extant of its having been found since that time.

Berkeley and Curtis were hardly justified in assuming this condition as evidence that the perfect form, when developed, would be a *Cordyceps*, and therefore, on this assumption, called it *Cordyceps Montagnei.*[1] Certainly it is probable ; but a name and position should not be based upon a probability, and that is all the evidence we have for *Cordyceps Montagnei*, the ascigerous condition of which Berkeley himself confesses has never been seen, and perhaps never will be. It is a common error, but we fear not a justifiable one, to give to an imperfect, or incomplete, fungus a name which it would bear if fully developed. It is at least misleading, and we imagine no one would contend that, upon an assumption, any organism should be placed in a genus of which it does not actually possess the essential generic character.

---

[1] "Fungi Cubensis," No. 747 ; Saccardo, "Sylloge," ii. No. 5048.

SPIDER TORRUBIELLA.

Torrubiella aranicida. Boud.[1]

This entomophyte, the type of a new botanical genus, was made known in 1885, on spiders in a rotten trunk in France. The perithecia are elongated conical, rather flexuous, sixty-five to seventy millimetres high, and half as broad; ochraceous, or tinged with orange; seated in company, either scattered or in clusters, on a thin white byssoid stroma, differing in this from *Cordyceps* that there is no stem or club. The long asci are similar to those in *Cordyceps*, and so are the thread-like spores, which are faintly septate, and granular, three or four hundred micromillimetres long, but apparently not breaking up into joints (plate 2, fig. 27). This peculiar fungus resembles some *Nectria* in appearance, with elongated necks, seated, as some species of *Nectria* are, upon a byssoid stroma, but possessing the long thread-like sporidia of *Cordyceps*. Although a technical point, we fail to recognize any sound generic distinction between this and *Ophionectria agaricicola*, found on putrid Agarics in Tasmania. The only apparent difference is a byssoid stroma. One may suffer from too much of a good thing, and a plethora of new genera portends a new disease.

---

[1] Boudier, in *Revue Mycologique* (1885), p. 227, pl. 56, fig. 4; Saccardo, " Sylloge," vol. supp., No. 7248.

Spider Hanger.

Laboulbenia armillaris. Berl.[1]

This entomophyte occurred on the body of living *Antennophorus caputcarabi* in Paraguay, the entire fungus being about three hundred micromillimetres high, and pale brown. The stem was clavate, attenuated at the base, and ending in an obconical nodule ; the perithecium elongated-ovoid, or rather cylindrical, ending in a black neck ; the pseudo-paraphyses furcately branched, with a black ring at the base of the branches. These superficial parasites are rather numerous on *Coleoptera*, but this is the solitary instance of one being found on *Arachnidæ*. We must direct attention to the figures given in an earlier portion of this volume to appreciate their habit and character. As already observed, they attach themselves externally to their host without penetrating the cuticle, but are fixed by a disc, or sucker, at the base, so that, although they may be more or less of an incumbrance, they inflict no direct injury. The most prominent difference presented by this species from all the rest consists in the black ring at the base of the branches of the furcate appendages.

---

[1] Berlese, "Laboulbenia," p. 14, pl. 11 ; Saccardo, "Sylloge," viii. No. 3608.

CLASSIFIED LIST OF ENTOMOPHYTES

ARRANGED UNDER THEIR RESPECTIVE FAMILIES.

———◆———

ORDER I.—ASCOMYCETES.

Definite perithecia ; sporidia produced in asci.

FAMILY I.—HYPOCREACEÆ.

Composite, or simple. Perithecia fleshy ; stroma soft.

GENUS I.—CORDYCEPS. Fries.

Stroma vertical, clavate ; sporidia filiform, breaking up into joints.

* *Capitulum globose or elliptical.*

Cordyceps entomorrhiza. Dicks. On larvæ and pupæ of *Lepidoptera.* England, N. America, Australia.
Cordyceps insignis. Cke. and Rav. On larvæ. N. America.
Cordyceps armeniaca. B. and C. On insects. N. America.
Cordyceps flavella. B. and C. On *Diptera* (?). Cuba.
Cordyceps dipterigena. B. and Br. On *Diptera.* Ceylon.
Cordyceps coccigena. Tul. On *Cocci.* New Guinea.
Cordyceps Lloydii. Fawc. On *Camponotus atriceps.* Guiana.
Cordyceps Sheeringii. Mass. On ants. Grenada.
Cordyceps Ditmari. Quel. On *Vespa crabro.* Jura.
Cordyceps myrmecophila. Ces. On ants, etc. Britain, Italy, Finland, N. America, Ceylon, Borneo.
Cordyceps Humberti. Rob. On *Icaria cincta.* Senegal.
Cordyceps helopis. Quel. On larvæ of *Helops.* Jura, France.
Cordyceps cinerea. Tul. On *Coleoptera* (*Carabus*). France.
Cordyceps unilateralis. Tul. On ants. Brazil.
Cordyceps australis. Speg. On *Formica.* Brazil.

Cordyceps curculionum. Tul. On *Curculio.* Peru, Brazil.
Cordyceps Odyneri. Quel. On *Odynerus.* Vosges.
Cordyceps Doassansii. Pat. On chrysalids of *Lepidoptera.* France.

** *Stroma furcate, capitulum subglobose.*

Cordyceps bicephala. Berk. On insects (?). Rio Negro.
Cordyceps sobolifera. Hill. On *Cicada,* etc. West Indies, Ceylon.
Cordyceps palustris. B. and Br. On larvæ. Carolina.

.*. *Stroma simple, clubs elongated.*

Cordyceps Gunnii. Berk. On larvæ of *Pielus.* Tasmania, Australia.
Cordyceps Hawkesii. Gray. On larvæ of *Pielus.* Tasmania.
Cordyceps sphecocephala. Klot. On wasps. West Indies, Brazil.
Cordyceps stylophora. B. and Br. On larvæ. S. Carolina.
Cordyceps gentilis. Ces. On *Sphecoideæ.* Borneo.
Cordyceps pistillariæformis. B. and Br. On *Cocci.* Britain, N. America.
Cordyceps militaris. Linn. On larvæ and pupæ. Britain, Sweden, Finland, Germany, Belgium, France, Italy, N. America, Ceylon, Borneo.
Cordyceps typhulæformis. B. and Cke. On larvæ. Java.
Cordyceps falcata. Berk. On larvæ. India.
Cordyceps sinensis. Berk. On larvæ. China.
Cordyceps Barnesii. Thw. On *Melolontha.* Ceylon.
Cordyceps melolonthæ. Tul. On *Melolontha.* N. America.
Cordyceps Forquignoni. Quel. On *Diptera.* France.
Cordyceps alutacea. Quel. Hab. uncertain. Jura.
Cordyceps sp. On *Elateridæ* larva. Cape.

.. *Stroma furcate; clubs elongated.*

Cordyceps caloceroides. B. and C. On larvæ. Cuba.
Cordyceps Taylori. Berk. On larvæ (*Hepialidæ*). Australia.
Cordyceps Sinclairi. Berk. On *Orthoptera.* New Zealand.
Cordyceps racemosa. Berk. On larvæ. India.

..* *Clubs various; perithecia free.*

Cordyceps acicularis. Rav. On larvæ. Carolina.
Cordyceps sphingum. Tul. On *Sphingides.* Brazil, N. America, Switzerland.

Cordyceps memorabilis. Ces. On *Staphylines.* Italy.
Cordyceps superficialis. Peck. On larvæ. N. America.
Cordyceps Robertsii. Hook. On larvæ *Hepialidæ.* New
　Zealand.
Cordyceps Ravenelii. Berk. On *Ancylonychus.* S. Carolina.

*** Species imperfect.

Cordyceps fuliginosa. Ces. On pupæ of *Bombyx.* Italy.
Cordyceps larvata. Mont. On — (?). Guiana.

GENUS 2.—TORRUBIELLA. Boud.

Stroma horizontal; perithecia free.

Torrubiella aranicida. Boud. On spiders. France.

GENUS 3.—DIALONECTRIA. Sacc.

Stroma absent ; perithecia free, fleshy ; sporidia subelliptical,
uniseptate.

Dialonectria coccorum. Speg. On *Cocci.* Argentina.

FAMILY 2.—LABOULBENIACEÆ.

Superficial, without mycelium. Receptacle stipitate ; stem
bicellular ; asci diffluent.

GENUS 1.—LABOULBENIA. Mont.

Perithecia mamillate ; pseudo-paraphyses filiform, jointed.

Laboulbenia Rougetii. M. and R. On *Brachinus, Staphylines,*
　etc. France, Germany.
Laboulbenia Guerinii. Robin. On *Gyretes.* Caraccas.
Laboulbenia flabellata. Peyr. On *Bembidium,* etc. Austria.
Laboulbenia armillaris. Berl. On *Antennophorus.* Paraguay.
Laboulbenia anceps. Peyr. On *Anchonemus.* Austria.
Laboulbenia fasciculata. Peyr. On *Chlænius.* Austria.
Laboulbenia luxurians. Peyr. On *Bembidium.* Austria and
　United States.
Laboulbenia vulgaris. Peyr. On *Bembidium.* Austria and
　United States.
Laboulbenia nebriæ. Peyr. On *Nebria brunnea.* Austria and
　United States.

Laboulbenia gracilis. Peyr. Host unknown. Austria.

Laboulbenia brachiata. Thax. On *Patrobus longicornis.* United States.

Laboulbenia fumosa. Thax. On *Platynus cincticollis.* United States.

Laboulbenia elongata. Thax. On *Platynus cincticollis.* United States.

Laboulbenia harpali. Thax. On *Harpalus pensylvanicus.* United States.

Laboulbenia elegans. Thax. On *Harpalus pensylvanicus.* United States.

Laboulbenia casnoniæ. Thax. On *Casnonia pensylvanica.* United States.

Laboulbenia truncata. Thax. On *Bembidium.* United States.

Laboulbenia arcuata. Thax. On *Harpalus pensylvanicus.* United States.

Laboulbenia conferta. Thax. On *Harpalus pensylvanicus.* United States.

Laboulbenia paupercula. Thax. On *Platynus extensicollis.* United States.

Laboulbenia scelephila. Thax. On *Platynus extensicollis.* United States.

Laboulbenia compacta. Thax. On *Bembidium.* Maine.

Laboulbenia variabilis. Thax. On *Omophron, Chlænius, Nebria, Platynus, Patrobus,* etc. United States.

Laboulbenia galeritæ. Thax. On *Galerita Janus.* United States.

Laboulbenia gyrinidarum. Thax. On *Gyrinus.* Connecticut.

Laboulbenia brachini. Thax. On *Brachinus.* Virginia.

Laboulbenia curtipes. Thax. On *Bembidium bimaculatum.* Washington.

Laboulbenia parvula. Thax. On *Platynus extensicollis* and *Bembidium.* United States.

Laboulbenia inflata. Thax. On *Bembidium.* Dakota.

Laboulbenia recta. Thax. On *Platynus extensicollis.* Connecticut.

Laboulbenia contorta. Thax. On *Platynus extensicollis.* Connecticut.

Laboulbenia gibberosa. Thax. On *Platynus extensicollis.* Connecticut.

Laboulbenia Schizogenii. Thax. On *Schizogenius lineolatus.* Connecticut.

Laboulbenia pedicellata. Thax. On *Bembidium.* Maine.

GENUS 2.—ACANTHOMYCES.   Thax.

Perithecia as in *Laboulbenia;* receptacle with a series of appendage-bearing cells on the inner side.

Acanthomyces lasiophora. Thax.   On *Atranus pubescens.* Connecticut.

GENUS 3.—PEYRITSCHIELLA.   Thax.

Pseudo-paraphyses arising from several different points on either side of the perithecium.

Peyritschiella curvata. Thax.   On *Platynus cincticollis.* United States.

Peyritschiella minima. Thax.   On *Platynus cincticollis.* United States.

GENUS 4.—STIGMATOMYCES.   Karst.

Perithecia thickened in the middle, ending in a thick neck.

Stigmatomyces Muscæ.   (Knoch.)   On flies.   Russia, Austria.

GENUS 5.—HELMINTHOPHANA.   Peyr.

Perithecia cylindrical, with a cylindrical neck ; pseudo-paraphyses basilar.

Helminthophana nycteribiæ.   Peyr.   On *Nycteribia.*   Austria.

GENUS 6.—APPENDICULINA.   Peck.

Perithecia globose, with a very long cylindrical neck ; pseudo-paraphyses inserted at base of perithecia.

Appendiculina entomophila.   Peck.   On *Drosophila.*   N. America.

GENUS 7.—CHITONOMYCES.   Peyr.

Perithecia three-lobed at the apex ; pseudo-paraphyses lateral, not jointed or appendiculate.

Chitonomyces melanurus.   Peyr.   On *Laccophilus.*   Austria.

GENUS 8.—HEIMATOMYCES.   Peyr.

Perithecia produced at the apex into a horn ; pseudo-paraphyses lateral.

Heimatomyces parodoxus.   Peyr.   On *Laccophilus.*   Austria and United States.

Heimatomyces simplex. Thax. On *Laccophilus maculosus*, etc. Connecticut.

Heimatomyces hyalinus. Thax. On *Laccophilus maculosus.* Connecticut.

Heimatomyces affinis. Thax. On *Laccophilus maculosus*, etc. Connecticut.

Heimatomyces appendiculatus. Thax. On *Laccophilus maculosus.* Connecticut.

Heimatomyces Halipli. Thax. On *Haliplus ruficollis*, ect. Connecticut.

Heimatomyces lichanophorus. Thax. On *Laccophilus maculosus.* Connecticut.

Heimatomyces rhynchostoma. Thax. On *Laccophilus maculosus.* Connecticut.

Heimatomyces uncinatus. Thax. On *Laccophilus maculosus.* Connecticut.

Heimatomyces marginatus. Thax. On *Laccophilus maculosus.* Connecticut.

GENUS 9.—CERATOMYCES. Thax.

Perithecia highly developed, with antheridial appendage at the base.

Ceratomyces mirabilis. Thax. On *Tropisternus glaber.* Connecticut.

Ceratomyces camptosporus. Thax. On *Tropisternus glaber.* Connecticut.

GENUS 10.—CORETHROMYCES. Thax.

Receptacle reduced to a basal, with two or three terminal cells.

Corethromyces cryptobii. Thax. On *Cryptobium pallipes.* Virginia.

GENUS 11.—CANTHAROMYCES. Thax.

Pseudo-paraphyses, one or more, arising from the supra-basal cell.

Cantharomyces bledii. Thax. On *Bledius assimilis.* Illinois.

Cantharomyces vorticillata. Thax. On *Sunius longicollis.* Illinois.

To these must be added—

Zodiomyces vorticellaria. Thax. On *Hydrocombus palustris.* United States.

Hesperomyces virescens. Thax. On *Chilocorus bivulnerus.* United States.

ORDER II.—PHYCOMYCETES.

Mycelium unicellular ; fructification agamic or sexual.

FAMILY I.—SAPROLEGNIACEÆ.

Aquatic. Threads producing zoosporangia. Agamic reproduction by zoospores ; sexual by oogonia and antheridia.

GENUS I.—SAPROLEGNIA. Nees.

Zoosporangia clavate ; oogonia mostly many-spored.

Saprolegnia monoica. Prings. On spiders, larvæ, etc. Germany, France, Belgium.
Saprolegnia asterophora. De Bary. On flies. Germany, Belgium.
Saprolegnia ferax. Gruith. On flies. Universal in Europe.

GENUS 2.—PYTHIUM. Prings.

Zoosporangia formed from the protoplasm ; zoospores always naked ; oogonia one-spored.

Pythium proliferum. De Bary. On insects. Germany, Belgium.

GENUS 3.—DIPLANES. Leit.

Zoosporangia perforated ; oogonia many-spored.

Diplanes saprolegnioides. Leit. On insects. Germany, France.

GENUS 4.—ACHLYA. Nees.

Zoospores disposed without order in zoosporangia, naked after exclusion ; oogonia many-spored.

* *Diœcious.*

Achlya prolifera. Nees. On insects. Germany.
Achlya dioica. Prings. On insects. Germany.

** *Monœcious.*

Achlya polyandra. Hilde. On flies. Germany.

GENUS 5.—APHANOMYCES. De Bary.

Zoosporangia very long, zoospores in a single series; oogonia one-, or rarely two-spored.

Aphanomyces stellatus. De Bary. On insects. Germany, Belgium.

Aphanomyces scaber. De Bary. On insects. Germany, Belgium.

FAMILY 2.—ENTOMOPHTHORACEÆ.

Threads producing conidia. Agamic reproduction by conidia and resting-spores, sexual by zygospores.

GENUS I.—EMPUSA. Cohn.

Mycelium evolved within the bodies of insects, soon broken into fragments; conidia-bearers simple.

Empusa muscæ. Fries. On *Musca.* Britain, Germany, Austria, Switzerland, Italy, Netherlands, United States, S. America.

Empusa culicis. Braun. On *Culex.* Germany, N. America.

Empusa grylli. Fresen. On *Culex, Locusta.* Germany, United States, Newfoundland.

Empusa aulicæ. Reich. On larvæ and chrysalids of *Euprepia, Trachea,* etc. Germany.

Empusa Jassi. Cohn. On *Jassus sexnotatus.* Germany.

Empusa Fresenii. Nowa. On *Aphis cracca,* etc. Germany, Poland, United States.

Empusa apiculata. Thax. On *Lepidoptera.* Maine, N. Carolina, U.S.

Empusa tenthredinis. Fres. On larvæ of *Tenthredo.* Germany, United States.

Empusa Planchoniana. Cornu. On *Aphides.* Europe, United States.

Empusa lageniformis. Thax. On *Aphides.* United States.

Empusa conglomerata. Sor. On *Tipula* and *Culex.* Europe, United States.

Empusa papillata. Thax. On *Diptera.* N. America.

Empusa caroliniana. Thax. On *Diptera.* N. Carolina.

GENUS 2.—ENTOMOPHTHORA. Fres.

Mycelium at first innate, then emitting threads from the dead body ; conidia-bearers branched.

Entomophthora sphærosperma. Fres. On larvæ of *Pieris* and *Limmophilus*, and various orders of insects. Germany, United States.
Entomophthora aphides. Hoffm. On *Aphides.* Germany, United States.
Entomophthora tipulæ. Fres. On *Tipula.* Germany.
Entomophthora muscivora. Schrot. On *Musca, Calliphora,* etc. France, Germany.
Entomophthora curvispora. Nowak. On *Simulia,* etc. Poland.
Entomophthora ovispora. Nowak. On *Lonchæa,* etc. Poland.
Entomophthora conica. Nowak. On *Diptera.* Poland, United States.
Entomophthora lampyridarum. Thax. On *Coleoptera.* N. Carolina.
Entomophthora virescens. Thax. On *Agrotis fennica.* Ottawa, Ontario.
Entomophthora geometralis. Thax. On geometrid moths. United States.
Entomophthora colorata. Sor. On grasshoppers. Europe.
Entomophthora rhizospora. Thax. On *Phryganidæ.* United States.
Entomophthora phryganeæ. Sor. On *Phryganea grandis.* Europe.
Entomophthora occidentalis. Thax. On *Aphides.* United States.
Entomophthora pelliculosa. Sor. On *Anthomyia.* Europe.
Entomophthora variabilis. Thax. On *Diptera.* United States.
Entomophthora sepulchralis. Thax. On *Tipulidæ.* United States.
Entomophthora gracilis. Thax. On *Diptera.* N. Carolina.
Entomophthora echinospora. Thax. On *Diptera.* United States.
Entomophthora montana. Thax. On *Chironomus.* N. America.
Entomophthora americana. Thax. On *Diptera.* United States.
Entomophthora dipterigena. Thax. On *Diptera.* N. America.

GENUS 3.—TARICHIUM. Cohn.

Mycelium evolved in the body of insects, simple, then branched; resting-spores formed at the end of branches of the mycelium.

Tarichium megaspermum. Cohn. On larvæ of *Agrotis segetum.* Germany.

? *Tarichia uvella.* Krask. On coleopterous larvæ. Russia.

GENUS 4.—MASSOSPORA. Peck.

Conidia loosely coherent, forming a powdery mass; mycelium evolved in the body of insects.

Massospora cicadina. Peck. On *Cicada.* United States.

ORDER III.—HYPHOMYCETES.

Superficial. Threads simple or branched, bearing naked conidia or spores.

FAMILY I.—MUCEDINEÆ.

Pale or bright coloured, rarely brown. Threads lax, not combined into a common stem.

* AMEROSPORÆ. *Spores continuous.*

GENUS I.—OOSPORA. Wallr.

Threads short, simple; conidia globose or oblong, produced in chains.

Oospora aphidis. Cke. and Mass. On *Aphides.*

GENUS 2.—CORETHROPSIS. Corda.

Threads decumbent; sporophores simple, capitate at the apex bearing sterigmata, each surmounted by a spore.

Corethropsis pulchra. Sacc. On putrescent insects. Italy.

GENUS 3.—STERIGMATOCYSTIS. Cram.

Threads inflated at the apex, the head bearing verticillately branched basidia, surmounted by chains of spores.

Sterigmatocystis ferruginea. Cooke. On pupæ of *Lepidoptera.* India.

Sterigmatocystis candida. Sacc. On larvæ of insects. Italy.

GENUS 4.—PENICILLIUM. Link.

Fertile threads unequally branched at the apex, bearing chains
of subglobose conidia.

Penicillium Fieberi. Corda. On dead *Pentatoma.*

GENUS 5.—SPOROTRICHUM. Link.

Threads vaguely and repeatedly branched, creeping; conidia
produced at the ends or sides.

Sporotrichum densum. Link. On *Coleoptera,* etc. Europe.
Sporotrichum globuliferum. Speg. On *Coleoptera.* Argentina.
Sporotrichum minutulum. Speg. On larvæ of *Cicadæ.* S.
America.
Sporotrichum minimum. Speg. On *Formica.* Argentina.

GENUS 6.—BOTRYTIS. Mich.

Fertile threads erect, branched; conidia loosely congregated
about the tips of the branches.

Botrytis Bassiana. Bals. On silkworms, very destructive.
Europe.
—— var. *tenella.* Sacc. On *Diptera, Vespa,* etc. Italy.

GENUS 7.—VERTICILLIUM. Nees.

Fertile threads erect, branched; branches and branchlets in
whorls; conidia terminal.

Verticillium minutissimum. Corda. On larvæ. Bohemia.

** PHRAGMOSPORÆ. *Spores septate.*

GENUS 8.—ROTÆA. Ces.

Sterile threads creeping; conidia erect, clavate, many septate,
united together in globose tufts.

Rotæa flava. Ces. On *Cossus.* Italy.

FAMILY 2.—DEMATIEÆ.

Threads brown or black, rigid.

GENUS 1.—CLADOSPORIUM. Link.

Threads simple or sparingly branched; conidia apical or lateral, sometimes produced in short chains, at first simple, then with 1–3 septa.

Cladosporium aphidis. Thum. On *Aphides.* Austria.

FAMILY 3.—STILBEÆ.

Fertile threads erect, combined into a stem or stroma bearing conidia at their apices.

GENUS 1.—STILBUM. Tode.

Stroma tapering, capitate, with a single head.

Stilbum Buquetii. Mont. and Rob. On various insects. Tropics.
Stilbum formicarum. Cke. and Mass. On dead ants (*Formica*). Australia.
Stilbum ramosum. Peck. On insect larvæ in rotten wood. N. America.
Stilbum Kervillei. Quel. On *Leria cæsia.* France. ·

GENUS 2.—ISARIA. Pers.

Stroma vertical, clavate or branched, bearing conidia everywhere, from the tips of the combined threads.

Isaria farinosa. Dicks. On chrysalids. Britain, Germany, Italy, France, Sweden.
Isaria truncata. Pers. On chrysalids. Germany.
Isaria crassa. Pers. On chrysalids. Germany.
Isaria corallina. Fries. On pupa of *Noctua instabilis,* etc. Germany, Italy.
Isaria velutipes. Link. On chrysalids. Germany, Sweden.
Isaria strigosa. Fries. On *Noctua ypsilon.* Germany.
Isaria floccosa. Fries. On larvæ and pupæ of *Bombyx Jacobeæ.* Britain, Germany.
Isaria exoleta. Fries. On larvæ of *Noctua exoleta.* Germany.
Isaria cinnabarina. Preuss. On pupa of *Sphinx ligustri.* Germany.

Isaria sphingum. Schwz. On imagines of *Sphinx* and other *Lepidoptera.* N. America, India, Britain.
Isaria nigripes. Schwz. On chrysalids. N. America.
Isaria furcata. Schwz. On chrysalids. N. America.
Isaria leprosa. Fries. On chrysalids. Germany.
Isaria tenuipes. Peck. On pupæ. N. America.
Isaria stellata. Cooke. On *Aphides.* India.
Isaria suffruticosa. Cooke and Mass. On hairy caterpillar. Australia.
Isaria sphecophila. Ditm. On *Vespa crabro.* Germany.
Isaria Saussurei. Cooke. On *Polistes Americana.* Antilles, Cayenne.
Isaria stilbiformis. Speg. On the body of *Pentatoma.*
Isaria eleutheratorum. Nees. On beetles (*Carabus*). Germany, Italy, France.
Isaria gigantea. Mont. On *Mygale.* Cuba.
Isaria arachnophila. Ditm. On spiders (*Epeira, Drassus, Mygale,* etc.). Italy, France, Holland, Germany, Belgium, Britain, N. America.
Isaria aranearum. Schwz. On spiders. N. America.
Isaria cicadæ. Miquel. On *Cicada.* Brazil.

FAMILY 4.—TUBERCULARIEÆ.

Stroma compact, rather thick, wartlike or subglobose, waxy or rather gelatinous ; conidia produced from the side or tips of the agglutinated threads.

PHRAGMOSPORÆ. *Conidia septate.*

GENUS I.—FUSARIUM. Link.

Stroma pulvinate ; conidia fusoid or falcate typically, three or more septate, hyaline.

Fusarium larvarum. Fckl. On chrysalids. Germany.

GENUS 2.—MICROCERA. Desm.

Stroma conical or pulvinate ; sporidia fusiform elongated, many septate, hyaline.

Microcera coccophila. Desm. On various *Cocci.* Britain, France, Italy, Austria, Belgium.
Microcera rectispora. Cke. and Mass. On *Cocci* of the orange. Australia.

ORDER IV.—SCHIZOMYCETES.

Minute, unicellular.   Multiplication by division ; spores of two forms.

GENUS I.—BACILLUS.   Cohn.

Cells cylindrical, usually combined in rows, transversely dividing.

Bacillus alvei.   Chesh.   On larvæ of bees.   Britain, Germany.

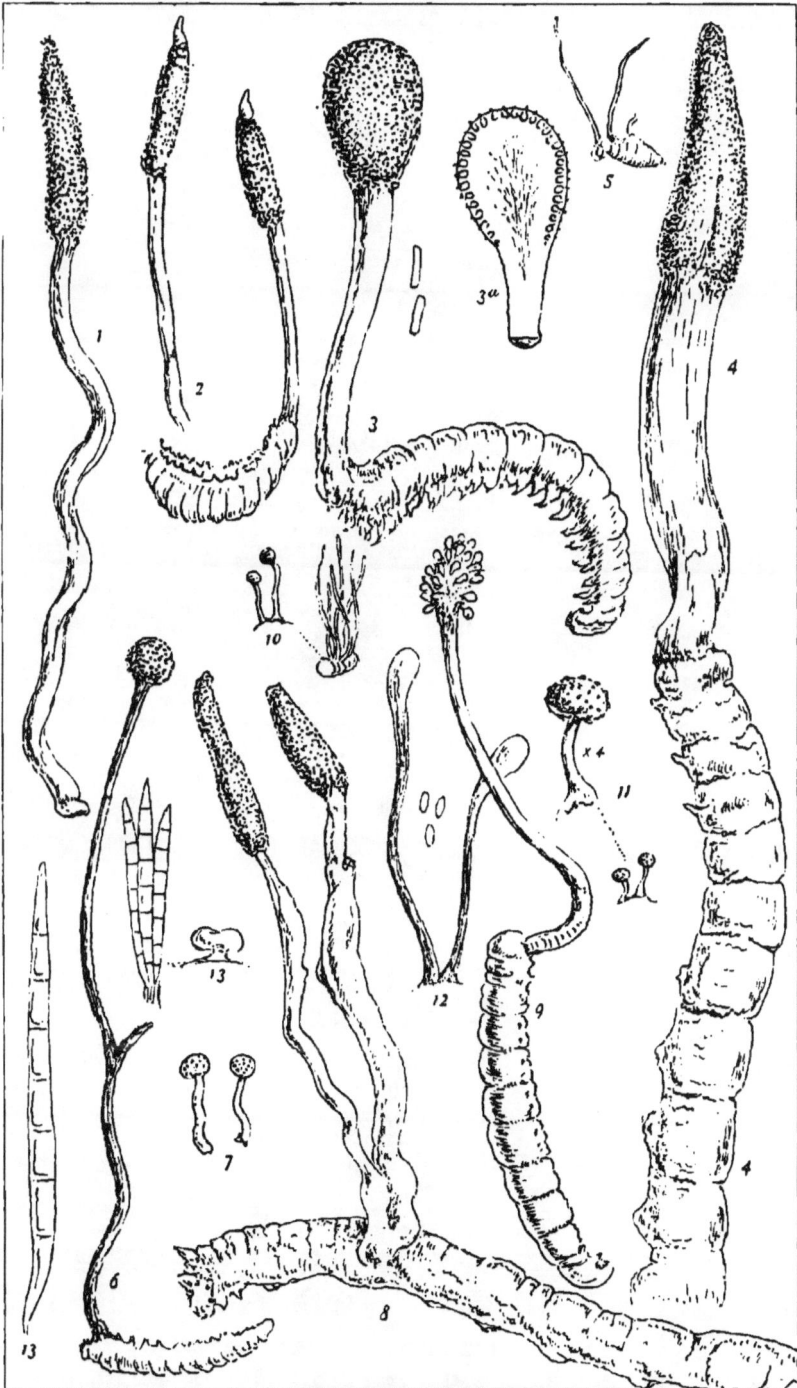

ENTOMOGENOUS FUNGI.

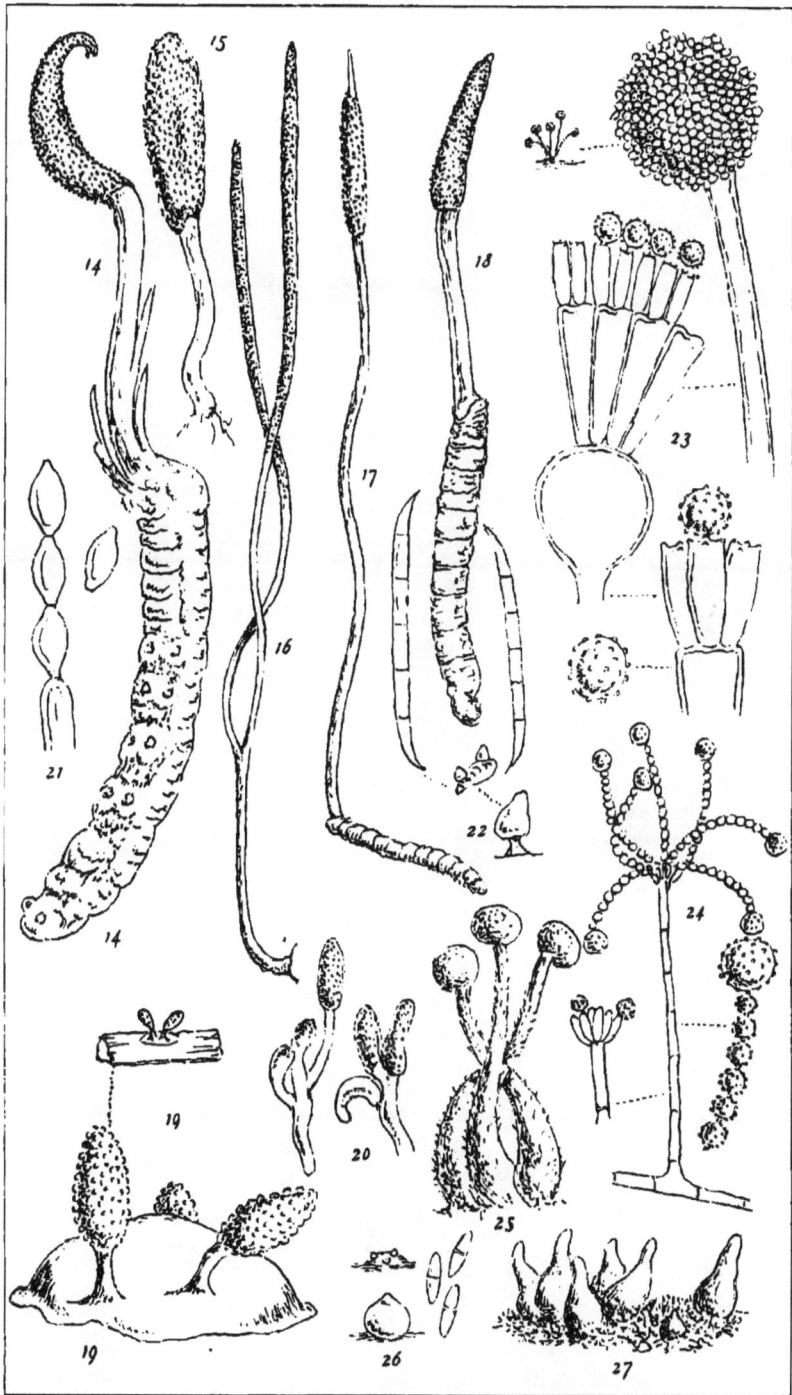

ENTOMOGENOUS FUNGI.

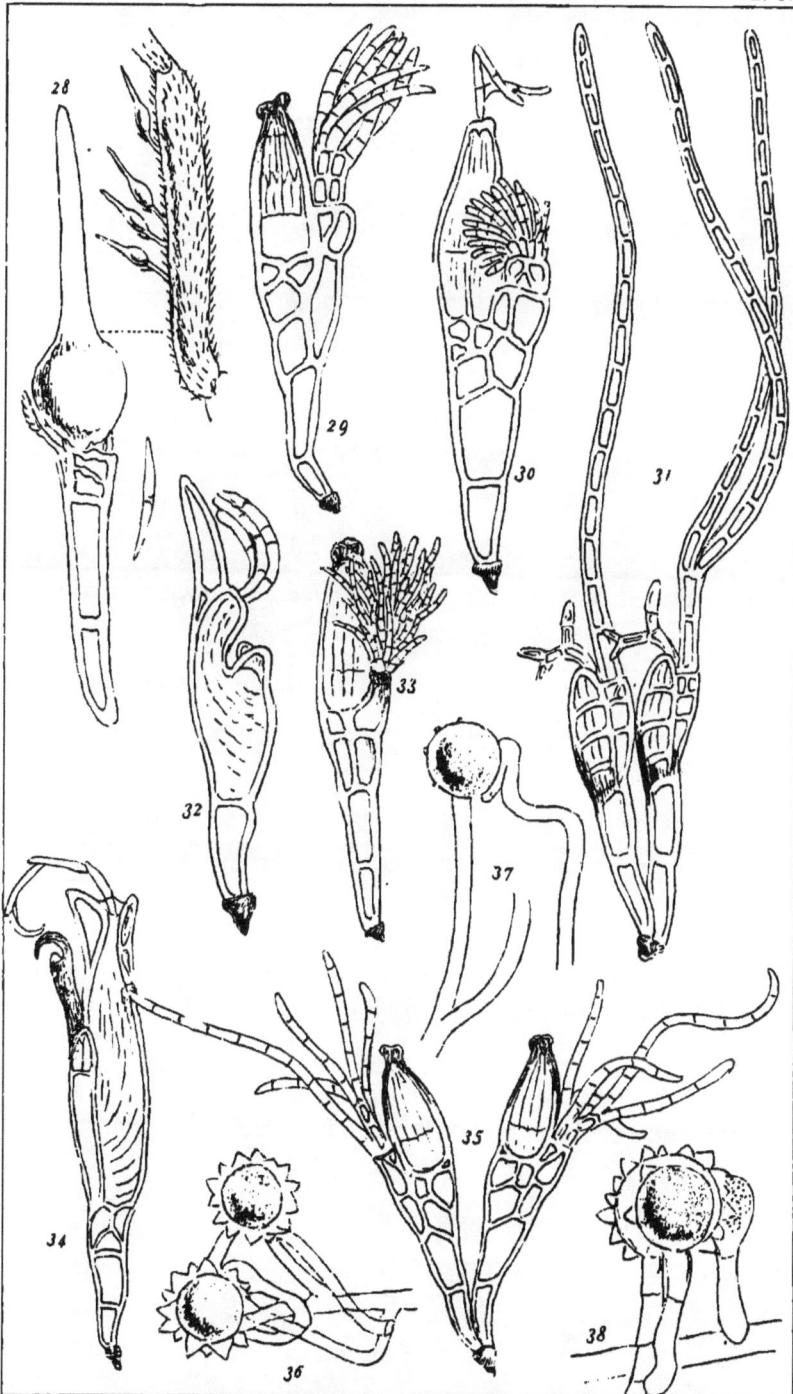

ENTOMOGENOUS FUNGI.

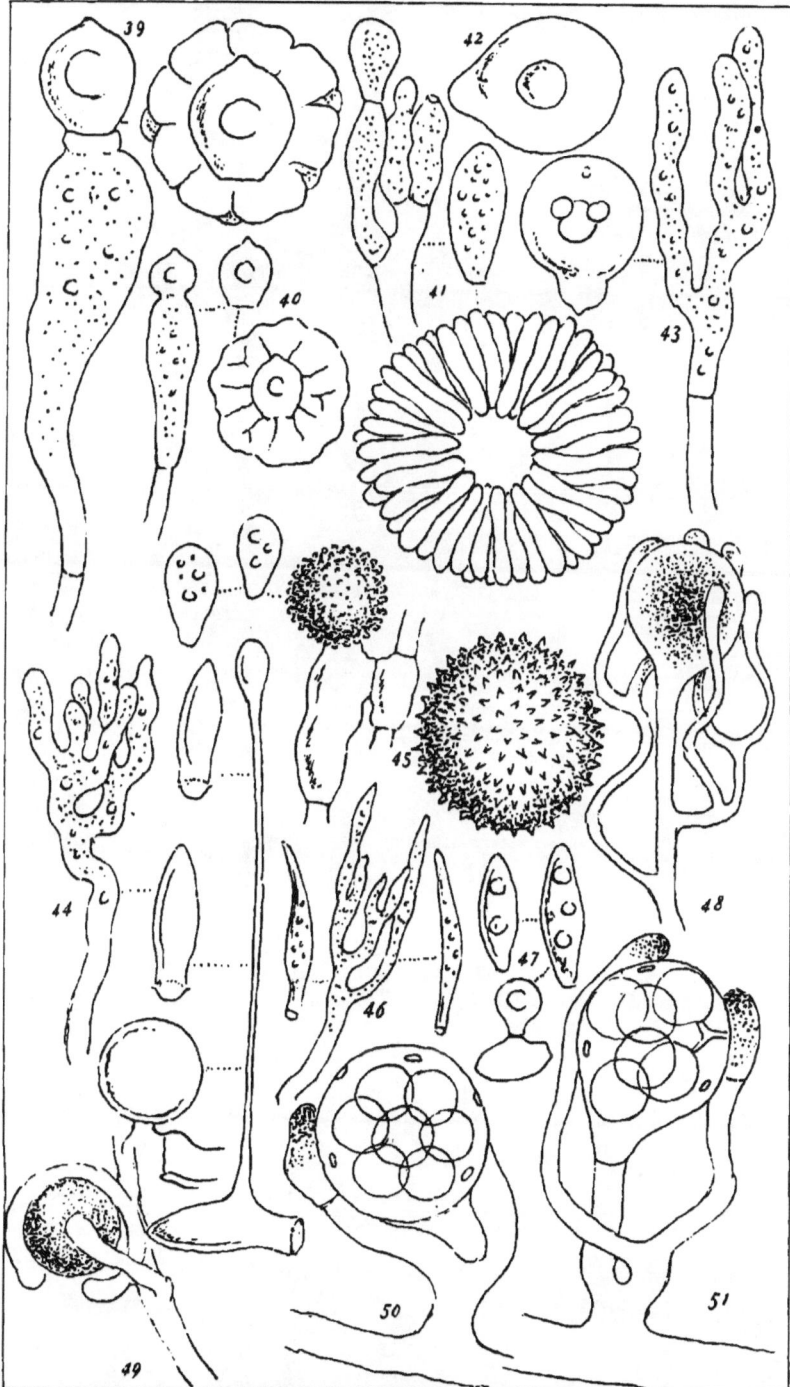

ENTOMOGENOUS FUNGI.

INDEX TO INSECT HOSTS.

GENERAL INDEX.

REFERENCES TO PLATES.

PLATE 1.

FIG.

1. Cordyceps Ravenelii, nat. size, after Berkeley.
2. Cordyceps Barnesii, nat. size, from specimens.
3. Cordyceps insignis, nat. size, from specimens, with section of capitulum and joints of sporidia.
4. Cordyceps Gunnii, nat. size, after Gray.
5. Cordyceps fuliginosa, nat. size, after Cesati.
6. Cordyceps cinerea, nat. size, from specimen.
7. Cordyceps armeniaca, nat. size, after Berkeley.
8. Cordyceps Hawkesii, nat. size, after Gray.
9. Cordyceps racemosa, nat. size, after Berkeley.
10. Cordyceps flavella, nat. size, and conidiophores, from specimens.
11. Cordyceps coccigena, nat. size and enlarged, after Tulasne.
12. Stilbum formicarum, enlarged, with conidia.
13. Microcera rectispora, nat. size, with conidia magnified.

PLATE 2.

14. Cordyceps falcata, nat. size, after Berkeley.
15. Cordyceps militaris, nat. size, from specimen.
16. Cordyceps caloceroides, nat. size, from specimen.
17. Cordyceps acicularis, nat. size, after Berkeley.
18. Cordyceps sinensis, nat. size, after Berkeley.
19. Cordyceps pistillariæformis, nat. size and enlarged, after Berkeley.
20. Cordyceps palustris, nat. size, after Berkeley.
21. Oospora aphidis, conidia × 350.
22. Microcera coccophila, nat. size, enlarged, and conidia magnified.
23. Sterigmatocystis ferruginea, nat. size, head enlarged, with conidiophores and conidia magnified.
24. Penicillium Fieberi, enlarged, with conidia further magnified, after Corda.

FIG.
25. Stilbum Buquetii, enlarged, after Robin.
26. Nectria coccorum, nat. size, perithecium enlarged, and sporidia, × 400.
27. Torrubiella aranicida, perithecia enlarged, after Boudier.

PLATE 3.

28. Appendiculina entomophila, after Peck.
29. Laboulbenia anceps, × 125, after Peyritsch.
30. Laboulbenia luxurians, × 250, after Peyritsch.
31. Laboulbenia nebriæ, × 115, after Peyritsch.
32. Heimatomyces paradoxus, × 250, after Peyritsch.
33. Laboulbenia fasciculata, × 125, after Peyritsch.
34. Chitonomyces melanurus, × 350, after Peyritsch.
35. Laboulbenia flagellata, × 125, after Peyritsch.
36. Aphanomyces stellatus, oogonia.
37. Aphanomyces scaber, oogonia.
38. Saprolegnia asterophora, oogonia.

PLATE 4.

39. Empusa muscæ, basidium with conidium, × 430.
40. Empusa culicis, basidium with conidium, × 430.
41. Entomophthora virescens, conidiophore, and conidium, × 430, with hyphal body germinating, × 230.
42. Empusa tenthredinis, conidium, × 430.
43. Empusa apiculata, conidiophore, × 230, with conidium × 430.
44. Entomophthora occidentalis, conidiophore, × 230, with conidia, and same germinating, with mature resting-spore, × 430.
45. Entomophthora echinospora, conidia with mature resting-spore, × 430.
46. Entomophthora gracilis, conidiophore, × 230, with conidia, × 430.
47. Entomophthora dipterigena, conidia, with one producing secondary conidium, × 430.
48. Achlya polyandra, oogonium with antheridia.
49. Aphanomyces lævis, oogonium with antheridia.
50. Diplanes saprolegnoides, oogonium with antheridia.
51. Saprolegnia monoica, oogonium with antheridia.
Figs. 39 to 47 after Thaxter.

PRINTED BY WILLIAM CLOWES AND SONS, LIMITED, LONDON AND BECCLES.

PUBLICATIONS

OF THE

Society for Promoting Christian Knowledge.

THE PEOPLE'S LIBRARY.

Crown 8vo, cloth boards, 1s. each.

A Chapter of Science ; or, What is a Law of Nature ? Six Lectures to Working Men. By Professor J. STUART, Cambridge. With Diagrams.

A Six Months' Friend. By HELEN SHIPTON, author of " Christopher." With several Illustrations.

Biographies of Working Men. By GRANT ALLEN, B.A.

Factors in Life. Three Lectures on Health—Food— Education. By Professor SEELEY, F.R.S.

Household Health. A sequel to " The Guild of Good Life." By B. W. RICHARDSON, M.D., F.R.S.

Hops and Hop-pickers. By the Rev. J. Y. STRATTON. With several Illustrations.

Life and Work among the Navvies. By the Rev. D. W. BARRETT, M.A. With several Illustrations.

The British Citizen : his Rights and Privileges. A Short History by the late J. THOROLD ROGERS, M.P.

The Cottage Next Door. By HELEN SHIPTON. With several Illustrations.

The Guild of Good Life. A Narrative of Domestic Health and Economy. By B. W. RICHARDSON, M.D., F.R.S.

Thrift and Independence. A Word for Working Men. By the Rev. W. LEWERY BLACKLEY, M.A.

Works by the late Mrs. EWING.

Snapdragons; a Tale of Christmas-Eve and **Old Father Christmas.** Illustrated by GORDON BROWNE. Small 4to, paper boards, 1s.

The Peace Egg, and a **Christmas Mumming Play.** With Illustrations by GORDON BROWNE. Small 4to, paper boards, 1s.

Mary's Meadow, and Letters from a Little Garden. Illustrated by GORDON BROWNE. Small 4to, paper boards, 1s.

Lob Lie-by-the-Fire; or, The Luck of Lingborough. With Illustrations by the late R. CALDECOTT. Small 4to, paper boards, 1s.

Story of a Short Life (The). With Illustrations by GORDON BROWNE. Small 4to, paper boards, 1s.

Daddy Darwin's Dovecot; a Country Tale. With illustrations by the late R. CALDECOTT. Small 4to, paper boards, 1s.

Dandelion Clocks, and other Tales. With Illustrations by GORDON BROWNE, and other artists. Small 4to, paper boards, 1s.

Jackanapes. With Seventeen Illustrations by the late RANDOLPH CALDECOTT. Small 4to, paper boards, 1s.

Old - Fashioned Fairy Tales. Foolscap 4to, with numerous Woodcuts, ornamental paper boards, 3s. 6d.

Brothers of Pity, and other Tales of Beasts and Men. Crown 8vo, with numerous Illustrations, cloth boards, 2s. 6d.
Library Edition of JACKANAPES; DADDY DARWIN'S DOVE-COT; and LOB LIE-BY-THE-FIRE in one volume. Small 4to, cloth, 5s.

Verse Books in Volumes. Coloured Illustrations :—
A SOLDIER'S CHILDREN, and Five other Tales.
BLUE BELLS ON THE LEA, and Ten other Tales.
MOTHER'S BIRTHDAY REVIEW, and Seven other Tales.
Small 4to, paper boards, 3s. each vol.

Juliana Horatia Ewing and Her Books. By HORATIO K. F. GATTY. With a portrait by GEORGE REID, R.S.A. Illustrated by facsimiles from Mrs. EWING's sketches, and a cover designed by the late R. CALDECOTT. Small 4to, paper boards, 1s.

BOOKS FOR BOYS

BY

G. MANVILLE FENN.

Crown 8vo, Illustrated, cloth boards, 5s. each.

TO THE WEST.
CROWN AND SCEPTRE. A West Country Story.
GIL THE GUNNER; or, The Youngest Officer in the East.
MASS' GEORGE; or, A Boy's Adventures in the Old Savannahs.

PENNY LIBRARY OF FICTION.

Demy 8vo, 32 pages, Pictorial paper cover, price 1d. each.

THREE TIMES TRIED.
By B. L. FARJEON.

GOLDEN FEATHER.
By S. BARING GOULD.

FOR DICK'S SAKE.
By Mrs. J. H. RIDDELL.

SLIPPING AWAY.
By the Author of "Victa Victrix."

SAVED BY THE SKIN OF HIS TEETH.
By HELEN SHIPTON.

LORD JOHN.
By G. MANVILLE FENN.

GONE.
By KATHERINE S. MACQUOID.

A TERRIBLE INHERITANCE.
By GRANT ALLEN.

IN MARINE ARMOUR.
By G. MANVILLE FENN.

MY SOLDIER KEEPER.
By C. PHILLIPS-WOLLEY.

BY TELEGRAPH.
By J. MACLAREN COBBAN.

"CONSTABLE A1."
By JESSIE M. E. SAXBY.

THE PLAGUE SHIP.
By G. A. HENTY.

STAUNCH: a Story of Steel.
By G. MANVILLE FENN.

A LIVING APPARITION.
By GRANT ALLEN.

BROUGHT TO LIGHT.
By Mrs. NEWMAN.

THE MUTINY OF THE "HELEN GRAY."
By G. MANVILLE FENN.

THE SOLE TRUSTEE.
By GRANT ALLEN.

FIFTEEN POUNDS.
By S. BARING GOULD.

SAVED FROM HIMSELF.
By Mrs. HENRY CLARKE, M.A.

THE RANCHE IN THE VALLEY.
By G. A. HENTY.

Volumes I. II. & III. each containing Six Stories, paper boards, 6d. each.

PENNY SERIES

OF

BIOGRAPHIES.

Demy 8vo, 32 pages. Pictorial Paper Wrapper.

A HERO; a Story of a Noble Life.
ABRAHAM LINCOLN: Farmer's Boy and President.
DAVID LIVINGSTONE: the Great African Pioneer.

PENNY SERIES

OF

POPULAR TALES.

Imperial 8vo, 16 pages, Illustrated. Paper Cover.

ROB NIXON, THE OLD WHITE TRAPPER; a Tale of British North
    America. By the late W. H. G. KINGSTON.
MOUNTAIN MOGGY. By the late W. H. G. KINGSTON.
THE TWO WHALERS. By the late W. H. G. KINGSTON.
THE LILY OF LEYDEN. By the late W. H. G. KINGSTON.
THE LOG HOUSE BY THE LAKE; a Tale of Canada. By the late
    W. H. G. KINGSTON.
WHITER THAN SNOW.
A DRIFT FOR LIFE, and other Stories.
AN EVENTFUL NIGHT, AND WHAT CAME OF IT.

HEROES OF SCIENCE.

The aim of these volumes is to show, by way of selected Biographies,
the progress of Science from the beginning of the inductive method
until the present day.

Crown 8vo, cloth boards, 4s. each.

ASTRONOMERS. By E. J. C. MORTON, Esq., B.A. With numerous
    diagrams.
BOTANISTS, ZOOLOGISTS, AND GEOLOGISTS. By PROFESSOR P.
    MARTIN DUNCAN, F.R.S., etc.
CHEMISTS. By M. M. PATTISON MUIR, Esq., F.R.S.E. With
    several diagrams.
MECHANICIANS. By T. C. LEWIS, M.A.
PHYSICISTS. By WILLIAM GARNETT, Esq., M.A., D.C.L.

NATURAL HISTORY RAMBLES.

A Series of Popular Handbooks of the Fauna and Flora of the British Isles.

Fcap. 8vo, numerous Woodcuts, cloth boards, 2s. 6d. each.

IN SEARCH OF MINERALS.
By the late D. T. ANSTED, M.A., F.R.S.

LAKES AND RIVERS.
By C. O. GROOM NAPIER, F.G.S.

LANE AND FIELD.
By the late Rev. J. G. WOOD, M.A.

MOUNTAIN AND MOOR.
By J. E. TAYLOR, F.L.S., F.G.S.

PONDS AND DITCHES.
By M. C. COOKE, M.A., LL.D.

THE SEA-SHORE.
By Professor P. MARTIN DUNCAN, M.B. (London), F.R.S.

THE WOODLANDS.
By M. C. COOKE, M.A., LL.D.

UNDERGROUND.
By J. E. TAYLOR, F.L.S.

THE ROMANCE OF SCIENCE.

A Series of Books which shows that Science has for the masses as great interest as, and more edification than, the romances of the day.

Post 8vo, with numerous Woodcuts, cloth boards.

COAL; and what we get from it.
By Professor R. MEDOLA. 2s. 6d.

COLOUR MEASUREMENT AND MIXTURE.
By Captain ABNEY. 2s. 6d.

DISEASES OF PLANTS.
By Professor MARSHALL WARD, 2s. 6d.

SOAP BUBBLES, and the Forces which Mould them.
By C. V. BOYS, A.R.S.M., 2s. 6d.

SPINNING TOPS.
By Professor J. PERRY, M.E., F.R.S. 2s. 6d.

TIME AND TIDE: a Romance of the Moon.
By Sir ROBERT S. BALL. 2s. 6d.

THE STORY OF A TINDER BOX.
By the late C. MEYMOTT TIDY, M.B.M.S. 2s.

THE BIRTH AND GROWTH OF WORLDS.
By Professor A. H. GREEN, M.A., F.R.S. 1s.

THE MAKING OF FLOWERS.
By the Rev. Professor GEORGE HENSLOW, M.A. 2s. 6d.

ATLASES.

	s.	d.
Handy General Atlas of the World. A comprehensive series of Maps, illustrating General and Commercial Geography. With Index.....................*Half Morocco*	42	o
A Modern Atlas; containing 30 Maps, with Indexes. *Cloth boards*	12	o
Bible Atlas. 12 Maps and Plans, with Explanatory Notes, Complete Index, &c. Royal 4to.....................*Cloth boards*	14	o
Star Atlas. Translated and adapted from the German of DR. KLEIN by the Rev. E. McCLURE. With 18 Charts. New Edition.....................*Cloth boards*	7	6
Handy Reference Atlas of the World, with complete Index and Geographical Statistics.....................*Cloth boards*	7	6
Student's Atlas of Ancient and Modern Geography, with 48 Maps and a copious consulting Index......*Cloth boards*	7	6
World (The), an Atlas. 34 Coloured Maps and Complete Index. Folded 8vo.....................*Cloth gilt*	5	o
Century Atlas and Gazetteer of the World. Containing 52 Maps and Gazetteer of 35,000 Names. 4to.........*Cloth*	3	6
National Atlas. 32 Coloured Maps and Index...*Cloth boards*	2	6
British Colonial Pocket Atlas. With Index...*Cloth boards*	2	6
Pocket Atlas of the World. With Index, &c....*Cloth boards*	2	6
Young Scholar's Atlas. 24 Coloured Maps, and Index. Imp. 4to...... ....*Cloth boards*	2	6
Physical Atlas for Beginners. 12 Coloured Maps. *Paper covers*	1	o
Sixpenny Bible Atlas. 16 Coloured Maps......*Paper covers*	o	6
Shilling Quarto Atlas. 24 Coloured Maps......*Paper covers*	1	o
Atlas of the British Empire, with Notes.........*Paper boards*	1	o
British Colonies, Atlas of the. 16 Coloured Maps. *Paper covers*	o	6
Threepenny Atlas. 16 Coloured Maps. Crown 8vo. *Paper covers*	o	3
Penny Atlas. 13 Maps. Small 4to.....................*Paper covers*	o	1

SERIES OF PHOTO-RELIEVO MAPS.

(Patented.)   Size 19 in. by 14 in.

ENGLAND AND WALES.—SCOTLAND.—EUROPE.—ASIA.

		s.	d.
Names and places of rivers left to be filled in by scholars	*each*	o	6
With rivers and names of places.................................	,,	o	9
With names of places and county divisions in colours......	,,	1	o
NORTH LONDON, with names of places, &c.............	,,	o	6
SOUTH LONDON, with names of places, &c.............	,,	o	6
Photo-Relievo Wall Map, ENGLAND AND WALES—56 in. by 46 in., on canvas, roller and varnished, plain 12s., coloured		13	o

EARLY BRITAIN.

A Series of Books which has for its aim the presentation of Early
Britain at Great Historic Periods.

Anglo-Saxon Britain. By GRANT ALLEN, B.A. With
Map. Fcap. 8vo, cloth boards, 2s. 6d.

Celtic Britain. By Professor RHYS. With two Maps.
Fcap. 8vo, cloth boards, 3s.

Norman Britain. By the Rev. W. HUNT. With Map.
Fcap. 8vo, cloth boards, 2s. 6d.

Post-Norman Britain. By HENRY G. HEWLETT.
Fcap. 8vo, cloth boards, 3s.

Roman Britain. By the Rev. PREBENDARY SCARTH.
With Map. Fcap. 8vo, cloth boards, 2s. 6d.

ANCIENT HISTORY FROM THE MONUMENTS.

This Series of Books is chiefly intended to illustrate the Sacred
Scriptures by the result of recent Monumental Researches in the
East.

Fcap. 8vo, cloth boards, 2s. each.

Babylonia (The History of). By the late GEORGE
SMITH. Edited by the Rev. Professor A. H. SAYCE.

Assyria : from the Earliest Times to the fall of Nineveh.
By the late GEORGE SMITH.

Egypt : from the Earliest Times to B.C. 300. By the late
S. BIRCH, LL.D.

Persia : from the Earliest Period to the Arab Conquest.
By the late W. S. VAUX, M.A., F.R.S.

Sinai : from the Fourth Egyptian Dynasty to the Present
Day. By the late HENRY S. PALMER, Major R.E., F.R.A.S.
A new and Revised Edition by the Rev. Professor SAYCE. With
Map.

MANUALS OF HEALTH.

Fcap. 8vo, 128 pp., limp cloth, price 1s. each.

Health and Occupation. By Dr. B. W. RICHARDSON.

Habitation in Relation to Health (The). By F. S. B. CHAUMONT, M.D., F.R.S.

On Personal Care of Health. By the late E. A. PARKES, M.D., F.R.S.

Water, Air, and Disinfectants. By W. NOEL HARTLEY, Esq., King's College.

MANUALS OF ELEMENTARY SCIENCE.

Fcap. 8vo, 128 pp., with Illustrations, limp cloth, 1s. each.

Physiology. By F. LE GROS CLARKE, F.R.S.

Geology. By the Rev. T. G. BONNEY, M.A., F.G.S., Fellow and late Tutor of St. John's College, Cambridge.

Chemistry. By ALBERT J. BERNAYS.

Astronomy. By W. H. CHRISTIE, M.A., the Royal Observatory, Greenwich.

Botany. By ROBERT BENTLEY, Professor of Botany in King's College, London.

Zoology. By ALFRED NEWTON, M.A., F.R.S., Professor of Zoology and Comparative Anatomy at Cambridge.

Matter and Motion. By the late J. CLERK MAXWELL, M.A., Trinity College, Cambridge.

Spectroscope, The Work of the. By the late RICHARD A. PROCTOR.

Crystallography. By HENRY PLAIN GURNEY, M.A., Clare College, Cambridge.

Electricity. By the late Professor FLEEMING JENKIN.

LONDON: NORTHUMBERLAND AVENUE, W.C.;
43, QUEEN VICTORIA STREET, E.C.
BRIGHTON: 135, NORTH STREET.

www.ingramcontent.com/pod-product-compliance
Lightning Source LLC
Chambersburg PA
CBHW030858270326
41929CB00008B/483